TIME LIFE ®
BOOKS

*This volume is one of a series that explains and demonstrates
how to prepare various types of food, and that offers in each
book an international anthology of great recipes.*

Shellfish

BY
THE EDITORS OF TIME-LIFE BOOKS

TIME-LIFE BOOKS/ALEXANDRIA, VIRGINIA

Cover: A golden butter sauce is poured over a mélange of shrimp, mussels, oysters and scallops poached together in a rich fish stock *(pages 34-35).* The shellfish were added to the pot in successive stages so that each type cooked only the number of minutes required to develop its full flavor.

Time-Life Books Inc.
is a wholly owned subsidiary of
TIME INCORPORATED

Founder: Henry R. Luce 1898-1967

Editor-in-Chief: Henry Anatole Grunwald
President: J. Richard Munro
Chairman of the Board: Ralph P. Davidson
Executive Vice President: Clifford J. Grum
Chairman, Executive Committee: James R. Shepley
Editorial Director: Ralph Graves
Group Vice President, Books: Joan D. Manley
Vice Chairman: Arthur Temple

TIME-LIFE BOOKS INC.

Editor: George Constable. *Executive Editor:* George Daniels. *Board of Editors:* Dale M. Brown, Thomas H. Flaherty Jr., William Frankel, Thomas A. Lewis, Martin Mann, Philip W. Payne, John Paul Porter, Gerry Schremp, Gerald Simons, Nakanori Tashiro, Kit van Tulleken. *Art Director:* Tom Suzuki; *Assistant:* Arnold C. Holeywell. *Director of Administration:* David L. Harrison. *Director of Operations:* Gennaro C. Esposito. *Director of Research:* Carolyn L. Sackett; *Assistant:* Phyllis K. Wise. *Director of Photography:* Dolores Allen Littles. *Production Director:* Feliciano Madrid; *Assistants:* Peter A. Inchauteguiz, Karen A. Meyerson. *Copy Processing:* Gordon E. Buck. *Quality Control Director:* Robert L. Young; *Assistant:* James J. Cox; *Associates:* Daniel J. McSweeney, Michael G. Wight. *Art Coordinator:* Anne B. Landry. *Copy Room Director:* Susan Galloway Goldberg; *Assistants:* Celia Beattie, Ricki Tarlow.

President: Carl G. Jaeger. *Executive Vice Presidents:* John Steven Maxwell, David J. Walsh. *Vice Presidents:* George Artandi, Stephen L. Bair, Peter G. Barnes, Nicholas Benton, John L. Canova, Beatrice T. Dobie, Carol Flaumenhaft, James L. Mercer, Herbert Sorkin, Paul R. Stewart

THE GOOD COOK

The original version of this book was created in London for Time-Life Books B.V.
European Editor: Kit van Tulleken; *Design Director:* Louis Klein; *Photography Director:* Pamela Marke; *Planning Director:* Alan Lothian; *Chief of Research:* Vanessa Kramer; *Chief Sub-Editor:* Ilse Gray; *Production Editor:* Ellen Brush

Staff for Shellfish: Series Editor: Windsor Chorlton; *Series Coordinator:* Liz Timothy; *Series Designer:* Douglas Whitworth; *Text Editor:* Tony Allan; *Anthology Editor:* Liz Clasen; *Staff Writers:* Gillian Boucher, Norman Kolpas, Anthony Masters; *Designer:* Rick Bowring; *Researcher:* Ursula Beary; *Sub-Editors:* Jay Ferguson, Nicoletta Flessati; *Permissions Researcher:* Mary-Claire Hailey; *Design Assistants:* Mary Staples, Elaine Maddex; *Editorial Department:* Anetha Besidonne, Pat Boag, Philip Garner, Margaret Hall, Joanne Holland, Debra Raad, Molly Sutherland, Julia West

U.S. Staff for Shellfish: Editor: Gerry Schremp; *Senior Editor:* Ellen Phillips; *Designer:* Ellen Robling; *Chief Researcher:* Barbara Fleming; *Picture Editor:* Adrian Allen; *Writers:* Patricia Fanning, Leslie Marshall; *Researchers:* Karin Kinney (techniques), Marilyn Murphy (anthology); *Assistant Designer:* Peg Schreiber; *Copy Coordinators:* Nancy Berman, Tonna Gibert, Bobbie C. Paradise, Katherine F. Rosen; *Art Assistant:* Mary L. Orr; *Picture Coordinator:* Alvin Ferrell; *Editorial Assistants:* Brenda Harwell, Patricia Whiteford; *Special Contributor:* Christine B. Dove

CHIEF SERIES CONSULTANT

Richard Olney, an American, has lived and worked for some three decades in France, where he is highly regarded as an authority on food and wine. Author of *The French Menu Cookbook* and of the award-winning *Simple French Food,* he has also contributed to numerous gastronomic magazines in France and the United States, including the influential journals *Cuisine et Vins de France* and *La Revue du Vin de France.* He has directed cooking courses in France and the United States and is a member of several distinguished gastronomic and oenological societies, including L'Académie Internationale du Vin, La Confrérie des Chevaliers du Tastevin and La Commanderie du Bontemps de Médoc et des Graves. Working in London with the series editorial staff, he has been basically responsible for the planning of this volume and has supervised the final selection of recipes submitted by other consultants. The United States edition of The Good Cook has been revised by the Editors of Time-Life Books to bring it into complete accord with American customs and usage.

CHIEF AMERICAN CONSULTANT

Carol Cutler is the author of a number of cookbooks, including the award-winning *The Six-Minute Soufflé and Other Culinary Delights.* During the 12 years she lived in France, she studied at the Cordon Bleu and the École des Trois Gourmandes, and with private chefs. She is a member of the Cercle des Gourmettes, a long-established French food society limited to just 50 members, and is also a charter member of Les Dames d'Escoffier, Washington Chapter.

SPECIAL CONSULTANTS

Joyce Dodson Piotrowski studied cooking while traveling and living around the world. A teacher, chef, caterer, food writer and consultant, she has been responsible for many of the step-by-step photographic sequences in this volume.

Derek Walker, a partner in a retail seafood market in Alexandria, Virginia, has been responsible for most of the step-by-step demonstrations in the introduction to this volume.

PHOTOGRAPHERS

Aldo Tutino has worked in Milan, New York City and Washington, D.C. He has received a number of awards for his photographs from the New York Advertising Club.

Alan Duns was born in 1943 in the north of England and studied at the Ealing School of Photography. He has undertaken many advertising assignments, but specializes in food photography. His work has appeared in major British publications.

INTERNATIONAL CONSULTANTS

GREAT BRITAIN: *Jane Grigson* has written a number of books about food and has been a cookery correspondent for the London *Observer* since 1968. *Alan Davidson* is the author of several cookbooks and the founder of Prospect Books, which specializes in scholarly publications about food and cookery. FRANCE: *Michel Lemonnier,* the cofounder and vice president of Les Amitiés Gastronomiques Internationales, is a frequent lecturer on wine and vineyards. GERMANY: *Jochen Kuchenbecker* trained as a chef, but worked for 10 years as a food photographer in several European countries before opening his own restaurant in Hamburg. *Anne Brakemeier* is the co-author of a number of cookbooks. THE NETHERLANDS: *Hugh Jans* has published cookbooks and his recipes appear in several Dutch magazines. THE UNITED STATES: *Judith Olney,* the author of *Comforting Food* and *Summer Food,* received her culinary training in England and in France. In addition to teaching cooking classes, she regularly contributes articles to gastronomic magazines. *José Wilson* wrote many books on food and interior decoration.

Correspondents: Elisabeth Kraemer (Bonn); Margot Hapgood, Dorothy Bacon, (London); Susan Jonas, Lucy T. Voulgaris (New York); Maria Vincenza Aloisi, Josephine du Brusle (Paris); Ann Natanson (Rome).
Valuable assistance was also provided by: Jeanne Buys, Janny Hovinga (Amsterdam); Hans-Heinrich Wellmann, Gertraud Bellon (Hamburg); Bona Schmid, Maria Teresa Morenco (Milan); Michèle le Baube, Cécile Dogneiz (Paris).

First printing. Printed in U.S.A.
Published simultaneously in Canada.
School and library distribution by Silver Burdett Company, Morristown, New Jersey 07960.

TIME-LIFE is a trademark of Time Incorporated U.S.A.

For information about any Time-Life book, please write:
Reader Information, Time-Life Books
541 North Fairbanks Court, Chicago, Illinois 60611

Library of Congress CIP data, page 176.

CONTENTS

Treasures from the Waters

As evidence of the generous bounty of the waters, consider the families of shellfish—abalone, clams and oysters thronging the seashores and shallows, armies of shrimp and lobster marching on the ocean floors, agile squid and octopus swimming through the deeps. These creatures and their relatives exist in thousands of varieties and countless numbers. The tastes of their flesh vary from sweet to briny, but all provide an incomparable subtlety of flavor. At its best, shellfish offers what the American essayist Eleanor Clark calls "a shock of freshness . . . some piercing intimation of the sea and all its weeds and breezes."

This book explores the apparently bewildering variety of shellfish types and teaches the ways in which each may be presented at its most delicious. The introduction to the first half of the volume includes a guide describing the different shellfish available to the cook and demonstrations showing how to detach each from its shell or otherwise ready it for cooking. On the following pages appear lessons in preparing complements to the shellfish—stocks, sauces and pastry doughs.

Each of the succeeding chapters is devoted to a different method of shellfish cookery. The first concerns poaching and steaming; it explains how to apply these basic methods to ensure moist and tender shellfish. The second chapter teaches the stewing techniques used to make such famous dishes as San Francisco's cioppino—mixed shellfish stew—and the Mediterranean's spicy squid and octopus preparations. The third chapter demonstrates frying techniques, from Western sautéing to the stir-fried recipes of Asia. A baking and broiling chapter explains how to make crisp-crusted shellfish pies, airy soufflés and stuffed assemblies. The last chapter shows the elaborate shellfish dishes of classic French cuisine—aspic-coated presentations, silky mousses, elegant quenelles and towering pastry cases that hold amalgams of shellfish and sauce.

The second half of the volume is an anthology of more than 200 recipes collected from cookbooks old and new. The anthology serves as another teaching tool: It shows specific applications of general techniques described in the first half of the volume.

Catching the shellfish

The major groups of shellfish include bivalves and univalves such as clams and conchs; crustaceans such as lobsters; as well as sea urchins, and cephalopods such as squid. All have served as human food for many millennia, as can be seen in the ancient kitchen middens of China, the Middle East, Europe and North America. Prehistoric man clearly had an ample and varied shellfish supply. A 10,000-year-old Danish midden composed mainly of clam and oyster shells is 200 feet [60 meters] wide and almost 1,000 feet [300 meters] long; a midden on California's Catalina Island dating from 4000 B.C. contains the shells of more than 20 species.

The enthusiasm of early hunters is not surprising: Shellfish are as prolific as they are delicious, and gathering them is an easy matter compared with hunting land animals. Most bivalves, univalves and sea urchins cling to rocks along the shore. Dull, stationary creatures, they are uncovered at low tide and can be gathered by hand. Crustaceans are more active, but some crawl on the shore and others can be caught by divers and by fishermen using nets and traps.

Because human populations remained relatively small for centuries, the shellfish supply seemed limitless until well into modern times. And many shellfish—left undisturbed until they had attained their full growth—reached prodigious size. Europeans coming from much-fished areas to unexplored America in the 1600s were astonished at what they found. Lobsters were not only fantastically plentiful, but reached 6 feet [180 cm.] in length and weighed as much as 30 pounds [15 kg.].

In time, the Americans, like the Europeans before them, discovered a sad truth: The more people there were to fish and eat the delectable creatures, the fewer there were and the smaller their size. The solutions, from ancient times to the present, have been two: to breed and farm certain kinds of shellfish and to limit the harvesting of the others.

Breeding is most effective with almost-motionless bivalves—and has been in practice since the Fourth Century B.C. As described by Aristotle, Greeks moved young oysters from wild beds to more convenient sites, using pottery shards as resting places; this is basically how oysters are farmed today. Similarly, mussels have been farmed on French coasts since the 1200s.

Farming also is feasible for small fresh-water crustaceans. Crayfish, for instance, are bred in Louisiana ponds and rice fields. And recently, shellfish breeders have begun to stock ponds with large, shrimplike prawns imported from Malaysia.

Restrictions on gathering animals of certain sizes and in certain seasons allow the shellfish to grow and multiply. The most famous restriction, first mentioned in 1599, is the "R Rule": Oysters are poisonous in months whose names lack the letter r. In fact, oysters are perfectly edible in those months, but they are spawning and their flesh is very soft and tastes watery. Other shellfish are legally protected. In some Eastern states, "berried" lobsters—those carrying visible eggs—may not be taken. Western states restrict the seasons during which abalone—once prolific but now relatively rare—can be caught.

These restrictions apply to amateur as well as commercial fishermen. Anyone who wishes to gather clams or abalone, catch crabs or trap lobsters must consult the state fish-and-game department to find out whether a license is needed and what fishing rules apply.

Getting shellfish to market

Freshness is vital in shellfish. Once out of the water, the animals die quickly and then rapidly deteriorate and become inedible. Therefore, shellfish gatherers must not only catch the creatures but keep them alive almost until the moment they are eaten. Until recent times, this usually meant that shellfish could be consumed only in coastal regions: There was no fast way to carry them inland.

The notable exceptions to the rule were oysters. These bivalves were greatly appreciated in Classical Rome, where the Emperor Vitellius, a notorious glutton, is said to have consumed 1,000 at a sitting. Rome supplied itself from oyster beds throughout the Empire—Britain, France and Africa. The oysters were transported in baskets packed with straw and snow; safe in their shells, they survived the trip.

Icy beds of straw still are used for keeping shellfish alive, but the Industrial Age has provided alternatives. Trapped lobsters, for example, are kept in underwater cages, then trans-

---

Some Sensible Precautions

Shellfish from clean waters is as safe to eat as it is delectable. However, in polluted waters, it readily absorbs bacteria and viruses that can cause dangerous diseases—including cholera, typhoid and hepatitis. Amateur shellfish gatherers should take care to avoid waters declared unsafe by local fish-and-game departments. Any shellfish purchased should, of course, come from a reputable dealer.

---

ferred to sea-water tanks for marketing. A like stratagem is used for that summer delicacy, soft-shell crabs. Crabmen trap them when they are about to molt their hard shells—they are identifiable by colored stripes on their back fins—and segregate them in underwater floats. When the crabs burst from their old shells, delectably soft and entirely edible after cleaning, they can be packed in sea grass and sold live.

Some shellfish are so difficult to keep alive that they rarely appear that way in the market. Sea scallops and geoduck clams, for instance, cannot close their shells completely and leak their life-sustaining fluids as soon as they are taken from the water; these are usually shucked by fishermen and their flesh preserved by refrigeration. Giant king crabs 6 feet wide that are trapped in the Bering Sea can be brought to Alaskan ports in huge sea-water tanks, but this is impractical for transportation over land: The crabs are cooked in port and frozen.

Care must also be given to shellfish caught by amateurs. Hard-shell clams, oysters and mussels will survive for 10 days if covered with a damp cloth and refrigerated. Crabs can be kept refrigerated for a day, but lobsters only for a few hours.

The eating of shellfish

Devotees of shellfish fall into two schools—purists and elaborators. Purists allow almost nothing to interfere with the clear taste of shellfish; elaborators marry the flesh with a host of other ingredients chosen to enrich or complement it.

As far as bivalves are concerned, the Walrus and the Carpenter in Lewis Carroll's *Alice in Wonderland* were classic purists: They ate their oysters straight from the sea—weeping over the little creatures' fate—and drank the briny juices from the shells. The Walrus and the Carpenter liked vinegar and pepper with their oysters; other diners choose lemon juice or freshly grated horseradish.

New England purists are apt to insist that lobsters be eaten only one way—boiled in sea water and served with lemon and melted butter. Crabmen say the same about crabs. (Actually, crustaceans should be gently poached, as shown on pages 30-35, to prevent toughness.)

Raw bivalves and poached crustaceans are undeniably delicious but, like all shellfish, lend themselves to delectable enhancement. Among the classics are sauces that include cream and white wine flavored with aromatic vegetables; dishes that feature these ingredients often are described as *à la bordelaise (recipe, page 123)*, after the French port of Bordeaux. Classic sauces for crustaceans include Nantua sauce *(recipe, page 164)*, a velvety preparation colored and flavored by the animals' own shells and named after a French city famed for its crayfish.

This is not to suggest that shellfish must be cooked with bland ingredients: Famous Mediterranean dishes include onions, tomatoes and garlic *(recipes, pages 112, 135, 147, 149)*; Asian shellfish preparations may be brightened with fresh ginger and scallions *(recipe, page 92)*. For these dishes—as for all shellfish cookery—discretion is the key to success: No matter what the ingredients, the most noticeable element must be the sweet taste and delicate texture of the shellfish itself.

Wine with shellfish

With a few exceptions, shellfish are best accompanied by dry white wines. The exceptions include robust stews flavored with tomato and garlic: These are excellently partnered by red wines. Light, dry Bardolino and richer Valpolicella, both from Italy, make good choices.

Suitable dry white wines for most shellfish dishes include Brittany's muscadet; light and fresh with faint musky undertones, it is perfect with oysters. Among white Burgundies, Meursault—dry but rather soft—and, for more depth, Montrachet are fine companions to poached crustaceans or steamed bivalves. For a drier Burgundy there is Pouilly Fuissé and, the classic choice for grand occasions, flinty Chablis.

For shellfish dishes with light, buttery sauces, many diners prefer fruitier wines, often with a hint of sweetness. Alsatian and German Rieslings belong in this category; California Rieslings have similar qualities. With rich assemblies such as lobster Newburg, an interesting accompaniment would be a sweet wine usually served for dessert—a Sauternes or a Barsac. This would be an adventurous choice, but in wine—as in the food it joins—adventurousness often produces the greatest rewards.

A Primer of Shellfish Cookery

The chart below shows the cooking methods most appropriate for various common forms of shellfish—and the minimum number of minutes to allow for each process. For live lobsters, the timing is given in the minutes per pound [½ kg.] required by each animal. Thus one or six 2 pound [1 kg.] lobsters require 50 minutes of poaching.

All other timings shown are for a potful of shellfish, regardless of the size of the specimens in the pot; where the sizes of whole or cut-up shellfish may differ widely, a range of times is shown. For example, one live blue crab or a dozen will require 20 minutes of poaching; and 1 or 5 pounds [½ or 2½ kg.] of shrimp will need one

to three minutes, depending on the size of the shrimp.

To use the chart, locate the kind of shellfish you wish to cook in the left-hand column and read across that line to determine what methods are suitable. Then consult the techniques demonstrated in this volume for guidelines to each method.

Shellfish	Minutes of Cooking According to Method							
	Poach	Steam	Stew	Sauté	Stir Fry	Deep Fry	Bake	Broil
Abalone, shucked and diced	—	—	15-20	—	—	—	—	—
Abalone, shucked, tenderized and sliced	—	—	—	1-2	1	—	—	2
Geoduck clams, shucked, sliced and tenderized	—	—	30	1-2	1	3-5	—	—
Hard-shell and Pacific littleneck clams, live	—	5-7	—	—	—	—	8-10	—
Hard-shell and Pacific littleneck clams, on the half shell	—	—	—	—	—	—	5-8	3-4
Hard-shell and Pacific littleneck clams, shucked	2-3	—	—	1-2	1	1-2	—	—
Razor clams, shucked and chopped	—	—	15-20	3-5	2-3	3-5	—	—
Soft-shell clams, live	—	5-7	—	—	—	—	—	—
Soft-shell clams, shucked	2-3	—	—	2-3	1	1-2	—	—
Conch, shucked, tenderized and diced	—	—	90-180	3-5	2-3	—	—	—
Blue crabs, live	20	—	20	—	—	—	—	—
Blue crabs, cut into pieces	—	—	7-10	4-5	2-3	—	—	—
Dungeness crabs, live	25-30	—	25-30	—	—	—	—	—
Dungeness crabs, cut into pieces	—	—	10-15	5-7	4-5	—	—	—
King, spider or stone crab legs or claws	—	—	—	—	—	—	7-10	2
Soft-shell crabs, live	—	—	—	5-7	—	3-5	10	5
Crayfish	5-7	—	5-7	3	2	1-2	10	2-3
Lobsters, American and spiny, live (per pound [½ kg.])	25	—	—	—	—	—	—	—
Lobsters, halved, in the shell	—	—	—	—	—	—	10-15	7
Lobster pieces, in the shell	10-15	—	10-25	5-7	3-4	—	—	—
Malaysian prawns	1-3	—	1-3	1-3	1-2	1-2	10	2-3
Mussels, live	—	5-7	—	—	—	—	7	—
Octopus, cleaned, tenderized and cut into pieces	—	—	45-90	1-3	1-2	2-3	—	—
Oysters, live	—	—	—	—	—	—	8-10	—
Oysters, on the half shell	—	—	—	—	—	—	5-8	½-4
Oysters, shucked	1-3	—	1-3	1-3	1	1-2	—	—
Periwinkles, live	1-3	—	—	—	—	—	—	—
Rock shrimp	1-2	—	1-2	2-3	1-2	1-2	5-8	2-3
Bay scallops, shucked	2	—	2	1-2	1-2	1-2	5-8	2-3
Sea scallops, shucked	4	—	4	2-3	2-3	2-3	5-8	3-4
Sea urchin roe	—	—	—	4	—	—	—	—
Shrimp	1-3	—	1-3	3-4	2-3	1-2	10	2-3
Squid, cleaned, tenderized and cut into pieces	2	—	20-45	1-3	1-2	1-2	—	—

A Marvelous Diversity of Mollusks

The 31 shellfish illustrated on these and the following pages—drawn to a sliding scale *(box, below)*—are a representative sampling of the hundreds of species that are available in North America. To indicate species that share common characteristics and often are interchangeable in cooking, the shellfish are grouped by type. Mollusks appear here, sea urchins and crustaceans on pages 10-11. There are three categories of mollusks—cephalopods, which recall prehistoric mollusks in having no shells, and the more highly evolved univalves and bivalves.

The shellfish are identified by their most common market names, although many also have local designations. In New England, for example, the hard-shell clam is sometimes called a little-neck if small, a cherrystone if medium-sized and a chowder clam if large.

The guide also shows where different species are found, when they are harvested, and characteristics of the flesh—taste, texture, tenderness—that help determine how they should be cooked.

In buying shellfish the most important guidelines are those that indicate freshness: Most species are highly perishable.

The best approach is to buy univalves and bivalves live. To test a conch or periwinkle, touch the movable disk, or operculum, at its shell opening. A live specimen will retract it. An abalone has a dark fringe around the edge of its shell that also retracts at a touch.

Oysters, mussels and most clams usually keep their shells tightly closed out of the water; a live animal will snap shut its shell if tapped. Soft-shell and geoduck clams are exceptions; their siphons, or necks, protrude from the shells and retract at a touch if the animals are alive. Scallops never totally close their shells, but live ones will move them slightly if tapped. Discard unusually light or heavy bivalves: They are probably dead—the heavy ones sealed shut with mud.

Cephalopods are never sold live. To determine freshness, you must use your eyes and nose. Fresh squid has cream-colored skin with mauve patches; octopus has even-colored, purplish black skin. Neither should smell fishy.

A Sliding Scale for Judging Size

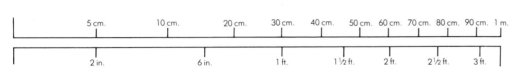

Gauging size. To show species of different sizes on the same pages, length is represented here according to the sliding scale at left. Thus the octopus and the long-finned squid below appear fairly close in length, but the average octopus is nearly 1 foot [30 cm.] longer than the average squid.

Cephalopods: A Family of Tentacled Swimmers

Octopus and squid. Octopus and long-finned squid are harvested on both coasts; short-finned squid on the Atlantic only. All are most available during autumn and winter. Both octopus and squid can grow as long as 55 feet [167 meters], but those marketed are usually no longer than a foot [30 cm.]. Both have mild-tasting body pouches and tentacles; their flesh is firm and somewhat chewy.

Octopus

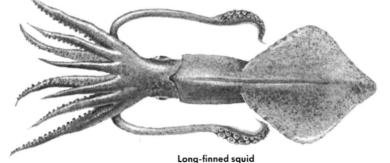

Long-finned squid

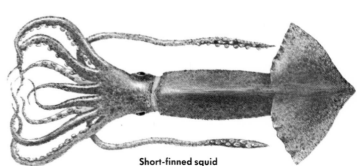

Short-finned squid

Among the univalves, conch and abalone are often sold shucked. Conch flesh should be white with overtones of red or purple; gray indicates deterioration. Abalone flesh should be creamy white or beige. Both should smell sweet.

Of the bivalves, scallops are almost always sold after shucking; clams and oysters are available shucked as well as in the shell. In all cases, the flesh should be plump, even in color and sweet-smelling.

Live or not, shellfish bought from a market must be kept in the refrigerator and used within 24 hours; tightly closed bivalves that you gather yourself can be kept for 10 days. Cover live specimens loosely, but store shucked meats or cephalopods in tightly closed containers.

Univalves: Snails of the Sea

Periwinkle, abalone and conch. The Atlantic yields the assertive, chewy periwinkle—and related, larger whelk—from spring to autumn in the North and the conch year-round in Florida. Milder abalone is harvested from the Pacific in spring and autumn.

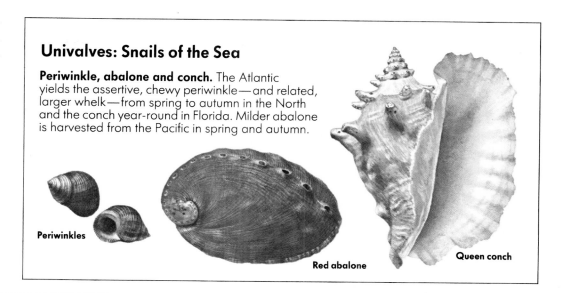

Periwinkles

Red abalone

Queen conch

Bivalves: Clams and Their Cousins

Sea scallop

Bay scallop

Scallops. The large sea scallop lives in Atlantic waters; the small bay scallop and similar calico scallop *(page 17)* inhabit Atlantic estuaries and bays. Related species of both sizes are found in the Pacific. Tender and sweet-tasting, scallops are harvested year-round.

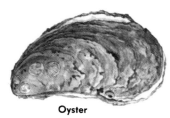

Oyster

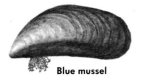

Blue mussel

Clams. Tender-fleshed hard-shell clams—quahogs—thrive in the Atlantic; tender littleneck and tough geoduck clams are Pacific species. All are available year-round. Tough razor clams (a Pacific variety is shown) and tender soft-shell clams—steamers—inhabit both oceans and are in peak supply in summer. All clam flesh is sweet-tasting.

Hard-shell clam
Quahog

Pacific littleneck clam

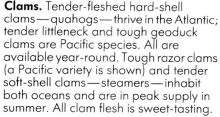

Soft-shell clam
Steamer clam

Geoduck

Oysters and mussels. Oysters live in shallow water along temperate and tropical coasts. Their tender, briny flesh is edible all year but usually tastes best from September through April. The blue mussel is harvested on the Atlantic and Pacific coasts year-round; its tender flesh has a distinctive, smoky taste.

Northern razor clam

Armored Denizens of Sea and Streams

Among the hundreds of crustaceans and lesser known sea urchins available in North America are the 15 specimens—representing a range of different types—displayed here in drawings made to the sliding scale shown on page 8. To shop for shellfish intelligently, the cook should understand how each type is sold and the signs of freshness it should display.

Seven of the shellfish pictured—red and green sea urchins, blue and Dungeness crabs, crayfish, and American and spiny lobsters—are sold live in areas near their native waters. (American lobster, the only one of the group that survives well in marine tanks, also is sold live throughout the country.) Once dead, these shellfish deteriorate quickly: They must remain active until they are used. You should be able to discern movement in a sea urchin's spines and around its mouth. Crabs should wave their claws energetically; lobsters should curl their tails tightly when lifted. After buying them, keep these shellfish refrigerated; use them the same day.

Shrimp and Malaysian prawns also are sold fresh, but they are seldom available live. When fresh, the flesh of these shellfish will feel firm and smell sweet: There should be no odor of ammonia, a sign of deterioration. Shrimp and prawns also are available frozen, or frozen and thawed. The same standards of quality apply to frozen and fresh specimens.

The edible parts of particularly perishable crustaceans are generally sold only in cooked, frozen form. These include stone-crab claws and the legs and claws of spider and king crabs; all are sold still in their shells to help retain the moisture of the flesh. Examine the exposed flesh at the joints for dull white patches, which indicate that the shellfish have been improperly handled and that their flesh has dried out. Claws and legs—like all frozen shellfish—should be defrosted thoroughly in the refrigerator before use.

It also is possible to buy only the flesh of some types of shellfish. Sea urchin roe is sold at Asian markets. Cooked crab meat is generally available at fish markets and supermarkets. Both should be sweet-smelling and must be used within one day of purchase.

Sea Urchins

Spiny orbs. Both the large Pacific red sea urchin and the smaller green sea urchin, which is harvested in the Pacific and Atlantic from autumn through spring, yield a mass of orange-colored granules that are the eggs and sperm, but are commonly referred to as the roe. This roe—the only edible part of sea urchins—has a fragile texture and distinctive, slightly briny taste, and can be eaten raw or sautéed.

Red sea urchin

Green sea urchin

Marine Crustaceans

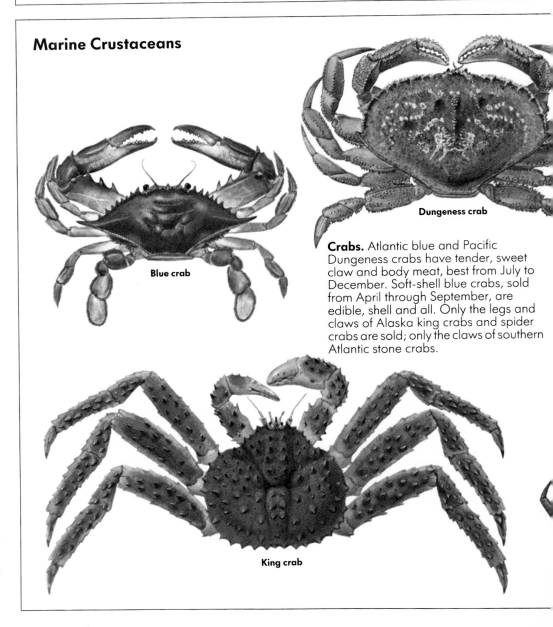

Blue crab

Dungeness crab

King crab

Crabs. Atlantic blue and Pacific Dungeness crabs have tender, sweet claw and body meat, best from July to December. Soft-shell blue crabs, sold from April through September, are edible, shell and all. Only the legs and claws of Alaska king crabs and spider crabs are sold; only the claws of southern Atlantic stone crabs.

Fresh-water Crustaceans

Prawns and crayfish. The delectable Malaysian prawn is now cultivated in the United States— notably South Carolina and Hawaii— and harvested in the autumn. Crayfish are harvested from rivers and ponds throughout the continent from spring through autumn. The tail meat of crayfish and prawn is edible. Both are similar to shrimp in texture but have a sweeter flavor.

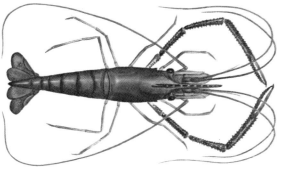

Malaysian prawn

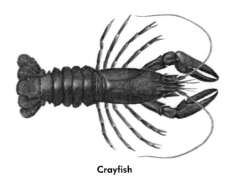

Crayfish

Shrimp. Brown, white and pink shrimp from the Gulf and southern Atlantic waters represent one among hundreds of similar species found year-round on every coast. All have firm flesh and a salty flavor. Florida's rock shrimp have a thicker shell and even firmer flesh.

Brown shrimp

White shrimp

Pink shrimp

Rock shrimp

Lobsters. The spiny lobster is found along the coasts of Florida, the Gulf of Mexico and California; only its tail is meaty. The American lobster, found in the Atlantic from Newfoundland to Cape Hatteras, yields meat from its claws as well as its tail. The meat of both lobsters is firm, and prized for its succulence.

Spiny lobster

Stone crab

Spider crab
Snow crab

American lobster

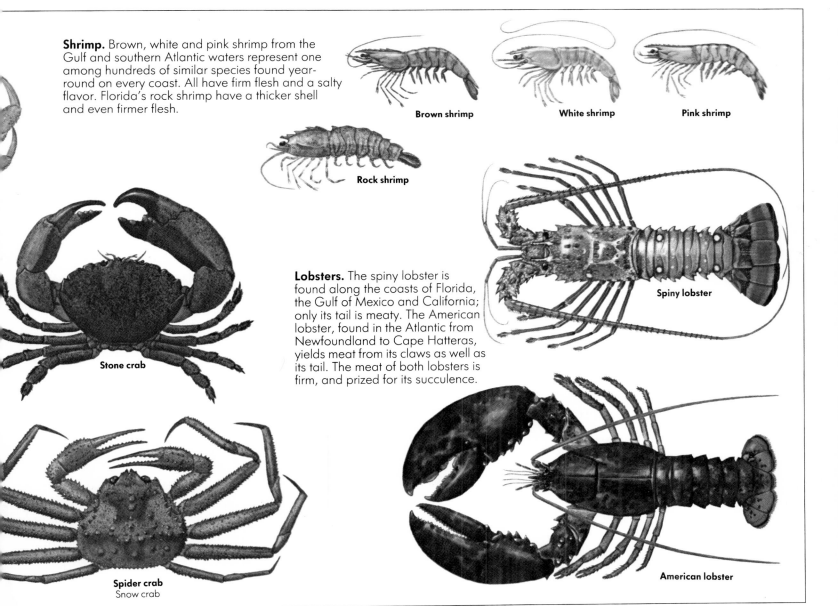

Making Cephalopods Ready for the Pot

The edible parts of both squid and octopus include a fleshy body pouch, long tentacles and—within the animals—an ink sac whose briny-tasting fluid sometimes is used as a flavoring *(page 53)*. Additionally, squid have edible fins. Separating the meat from the inedible parts of the cephalopods takes little effort, although the natures of the animals dictate minor variations in technique. The cleaning of a squid, for instance, begins with the removal of a shell-like support structure called a pen from within its body; an octopus has no pen.

Except for this initial step, the cutting up of either creature proceeds in much the same way: The tentacles are separated from the body pouch, and the viscera and other organs removed and discarded. Within the viscera of each animal lies the ink sac *(Step 2, opposite, below)*.

After they have been separated into segments, the cephalopods must be skinned. The thin, translucent skin of a squid is easily peeled by hand. If the squid is longer than 8 inches [20 cm.], the suckers that lie under the tentacle skin should be scraped off with a knife: They are sharp in large squid.

The skin of an octopus clings. Rub the flesh with salt, which abrades the skin so that it can be peeled by hand. After peeling, soak the flesh in cold water for about 20 minutes to remove the salt. Alternatively, cover the octopus flesh with simmering water and poach it for two minutes to loosen the skin for peeling. You need not remove octopus suckers.

Most American cooks find the pouch meat of squid and octopus tough and prefer to tenderize it before cooking. To break down tough fibers, cooks pound the outside of a squid's pouch with a mallet; tougher octopus pouches must first be pounded on the outside, then turned inside out and pounded again.

Cooking methods chosen for squid and octopus also will affect tenderness. Both are tender if fried or poached for no longer than two minutes, but require relatively longer cooking if braised *(pages 52-53)*. The explanation of this paradox is simple: After two minutes of cooking, squid and octopus flesh begins to dry and toughen and lengthy cooking in liquid is needed to moisten and tenderize it again.

Separating Squid into Edible Segments

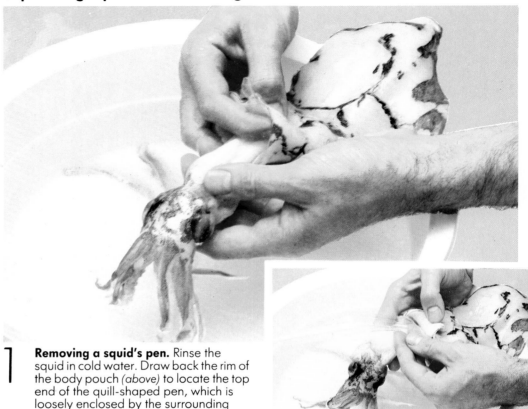

1 **Removing a squid's pen.** Rinse the squid in cold water. Draw back the rim of the body pouch *(above)* to locate the top end of the quill-shaped pen, which is loosely enclosed by the surrounding flesh. Grasp the pen by its tip and gently pull it free *(inset)*. Discard the pen.

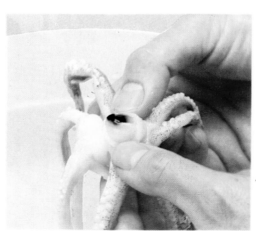

5 **Removing the beak.** Within the rim of edible flesh that connects the tentacles lies a bony, beaklike mouth, complete with rasping teeth. With your fingers, squeeze the beak out of the fleshy rim; discard the beak.

6 **The end result.** Spread on a plate, ready for cooking *(page 52)*, the four edible pieces of squid flesh: the pouch, the tentacles and the two triangular fins. Frozen squid that has been thawed and cleaned should be used immediately; covered with plastic wrap, fresh squid can be stored in a refrigerator for one day.

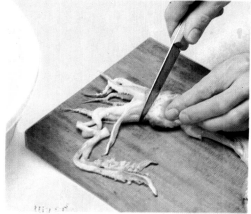

2 **Freeing the pouch.** Hold the body pouch in one hand; with the other, grasp the head just below the eyes. Gently pull the two sections apart. The viscera, including the ink sac, should come away with the head and the tentacles, if not, scrape out the viscera. Rinse the pouch in cold water and pull away the mucous membrane that lines it.

3 **Skinning the pouch.** Translucent skin, irregularly patterned with mauve patches, covers the creamy white flesh of the squid's pouch. Slip a finger under the skin and peel it off. Carefully pull the edible, triangular fins from either side of the pouch. Skin the fins.

4 **Severing the tentacles.** Using a sharp knife, cut off the tentacles from the rest of the head, slicing just below the eyes. The tentacles should come away together, connected by a narrow rim of edible flesh. If you plan to cook the squid in its ink, separate the silvery gray ink sac from the viscera. Discard the head and viscera.

Cutting Octopus without Breaking the Ink Sac

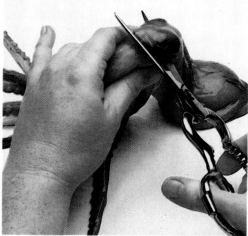

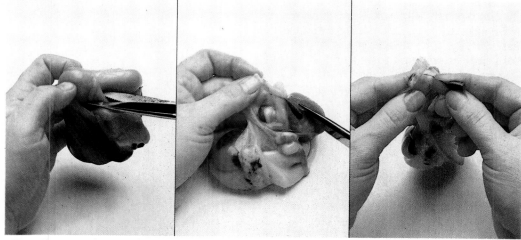

1 **Severing the tentacles.** Rinse the octopus in cold water. Grasping the tentacles of the octopus below its head in one hand, sever the tentacles by using kitchen shears to cut through the flesh just below the eyes. Invert the tentacles and squeeze out the beak in the same way as for squid *(Step 5, left)*. Then discard the beak.

2 **Cleaning the pouch.** Turn the pouch inside out to expose the membrane that holds the viscera in place. Pierce the membrane near the opening of the pouch *(above, left)* and cut completely around its edge, severing the membrane and freeing the viscera and the eyes. Remove the viscera from the pouch and locate the ink sac, which lies adjacent to the liver, a large, reddish brown organ. The ink sac is encased in several membranes; cut through them to free the sac *(center)*. Avoid puncturing or squeezing the delicate sac. Carefully lift out the ink sac *(right)* and then discard the viscera and the eyes. Rinse the pouch and turn it right side out.

Preparing Univalves and Sea Urchins

The heavy shell of abalone, the convolutions of a conch and the spiny covering of a sea urchin would suggest that extracting the flesh of these univalves is a formidable task. In fact, once the structure of each animal is understood, the process is not at all difficult.

An abalone consists of a mushroom-shaped piece of flesh. The stem section is a muscle that attaches the flesh to its single, bowl-shaped shell. The cap section—actually the creature's foot—includes a solid piece of flesh perforated by a mouth and an intestinal vein and covered with tough skin. The flesh is simply pried away from the shell with the aid of a wooden spatula or an abalone shucker—a short-handled, spatula-like implement sold at diving-equipment shops on the West Coast. After the flesh is skinned and cleaned *(right, top)* and before it can be used, it must be tenderized by pounding *(pages 56-57)*, which breaks down the tough muscle fibers.

Conch flesh is an elongated mass hidden within a whorled, conical shell. The flesh and organs are covered by a tough skin and attached by a muscle to the spiked top of the shell—the so-called crown of the conch. The flesh near the shell opening tapers into a tough claw-like shape known as the operculum; this is the animal's door, used to shut the shell when necessary. You must break a hole in the shell near the crown so that you can sever the attaching muscle. After this, you can pull out the flesh and clean it *(right, below)*. Conch flesh must be tenderized by pounding and parboiling *(pages 46-47)*.

A sea urchin shell is a spine-covered sphere containing viscera and the urchin's edible roe. You must protect your hand with a cloth when holding the shell: The spines can cause painful wounds. To extract the contents, cut open the top of the shell—the animal's round mouth—as if removing the lid from a pumpkin; once the viscera are shaken out, the roe is clearly visible *(opposite, top)*. Sea urchin roe is highly perishable and should be used within eight hours. It is most often eaten raw, with a little lemon juice for flavor; however, it also can be steamed or fried *(page 56)*.

Prying Out Abalone Flesh

1 **Extracting the flesh.** Slide the blade of an abalone shucker, as here, or a sturdy wooden spatula under the edges of the abalone flesh around the rim of the shell and pry up the flesh. When you have freed the flesh around the edges, work the shucker underneath the stemlike muscle to sever it.

2 **Cleaning the abalone.** With a small, sharp knife, cut away the soft viscera that surround the abalone's stemlike muscle. Discard them. Cut away and discard the dark skin from around the edges and across the surface of the abalone flesh. Cut away and discard the mouth and dark intestinal vein at one end of the flesh.

Severing a Conch's Hidden Muscle

1 **Opening the shell.** Hold a conch crown side up, and with a hammer knock a hole in the shell at a point about 1 inch [2½ cm.] below the top. Make the hole large enough to accept the blade of a small knife.

2 **Severing the muscle.** Fit the blade of a small, sharp knife through the hole in the shell. Angle the blade toward the top of the conch and move the blade back and forth to sever the muscle that attaches the flesh to the crown.

Preparing Sea Urchin

1 **Cutting an opening.** Hold the sea urchin with its dimpled mouth uppermost, using a cloth to protect your hand. Insert the tips of kitchen shears into the center of the mouth and make a cut to the edge. Then cut around the edge of the mouth to form a removable lid.

2 **Lifting out the lid.** Grasp the mouth between the tips of the shears, lift it out and discard it. Invert the sea urchin and shake it gently to empty the viscera from the shell.

3 **Removing the roe.** With a spoon, scoop out the orange roe, which lies in a star formation at the bottom of the urchin's shell. Place the roe in a bowl, cover it and refrigerate it. The roe can safely be kept for up to eight hours.

3 **Extracting the flesh.** Grasp the flat, hard operculum that protrudes from the mouth of the shell and pull on it to extract the freed flesh.

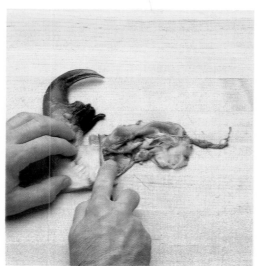

4 **Removing viscera.** Using a sharp knife, cut away and discard all the soft parts — the viscera and eyes — from the crown end of the conch's flesh. Find the intestinal vein that runs down the length of the conch and cut it out. Under cold running water, rinse the channel where the vein was removed.

5 **Removing the skin.** Starting from the channel where the vein was removed, peel off and discard the conch's skin. Use the knife to cut away any tough, stubborn bits of orange membrane and the operculum.

Preparing the Various Bivalves

Although the techniques are adjusted to suit the characteristics of particular types of shellfish, most live bivalves are opened in essentially the same way—the two half shells are pried apart and the flesh within is cut free. But before cooking whole oysters, mussels or clams—or before serving them raw—you must sort through all the specimens to ensure that each one is alive—signs are described on pages 8-9—and, if the bivalves are to be cooked in their shells or half shells, you must clean them thoroughly.

For most bivalves, a thorough scrubbing with a stiff brush under cold running water is necessary (right, top). Because the brittle shells of soft-shell clams are easily broken, these are best rinsed and rubbed clean with your hands. And mussels have barnacles and the fibrous strands called beards attached to their shells; both must be removed just before cooking (right, center).

Controversy exists about the further cleaning of these shellfish. Some cooks maintain that bivalves should be soaked so they will expel sand and grit. This can be done in one or two hours using several changes of salted water made with ⅓ cup [75 ml.] of noniodized salt for each gallon [4 liters] of cold water—or in up to 24 hours using salted water mixed with a small amount of cornmeal. Other cooks insist that any soaking diminish-es the natural flavors of the shellfish.

Whether soaked or not, both clams and oysters will be easier to open if refrigerated for two or three hours or frozen for up to one hour.

Different tools are needed to pry open the various bivalve shells. Scallops (opposite, bottom) and mussels—the latter are opened only for stuffing, as demonstrated on page 51—can be opened with any sturdy kitchen knife. For clams (right, top), most cooks prefer a clam knife with a straight blade and rounded tip: The blunt tip diminishes the chances of slicing up the clam flesh as you sever the two muscles that bind it to its shells. For oysters (below), use an oyster knife with a short, strong blade, a pointed tip and a heavy hand guard at the base of the handle. The tip will pierce the oysters' thick hinges; the rigid blade and hand guard serve as protections while opening the oysters, a process that often requires considerable force. Both types of knives are sold at kitchen-equipment shops and seafood markets.

Two clams require additional cleaning after they are opened and the flesh is detached from the shells; the tough, dark membrane that covers the necks of soft-shell and geoduck clams must be peeled away (opposite, bottom). Scallops contain inedible viscera that must be removed before the flesh and roe are eaten.

Shucking a Hard-shell Clam

1 **Cleaning.** Using a stiff vegetable brush, scrub the clam shells under cold running water to remove any surface mud or grit.

Debearding a Mussel

Removing beards. Scrub the mussels under cold running water. Pull out the strands that emerge from the shells. Scrape off surface encrustations.

Forcing Open an Oyster

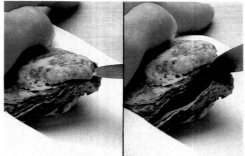

1 **Opening.** Hold the oyster in a heavy cloth, flatter shell upward. Insert the tip of an oyster knife into the hinge (above, left) and twist it to open the shells (right).

2 **Severing the muscle.** Slide the knife along the inside of the upper shell to cut the muscle that attaches it to the flesh. Pull off and discard the upper shell.

3 **Cutting the oyster loose.** Slide the knife under the oyster to free it from the lower shell. Remove any bits of broken shell with the point of the knife.

2 **Opening.** Slide the blade of a clam knife between the shell halves at a point opposite the hinge *(above, left)*. Twist the blade to force the halves apart *(right)*.

3 **Freeing one half shell.** Slide the cutting edge of the blade along the inside of one half shell to sever the ends of the two muscles that hold it.

4 **Cutting the clam loose.** Twist off the freed half shell. Run the blade under the clam to sever the other ends of the muscles holding it to the other half shell.

Peeling the Neck of a Soft-shell Clam

1 **Opening the shells.** Insert a clam knife into the shell just above or below the protruding neck and sever the muscle that attaches the clam to one half shell.

2 **Cutting the clam loose.** Twist off and discard the freed shell. Slide the knife blade under the clam to cut it free from the remaining half shell.

3 **Skinning the neck.** Pull off and discard the blackish skin that covers the neck of the clam and the trailing membrane around the edge of the shell.

Opening and Cleaning a Scallop

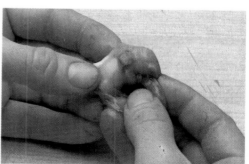

1 **Opening.** Insert a blade between the scallop's half shells—here, a calico scallop—to part them. Run the blade inside one shell to cut the muscle.

2 **Cutting the scallop loose.** Break the hinge open and discard the freed shell. Run the knife under the scallop to free it from the remaining shell *(above)*.

3 **Cleaning.** Pull apart the white flesh and the orange coral, or roe, from the grayish viscera. Discard the viscera. Both flesh and coral are edible.

Preparing Lobster, Shrimp, Crayfish and Prawns

Lobsters, shrimp, crayfish and prawns usually are poached whole in their shells, but a number of recipes—including lobster *à l'américaine (page 50)*—call for these crustaceans to be cut up or shelled before cooking. The object is to clean the meat of unpalatable debris and divide it into neat pieces.

Spiny lobster and American lobster are sold live, and when cooked whole, are killed by the heat; if you plan to cut up these lobsters before cooking, you must kill them *(Step 1, opposite and Step 1, below)*. Either type of lobster then may be halved and cleaned of viscera. Both types contain gray green tomalley, or liver, that should be removed and reserved for flavoring. Female lobsters—

which are distinguishable from males because the pair of appendages just behind their legs are soft rather than hard—contain masses of dark green to black roe that also should be reserved.

After cleaning, the tail of a spiny lobster may be cut into sections for cooking. American lobster tails and claws also may be cut up. The shells generally are left on both crustaceans to keep the meat moist and flavorful.

Shrimp usually have been beheaded; if you should purchase shrimp with heads, simply twist them off. The entire body —actually the shrimp's tail—is edible and cleaning is a matter of peeling off the shell and cutting out the often gritty intestinal vein *(bottom left)*. Most spe-

cies of shrimp are peeled with the fingers; the tougher shells of rock shrimp require scissors.

Crayfish are sold live and are cooked in their shells; the tails contain both the meat and the intestinal veins, and there is disagreement about cleaning them. Many cooks find the vein bitter and remove it before cooking *(bottom right)*; others remove it after cooking in the manner used for shrimp. Some cooks do not devein crayfish at all.

Malaysian prawns also are most often cooked whole, and their tails do not need deveining. For certain dishes prawns as well as shrimp *(pages 74-77)* are peeled and butterflied to flatten them for even cooking *(opposite, bottom)*.

Sectioning an American Lobster

1 **Killing the lobster.** Steady the lobster right side up. With a knife tip, pierce the shell and flesh at the center of the cross-shaped mark behind the head.

2 **Splitting.** Halve the lobster *(Step 2, opposite, top)* and locate the gravel sac near the head, the tomalley, the intestinal vein in the tail and the roe, if any.

3 **Cleaning.** Discard the gravel sac *(above)* and intestinal vein. Spoon out and reserve the tomalley and roe; they can be added to a sauce *(page 50)*.

Peeling a Shrimp

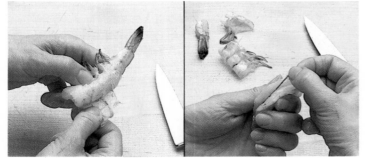

Peeling and deveining. Starting from the head end, use your thumbs to peel off the shrimp's shell and attached legs *(above, left)*. Pinch off the tail shell. Slit the shrimp down its back and lift out the intestinal vein *(above, right)*.

Deveining a Crayfish

Deveining. Press the body of a live crayfish flat against the work surface with one hand as you lift the center tail flap and twist it gently to free it *(above, left)*. Pull the freed tail flap away from the body to remove the intestinal vein *(right)*.

Dividing a Spiny-Lobster Tail

1 **Killing the lobster.** Steady the lobster on its back and stab the point of a heavy, sharp knife into its mouth to sever the spinal cord.

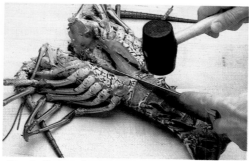

2 **Splitting the lobster.** Halve the lobster lengthwise: Place the knife along the underside and tap on the blade with a mallet to force it through the body.

3 **Cleaning.** Hold each lobster half under cold running water to rinse the viscera from the body and the intestinal vein from the tail.

4 **Dividing the halves.** Twist off and reserve the claws. Using a knife, sever each lobster half between the tail and the body *(above)*.

5 **Dividing the tail.** Slice the lobster's tail between each two segments of shell *(above)* to divide it into sections, but leave the shell in place.

6 **Cracking the claws.** Crack open the claws and their adjacent joints—with pincers, as here, or with a wooden mallet—but do not extract the meat.

Butterflying a Malaysian Prawn

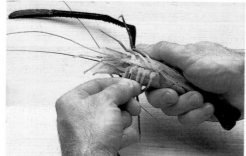

1 **Removing claws.** With your hands, twist off and discard the claws. Snip the feelers off with scissors. The prawn may now be cooked.

2 **Separating the tail.** Peel off all but the last section of the tail shell. Then twist the body and tail sections apart. Discard the body.

3 **Butterflying the tail.** With a knife, slice down the back of the tail, cutting almost but not quite all the way through. Flatten the tail slightly.

Preparing Crabs

The preparation required for live crabs depends on whether they are soft-shell, harvested during their molting period, or hard-shell varieties and—for hard-shell crabs—on how they are to be cooked. In any case, cleaning is a simple affair.

Soft-shell crabs should be held under cold running water to rinse off any bits of sea grass or moss, and their inedible parts should be removed. When this is properly done *(right)*, the body will remain in one piece and every bit, including the shell, can be eaten after the crab is fried or broiled *(pages 56-57)*.

Hard-shell crabs should be scrubbed clean under cold running water; they then may simply be poached or steamed whole. However, many stewing and stir-frying recipes call for cut-up crabs. To produce neat pieces, you must kill the crabs and remove inedible parts before dividing the bodies into segments. The technique is demonstrated here with a Dungeness crab *(bottom)*, but the same process applies to hard-shell blue crabs.

Cleaning a Soft-shell Crab

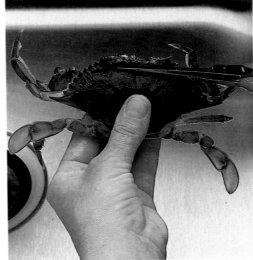

1 **Killing the crab.** Grasp the crab body between the back legs and hold it over a sink. With kitchen shears, cut across the body just behind the crab's eyes to remove the face and thus kill the crab. With your fingers, reach into the cavity revealed by the cut and pull out the grayish, pouchlike stomach—called the sand bag. Discard the sand bag.

2 **Lifting the apron.** Turn the crab over. With your fingers pry up the narrow tip of the flap, or apron, on the crab's underside. On a female crab, the apron will be triangular; on a male crab, as shown here, the apron will be T-shaped. Fold the apron down, away from the crab's body.

Splitting a Hard-shell Crab

1 **Killing the crab.** Grasp the crab firmly between the hind legs and steady it, right side up, against the work surface. With the point of a sharp knife, stab the crab once—forcefully—just behind the eyes to kill it instantly.

2 **Removing the apron.** Turn the crab over. Pry up the tip of the tail flap, or apron, and fold it back. Then twist off and discard the apron, along with the attached intestinal vein.

3 **Removing the top shell.** Turn the crab right side up. Grasp the top shell at the back where the apron was removed; pry up and tear off the top shell.

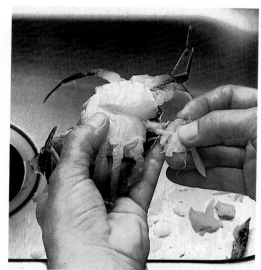

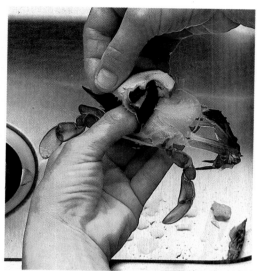

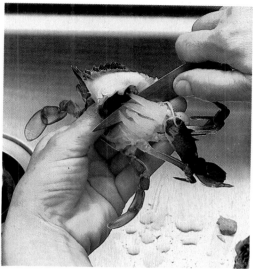

3 **Removing the intestinal vein.** Pull the apron gently out from the crab's body to remove the apron and the intestinal vein attached to it. Discard the apron and intestinal vein.

4 **Exposing the gills.** Turn the crab right side up. Gently lift the tapering point on one side of the top shell and fold it back to expose the spongy gills—called dead-man's fingers.

5 **Removing the gills.** With a small, sharp kitchen knife, scrape off and discard the exposed gills (above). Fold back the tapering point on the other side of the top shell to expose the gills; remove and discard them.

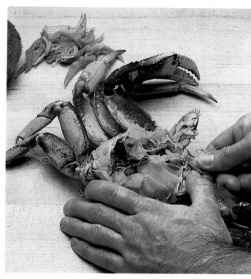

4 **Removing the gills.** Using your fingers, as here, or a small knife, remove and discard the spongy gills from each side of the crab's exposed top and the grayish sand bag from its center. With a Dungeness crab, as here, pull out and discard the mouth and its appendages—called the mandibles—from the front of the crab.

5 **Splitting the crab.** Grasping the crab's body at the sides where the legs are attached, apply pressure so that the crab will crack in half along the center of its body.

6 **Dividing the halves.** Fold the crab halves back and twist them apart (above). Starting at the end with the smallest leg, break one crab half into three segments, with two legs or the claw attached to each piece of the body. Crack every joint of the legs and claw with a nutcracker. Repeat to divide the other crab half into segments.

An Aromatic Base of Many Uses

Although shellfish often are steamed, poached or stewed in plain or salted water, their tastes will be greatly enhanced if the water has been flavored with other ingredients to make the aromatic fish stock demonstrated here *(recipe, page 163)* or the simpler court bouillon shown in the box on the opposite page. Both of these preparations offer a bonus as well: They can form the bases of the aspic that garnishes cold shellfish presentations *(pages 82-83)* and of the sauces used to swathe hot ones *(pages 24-25)*.

A classic fish stock consists of water simmered with fish trimmings—heads, bones and skin—as well as dry wine and aromatic vegetables and herbs. The fish should be of a lean variety: Use flounder, sole, whiting or bass. Oily fish such as salmon or mackerel would produce too strong-tasting a stock. For clear stock, rinse blood clots from the trimmings under cold water. For extra flavor, add crushed raw or cooked crustacean shells.

Other flavorings for the stock may be chosen at the cook's discretion. The wine may be white or red, and added in the quantity you prefer. For a mild taste, add the wine at the beginning of cooking so that its alcohol will evaporate. For a more assertive taste, add the wine halfway through cooking. Suitable aromatic vegetables include onions, leeks, garlic, celery and carrots. Among the herbs that complement shellfish are parsley, bay leaves, thyme, dill and fennel; the quantities depend on how emphatic you want the fragrance to be.

To extract the most flavor from stock ingredients, simmer them very gently— never boil them lest they disintegrate and cloud the liquid—for 30 minutes, no longer. If overcooked, fish trimmings will make the stock bitter.

After straining, the stock is ready for use as a cooking medium or sauce base. If you wish to use the stock for aspic, you must reinforce it with gelatin, which gives it enough body to set when chilled. And, for aspic of sparkling clarity, you must clarify the fish stock by cooking it with beaten egg whites and crushed eggshells: They both contain proteins called albumin, which attract and trap impurities in the stock that then can be removed by straining.

1 Assembling ingredients. Slice carrots and onions, split and rinse a leek, and dice a celery rib. Rinse fish trimmings—in this case, the heads and the bones of sole and whiting; remove and discard the bitter gills. Break up the skeletons. Put the ingredients into a large pan with parsley, thyme and a bay leaf. Cover them with cold water; salt lightly.

2 Skimming. Bring the liquid to a boil, skimming the scum that forms on the surface as the liquid reaches a simmer. Reduce the heat and simmer for 15 minutes, uncovered. Add dry white wine—up to one part of wine to one part of water. Simmer for 15 minutes more, but do not overcook, lest the fish bones make the liquid bitter.

5 Adding gelatin. Decant the clear liquid into a pan, leaving the solids behind, and warm it over medium heat. In a small bowl, soften powdered gelatin by soaking it in cold water for a few minutes. Stir in some of the heated stock to dissolve the gelatin, then stir the mixture into the rest of the stock. To make sure the stock will jell, test it by refrigerating a spoonful; if it fails to set within 10 minutes, add more dissolved gelatin to the stock.

6 Clarifying. Beat egg whites to soft peaks. Add the whites and crushed eggshells to the stock and whisk over high heat. As the stock comes to a boil, the whites will rise and coagulate. After the stock bubbles up through the egg layer, take the pan off the heat for 10 minutes to let the foam settle and bond with the particles. To make sure the stock is absolutely clear, repeat the boiling and resting steps twice.

3 **Straining.** Pour the stock through a colander set in a deep bowl. If the stock is intended for a clear sauce or an aspic, do not press the solids—you will cloud the liquid. The stock is now ready for use in poaching, steaming or stewing.

4 **Removing particles.** If the stock is to be used for aspic, strain the liquid again, using a sieve lined with dampened cheesecloth or muslin. Refrigerate the stock for several hours to allow the fine solids it contains to settle.

7 **Straining the aspic.** Line a sieve with four layers of dampened cheesecloth or muslin. Place it over a deep bowl and slowly pour in the stock. Let the liquid drip through the cloth. Refrain from squeezing the cloth to hasten the process; you might force impurities through. Let the strained stock cool to room temperature. Store the aspic in the refrigerator.

A Wine-scented Court Bouillon

A court bouillon for shellfish consists of nothing more than water cooked with an acidic liquid—either dry wine or wine vinegar—and aromatic vegetables and herbs. The wine may be red or white and may be used in whatever quantity you prefer. If you use wine vinegar, whether red or white, keep its proportions to no more than ¼ cup [50 ml.] for each 2 cups [½ liter] of water; otherwise the court bouillon will have a harsh taste. The suitable vegetables and herbs are the same as for fish stock.

The ingredients are simmered together for 30 to 40 minutes to draw out their flavors, then the solids are strained out to ready the court bouillon for use in poaching or steaming. After it has been used to cook shellfish and has absorbed their flavor, it will be rich enough to be turned into aspic *(Steps 5-7, left)* or a sauce base.

Adding wine. Prepare vegetables and herbs as for a fish stock *(Step 1, opposite, top)*. Add them to a pan of cold water and salt lightly. Simmer, uncovered, for 15 minutes, then pour in wine—here, dry white wine. Simmer, uncovered, for 15 minutes more, adding a few peppercorns at the end of cooking. Strain before using.

A Gallery of Garnishes

The sauces used for garnishing shellfish assemblies *(recipes, pages 163-166)* all are based on simple ingredients—butter, eggs, flour, oil and vegetables—and none are difficult to make. The quality of each sauce, however, depends on attention to particular details of preparation.

For white butter sauce *(right, top)*, success lies in carefully regulating the temperature of the ingredients. The sauce is formed by whisking butter into acidic liquid, usually a mixture of white wine and either vinegar or fish stock, flavored with shallots. So that the butter forms a creamy emulsion instead of melting to oil, the butter must be very cold and the cooking done over extremely low heat.

A properly creamy shellfish butter *(opposite, top)* depends on careful straining. To make it, butter is whisked with puréed crustacean shells or—for a more intense taste—shells and meat. Once it has absorbed their flavor, the butter has to be put through a sieve to eliminate every shell fragment.

White sauce and fish velouté sauce *(right center, and opposite, center)* are prepared in essentially the same way: A mixture of butter and flour known as a roux is first thinned with liquid—milk for white sauce, fish stock for velouté sauce—and then cooked. Long, slow simmering is necessary to give these sauces their thick rich consistency and to eliminate any taste of raw flour.

Flavored mayonnaise such as tartar sauce *(right, bottom)* is based on a simple emulsion of egg yolks and oil, but patience is required if the yolks are to accept the oil. All ingredients for a mayonnaise should be brought to room temperature ahead of time, and the oil must be added to the yolks gradually.

Spicy cocktail sauce *(opposite, bottom)* ideally uses only the tomato flesh: Skins or seeds spoil the texture, and seeds also have a bitter flavor. To prepare tomatoes, plunge them into boiling water for 20 seconds to loosen the skins; drain, peel and halve them and scoop out the seeds. Long simmering with ingredients such as onions and peppers reduces the tomatoes to a chunky sauce that may simply be chilled, or—for a satiny texture—puréed and simmered to reduce it further.

White Butter Sauce

Whisking in butter. Mix chopped shallots, wine and vinegar *(above, left)*. Boil until syrupy—about five minutes—then cool. Over very low heat, whisk in a few chunks of cold butter *(center)*. As they melt, whisk in more. Repeat until the sauce is creamy *(right)*.

White Sauce

Thinning a roux. Over low heat, melt butter *(above, left)*, then stir in flour *(center)* to make a smooth paste. Cook this roux for two minutes. Whisk in milk *(right)* and bring the liquid to a boil. Simmer, uncovered, over low heat for 40 minutes.

Mayonnaise-based Tartar Sauce

1 **Adding oil.** Whisk egg yolks with salt, pepper and vinegar. Whisk in oil drop by drop; as the mixture thickens, pour in the oil in a thin stream.

2 **Flavoring.** When the mayonnaise is creamy, stir in chopped capers, sour gherkins and fresh herbs—here, tarragon, chervil, chives and parsley.

Shellfish Butter

1 **Crushing shells.** Pull the tails from poached crayfish *(page 49)*; shell the tails, reserving the flesh for another use. In a mortar, crush the shells and bodies.

2 **Incorporating butter.** A spoonful at a time, pound softened butter into the crushed crayfish shells, until the mixture forms a grainy paste.

3 **Sieving.** Using a scraper, force the paste through a fine-meshed sieve. Discard cartilage and shell remaining on the mesh. Refrigerate the paste.

Fish Velouté Sauce

1 **Whisking.** Melt butter, then whisk in flour to form a paste; cook this roux briefly. Whisking continuously, add fish stock and bring the sauce to a boil.

2 **Cleansing.** Reduce the heat so that the sauce barely simmers, and set the pan half off the heat. Repeatedly skim off the skin that forms on the cooler side.

3 **Reducing.** Simmer and cleanse the sauce for 40 minutes, or until no more skin forms and the mixture is reduced by half. Adjust seasonings.

Tomato Cocktail Sauce

1 **Making a base.** Simmer prepared tomatoes for 30 minutes. Stir in sugar, spices, onions and peppers. Simmer for an hour to reduce the mixture by half.

2 **Puréeing.** Add vinegar and bring the mixture to a simmer. For a smooth sauce, purée the ingredients through a food mill or sieve into another pan.

3 **Finishing.** Stirring often, simmer the purée for 30 minutes until creamy. Ladle the sauce into a bowl. When it cools, stir in prepared horseradish.

Pastries for Cases and Coverings

The doughs that form the pastry casings for shellfish assemblies—puff pastry and short crust *(recipes, page 167)*—are made from flour, salt, butter and water. The character of the resulting pastry depends upon how you handle these ordinary ingredients.

Short-crust dough is the simplest to make. Butter is distributed in small bits throughout all-purpose flour and then the mixture is moistened with water. The liquid activates gluten proteins in the flour; these form strands that bind the particles into a mass. The butter waterproofs some of the flour particles, preventing excessive gluten development, which would toughen the dough.

The rules for handling short crust apply to any pastry dough: The ingredients must be kept ice-cold and must be handled as little and as quickly as possible. If the butter softens, it will coat too many flour particles, and the dough will not bind properly. Handling encourages gluten development. To ensure tenderness, the dough should be refrigerated for an hour before it is rolled out, to firm the butter and relax the gluten strands.

Puff-pastry dough is formed by repeatedly rolling and folding a sheet of dough around a sheet of butter, creating hundreds of layers of dough interspersed with butter. During baking, steam in the butter and dough puffs the layers into high, airy pastry.

Because puff-pastry dough is handled so much, part of the flour should be cake flour, which is lower in gluten than all-purpose flour. Compared to short crust, less butter is used for the dough base: The richness of the pastry is determined by the sheet of butter incorporated later.

The butter to be enclosed in the dough base requires preparation: Most butter contains excess water that could make the finished pastry gummy. Knead the butter on a floured surface for about five minutes to force out excess water. Chill the butter before shaping it into a sheet.

Because puff pastry is extensively handled, chilling is particularly important. Each time the dough-and-butter package is rolled and folded, it must be refrigerated for longer and longer periods to firm the butter and relax the gluten. The entire process may take up to eight hours.

The Elementary Short-Crust Dough

1 Preparing ingredients. Cut chilled, unsalted butter into pieces. Drop ice cubes into a bowl of water and set it aside. Measure all-purpose flour, add salt and sift them into a large bowl.

2 Rubbing in butter. Add the butter to the flour and salt. Using your finger tips and thumbs—not your warmer palms—lightly rub together a small amount of the butter and flour, and let the mixture fall back into the bowl. Continue until all of the butter is incorporated and the mixture resembles coarse bread crumbs.

The Many-layered Puff-Pastry Dough

1 Preparing the dough base. Mix all-purpose flour, cake flour, salt, chilled butter and ice water to form a compact ball of dough *(Steps 1 to 4, above)*. Refrigerate the dough for about 30 minutes. On a lightly floured cold surface, roll the dough with quick, light strokes to form a square about ½ inch [1 cm.] thick.

2 Enclosing butter. Place chilled, kneaded butter between two pieces of wax paper and roll it out into a square about ¾ inch [2 cm.] thick. Place this square diagonally on the square of dough. Fold the corners of dough over the butter, leaving a ½-inch [1-cm.] margin around the butter. Press the seams of the package together gently.

3 **Adding water.** Make a well in the flour-butter mixture and spoon in a little of the ice water. Because the ability of flour to absorb water varies with the kitchen's temperature and humidity, always start with a minimum amount. Too much water will produce a sticky dough and tough pastry; too little water, a mealy dough and crumbly pastry.

4 **Finishing the dough.** Quickly stir the mixture with a knife to distribute the water evenly. Gather the dough together with one hand *(above, left)*; if it is crumbly and dry to the touch, add more water gradually until the dough begins to cohere. Press the dough into a ball *(right)*, enclose it in plastic wrap or foil, and refrigerate it for at least an hour.

3 **Rolling the dough package.** Roll the package into a rectangle three times as long as it is wide, pressing lightly but evenly to avoid squeezing out the butter. Pat the edges of the dough with the sides of your hand to keep the edges neat. Do not sprinkle on flour: It would make the pastry tough and dry.

4 **Folding the dough.** Fold one end of the rectangle over the center, then fold the other one over the first, aligning them so that they form a three-layered package of dough that is about one third the size of the original rectangle. Seal air in the layers by pressing the edges down lightly with the rolling pin.

5 **Finishing.** Turn the dough so that its folded edges are at right angles to the rolling pin, and repeat Steps 3 and 4. Wrap the dough and chill it for an hour. Repeat the rolling and folding process twice more, then chill the dough for two hours. Roll and fold the dough two more times, then chill it for four hours.

1
Poaching and Steaming
Simple Methods Carefully Monitored

Tender treatments for crustaceans
Gleaning each morsel of lobster and crab
Sequential cooking for mixed shellfish
Juices captured by steaming
Delicate sausages and custards

Dollops of flavored mayonnaise give a golden finish to steamed mussels on the half shell, artfully displayed in concentric rings. The mussels have been cooked with wine, onions and herbs, then allowed to cool. Their cooking liquid, meanwhile, has been strained and boiled down to concentrate it into an essence for enhancing the mayonnaise.

Shellfish that are naturally tender and juicy—most notably crustaceans and bivalves—need only enough cooking to develop their full flavor and to coagulate the proteins of their meat, thus firming it and making it opaque. Poaching and steaming are ideal techniques: They do the job quickly, simply and with delectable results.

Success with either method requires careful control of temperature. For poaching, the shellfish are immersed in liquid that is kept at a constant temperature of 180° F. [80° C.], the point at which the liquid barely trembles. In steaming, the shellfish are cooked above a shallow layer of vigorously boiling liquid. To enhance the taste of the meat, the liquid may vary from salted water to a more assertive court bouillon or fish stock *(pages 22-23)*.

Whether to poach or to steam depends largely on the type of shellfish. Whole crustaceans—lobsters, crabs, shrimp, crayfish and Malaysian prawns—are candidates for poaching because their shells seal in their juices. Live bivalves, however, open their shells as they are heated, allowing juices to escape. For this reason tender varieties in their shells, such as mussels or soft-shell clams, are most often steamed to preserve their juices, which then blend with the cooking liquid to form a broth for enriching a sauce or for use as a soup *(pages 38-41)*. The exception is live oysters: Their shells are too heavy and bulky to be managed in a steamer—and are hard to clean well enough to yield a potable broth.

Although poaching and steaming are generally associated with straightforward presentations that emphasize the distinctive shapes and flavors of whole shellfish, both methods also can be applied to shucked and shelled specimens. Shucked oysters, for instance, or scallops—tender bivalves that are rarely available in their shells—are never more succulent than when poached in a bath of gently simmering liquid. And a unique harmony of taste and texture is easily achieved by adding a mélange of small shellfish such as these to the poaching pot in consecutive stages, thus ensuring that each component will be done to perfection *(pages 34-35)*. For more elegance, morsels of shellfish can be mixed with fish purée, then poached in parchment paper to create sausages *(pages 36-37)* or combined with eggs and stock, then steamed to produce delicate custards *(pages 42-43)*.

Gentle Simmering for Lobster

The old-fashioned way of preparing a live lobster for the table is to plunge it into boiling liquid, which kills it almost instantly and cooks it quickly. But sudden exposure to high heat makes the creature constrict its muscles with a violence that results in tough meat, and boiling leaches out flavor. In the modern method demonstrated here, the lobster's sweet taste and natural tenderness are preserved by immersing it in simmering liquid—which numbs, then kills the creature—and poaching it over gentle heat.

As it cooks, the lobster absorbs seasoning from the poaching liquid, which may be simply salted water or a mild-flavored court bouillon *(pages 22-23)*.

The essential requirements are to use liquid enough to submerge the lobster completely and to bring the liquid to a slow simmer—about 180° F. [80° C.]—before adding the lobster. It will take up to 10 minutes for the liquid to return to a simmer. At this point, the timing for each lobster begins—approximately 25 minutes per pound [½ kg.].

Like that of all crustaceans, the shell and adjacent flesh of lobsters contain pigments that redden when subjected to heat. However, the color changes before the flesh is cooked through. To test for doneness, insert a rapid-response thermometer into the vent hole at the end of the tail; the thermometer will register 165° F. [74° C.] when the lobster is fully cooked. Alternatively, remove the lobster with tongs and jerk one small leg sharply; it should come off readily.

Poached lobster can be served hot and in its shell, with a dipping sauce of melted butter—flavored, if desired, with lemon juice or chopped fresh herbs. Or it can be chilled and served whole or shelled, accompanied by tangy mayonnaise.

In either case, the final challenge is to glean every morsel of meat, including the greenish tomalley, or liver, and—in female lobsters—the reddish coral, or roe. Two strategies for extracting the meat of American lobster are shown; spiny lobster can be handled in the same ways, but only the tail has meat. In the tactic shown at top, the body is neatly halved to expose the tail meat; in the other, admittedly messier approach, the tail is removed in one piece.

Picking the Meat from Lobster Halves

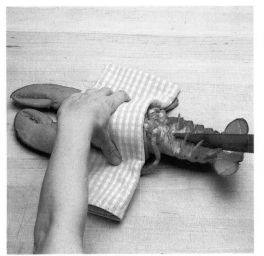

1 **Poaching.** Fill a large pot half-full with salted water and bring it to a simmer over medium heat. Grasp each lobster by its tail and plunge it headfirst into the pot. Return the water to a simmer, and simmer the lobsters uncovered for 25 minutes a pound [½ kg.] apiece—or until a leg can be easily jerked out. Remove and drain.

2 **Halving a lobster.** Lay each lobster on its back. Steady it and cut through the center of the tail from the midsection of the body to the flippers. Turn the lobster around, steady the split tail and halve the body. If desired, remove and discard the intestinal vein in the center of the cut surfaces of one—or both—tail halves.

Extracting Tail Meat in One Piece

1 **Breaking off the tail.** Poach lobster *(Step 1, above)* and prepare melted butter. Twist off the claws, break their shells, and extract and eat their meat *(Steps 3 and 4, above)*. Then separate the tail from the body of the lobster by twisting them apart.

2 **Removing the tail meat.** Break the flippers off the narrow end of the tail; extract and eat the meat inside each one. Insert a small fork into the narrow tail opening and push the meat out through the wide end of the tail. Slice the meat with the fork, or with a knife, and remove the intestinal vein. Dip each piece in the butter before eating it.

3 **Removing the claws.** Arrange the pairs of lobster halves on individual plates and serve them hot, accompanied by melted butter. To eat the lobster, first grasp a lobster half with one hand and twist off the claw at the joint between the claw and the body. Twist off the other claw similarly.

4 **Extracting claw meat.** Using a nutcracker, break the shells of both claws as well as each of the joints attached to them. With a small fork, extract claw meat pieces and dip them into the butter just before eating them. Break off the legs and suck out the juice and meat from their first and second joints.

5 **Extracting the tail meat.** With the fork, lift the meat from the tail section of each lobster half. Slice the meat with the fork, or with a knife, and dip each bite in the melted butter. From the body, lift out and eat the greenish tomalley and, in a female lobster such as the one shown, the reddish coral.

3 **Removing the back shell.** Pull on the legs and inner section of the body to unhinge it from the back shell. Pick out and eat any morsels adhering to it.

4 **Splitting the body.** Set the back shell aside with the other empty shells. With your hands, crack the body in half to expose its interior (above). Eat the red coral, if there is any.

5 **Eating the tomalley.** With a fork, lift out and eat the pieces of the greenish tomalley from each half of the body. Extract any meaty tidbits beneath the tomalley. Finally, break off the legs and suck out their juice and meat.

Making the Most of Hard-shell Crabs

Like lobsters *(pages 30-31)*, hard-shell crabs, periwinkles, crayfish, shrimp and prawns are at their best when poached whole in their shells. Their rich meat can be subtly enhanced by poaching them in salted water or court bouillon *(pages 22-23)*. Or they can be given a spicy tang by adding the seasoning blend called crab or shrimp boil *(recipe, page 162)* to a mixture of beer and water *(right)*.

For crabs, there is no foolproof doneness test and the poaching time must be monitored carefully. Blue crabs tend to be similar in size, so one—or a batch—requires exactly 20 minutes. Dungeness crabs, which weigh from 1¾ to 4 pounds [875 g. to 2 kg.] each, need 25 to 30 minutes. Periwinkles, shrimp and prawns poach in one to three minutes, crayfish in about five. The small crustaceans are done when the meat becomes opaque, the periwinkles when the disks that seal in the meat fall out or open.

After poaching, the periwinkles and small crustaceans slip easily out of their shells. Removing the meat from crabs is a somewhat more demanding chore.

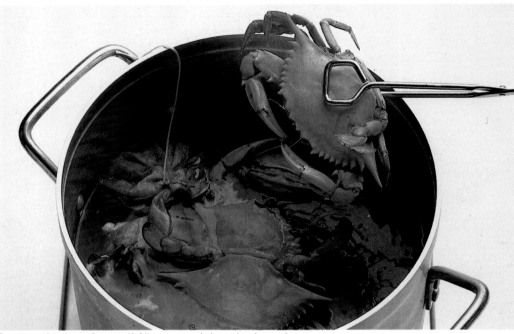

1 **Poaching crabs.** Half-fill a pot with liquid—here, beer, water and crab boil seasoning—and bring it to a simmer. Grasp each crab—blue crabs are shown—behind the back fin and plunge it headfirst into the pot. Simmer the crabs, uncovered, for 20 minutes after the liquid returns to a simmer. Remove them with tongs.

4 **Removing the gills.** Pull off and discard the feathery, grayish-white gills—often called the devil's or dead-man's fingers—from both sides of the body. The yellowish substance above the stomach sac is called the fat, and is considered a delicacy by many.

5 **Removing the sand bag.** Use a twisting motion to break off the crab's claws where they join the body. Pull out and discard the spongy stomach, or sand bag, from the area behind the crab's eyes. Twist off and discard the legs, saving any meat that adheres to them. Grasp the crab's body along its sides and snap it in half.

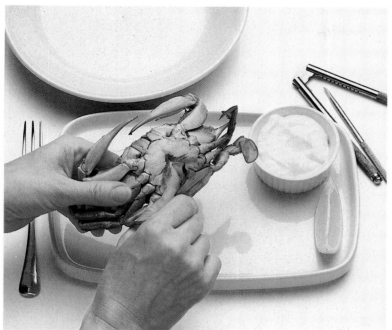

2 **Removing the apron.** Present each crab on a plate, with dipping sauce—mayonnaise *(page 24)* is shown—and a lemon wedge. Provide a dish for shells. To prepare a crab for eating, first turn it upside down and pry off the tail flap, or apron. Here the apron is triangular, indicating that the crab is female.

3 **Removing the top shell.** Turn the crab right side up and grasp the top shell in the space left by removing the apron. Pry up and tear off the top shell. Discard the shell or, if you like, reserve it for future use as an individual serving container.

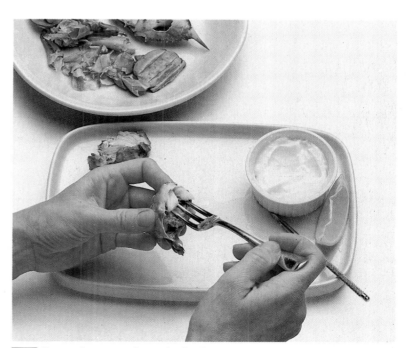

6 **Extracting the claw meat.** Use a nutcracker, as here, or a mallet to break the claw shells in several places. Extract the claw meat with a nut pick, a small fork or your fingers. Moisten each bite with lemon juice and dip it in sauce before eating it.

7 **Extracting meat from the body.** Use a small fork or nut pick to remove the lumps of back-fin meat from along the split edges of the body. Then break through the membrane with your fingers, or slice each half lengthwise, to expose the meat in the deeper pockets of each half. Pick out and eat the meat.

A Medley of Small Shellfish

Poaching will cook small shelled crustaceans or shucked bivalves in a few minutes and, as a bonus, produce a fragrant broth that can be thickened into a creamy sauce. Delectable when poached alone, different types also can be poached together and married with cooked vegetables to create a shellfish extravaganza of the sort shown here *(recipe, page 155)*.

Shrimp, Malaysian prawns, crayfish, oysters, scallops, hard-shell clams and Pacific littlenecks are all prime candidates for brief poaching—singly or in combination. Here, shrimp, oysters and bay scallops are poached with mussels, which have been left in their shells because they cannot be shucked without splitting their flesh in half *(page 51)*.

The liquid chosen may be salted water or water mixed with white wine, lemon juice or wine vinegar and flavored, per-haps, with finely chopped aromatics and fresh herbs. Onions, parsley, dill and fennel are all versatile shellfish seasonings. For more pronounced flavor, you also can use a court bouillon or fish stock *(pages 22-23)*; in this case, fish stock has been boiled down to concentrate its essences and is supplemented by liquor from the shucked oysters as well as by the juices that the mussels release. To preserve the texture of the shellfish, the poaching liquid must be kept at a gentle simmer. And to intensify the flavor of the finished broth, the level of the liquid should be kept low, barely covering the assembly.

Various types of shellfish may need slightly different poaching times *(chart, page 7)*. When poaching a combination of shellfish, start with the variety that cooks the longest and add others to the pot at appropriate intervals.

Because the timing of the shellfish must be monitored so carefully, vegetable garnishes should be prepared before the poaching begins. In this demonstration, julienned carrots, celery and leeks are simmered in a mixture of white wine and butter until tender but still crisp enough to counterpoint the texture of the shellfish. Parboiled and lightly sautéed whole shallots or sliced green beans or snow peas, sautéed tomato chunks or boiled green peas could also be used.

When the shellfish are cooked, the vegetable garnish is added to the pot and quickly combined with the other ingredients. Just before serving, the poaching broth is thickened lightly with white butter sauce or fish velouté *(pages 24-25)*, *beurre manié* made by kneading together equal amounts of butter and flour, or the simple whisked butter sauce shown here.

4 **Adding scallops and oysters.** Add shucked scallops to the mussels and shrimp, shaking the pan to distribute the shellfish evenly. Cover the pot and cook for one minute. Then add shucked oysters, along with their liquor. Cover the pot and cook for one minute more. Watch the timing at each stage carefully, lest overcooking toughen the shellfish.

5 **Adding vegetables.** Add the julienned vegetables to the shellfish, and season the mixture to taste with salt and pepper. Cover the pot, and let the mixture simmer for about a minute to allow the various flavors to blend.

1 **Preparing vegetables.** Cut celery ribs and carrots into julienne —or matchsticks—about 3½ inches [9 cm.] long. Cut off and discard the bases and leafy green tops from leeks; rinse the leeks well in cold water. Slice the leeks into thin strips of about the same length as the carrots and celery.

2 **Cooking vegetables.** In a small pan, bring butter and wine to a boil. Add the julienned vegetables, cover the pan and cook over low heat for about five minutes. Meanwhile, prepare a white butter sauce *(page 24)*. Set the sauce and vegetables aside off the heat.

3 **Poaching mussels and shrimp.** In a large pot, boil fish stock until it has reduced by half. Lower the heat to maintain a bare simmer and add cleaned mussels *(page 16)*. Cover the pot and cook the mussels for two minutes. Then add peeled, deveined shrimp, cover and cook for one minute.

6 **Serving.** Just before serving, pour the whisked butter sauce over the shellfish and vegetables, and stir gently to coat them well. Serve the shellfish directly from the pot or transfer to a warmed deep platter.

A Delectable Surprise: Shellfish Sausages

For a particularly eye-catching presentation, nuggets of tender shellfish can be folded into a creamy fish purée and the mixture packaged as sausages. Gentle poaching will then firm the sausages and cook them through while preserving the delicacy of the meat.

When sliced, the sausages reveal a mosaic of contrasting textures and colors. In this demonstration, pieces of shrimp and scallop stud an herb-flecked purée of sole *(recipe, page 156)*. Crayfish, Malaysian prawn, crab or lobster meat could be substituted for the shrimp and scallops. Any firm-fleshed fish—pike, trout, whiting or salmon—might be used for the purée; green peppercorns, chopped truffles or pistachios could replace or supplement the herbs.

The shellfish may be raw or cooked and need only to be shelled, trimmed and cut into chunks of ¼ to ½ inch [6 mm. to 1 cm.]. The fish must be raw and absolutely fresh so that its collagen proteins will become gelatinous in cooking and thus bind the sausage ingredients together.

To purée the fish fillets, you can use a mortar and pestle, as shown here; however, a food processor will make the chore easier. In either case, the purée must be sieved to silky smoothness and then be lightened with heavy cream in two stages—plain cream to soften the purée, whipped cream to aerate it.

Once assembled, the fish-and-shellfish mixture is simply rolled up in strips of buttered parchment paper or aluminum foil to form sausages. Here the mixture is shaped into two 9-inch [23-cm.] sausages about 3 inches [8 cm.] in diameter, but the number and size of the sausages can be varied as desired.

Because their filling is so soft and light, the sausages will tend to float in the poaching water and thus may cook unevenly. For perfect results, weight the sausages with a plate or pan lid to keep them fully submerged.

The poached sausages may be served with a fish velouté or white butter sauce *(pages 24-25)*. Or, to take advantage of the flavor of crustacean shells, the shellfish trimmings may be simmered in fish stock while the sausages poach and the resulting liquid then is turned into buttery shellfish sauce *(opposite)*.

1 Preparing the shellfish. Shell and devein shrimp *(page 18)*, reserving the shells. Cut the shrimp into ½-inch [1-cm.] pieces. Rinse shucked scallops— here, sea scallops—and cut off the light-colored, fibrous membrane that runs along one side of each scallop. Slice the scallops ¼ inch [6 mm.] thick and cut the slices into cubes.

2 Puréeing fish. Skin sole fillets and cut them into small pieces. Using a mortar and pestle or food processor, purée the sole. With a plastic scraper or wooden pestle, push the purée through a fine-meshed sieve into a large bowl; discard any bone or fiber on the mesh. With a rubber spatula, fold heavy cream into the purée to soften it.

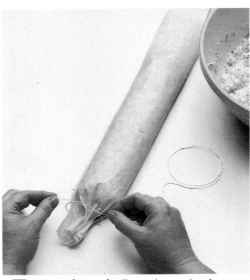

5 Tying the ends. Twist the ends of the rolled paper shut and tie them with pieces of kitchen string. Roll the remaining sausage mixture in another strip of paper and secure the ends with string. To make the sauce, crush the reserved shrimp shells in a mortar or food processor, combine them in a pot with fish stock *(pages 22-23)* and let the mixture simmer gently while you poach the sausages.

6 Poaching. Place the sausages in a deep sauté pan large enough to hold them easily and cover them with cold water. Weight the sausages with a small plate or lid. Cover the pan and heat the water until it simmers—about 180° F. [85° C.]. Poach the sausages for 15 to 20 minutes, or until they are firm. Then remove the pan from the heat, and let the sausages cool in the water for approximately 10 minutes.

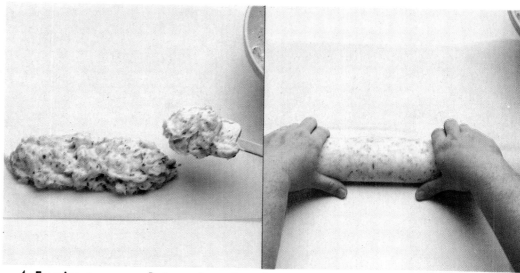

3 **Combining the ingredients.** Whip additional heavy cream until it forms soft peaks, then fold it gently into the purée mixture. Fold in the shrimp and scallops. Sprinkle on chopped herbs—in this case, parsley, tarragon, chives and chervil—salt, pepper and a pinch of cayenne pepper, and incorporate them gently but thoroughly.

4 **Forming a sausage.** Butter a piece of parchment paper about 15 inches [38 cm.] long and 12 inches [30 cm.] wide. Spread half of the sausage mixture in a strip across one long edge of the paper, leaving a margin of about 2 inches [5 cm.] at the edge and margins of about 3 inches [8 cm.] at the ends. Fold under the front edge of the paper by about an inch [2½ cm.], then lift the fold over the sausage mixture and roll up the mixture in the paper— pulling the paper tight to compress the sausage *(above, right)*.

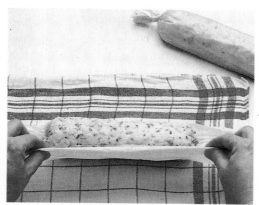

7 **Removing the wrapping.** Unwrap the sausages carefully on a clean kitchen towel and pat them dry. Cut the sausages into slices about ½ inch [1 cm.] thick and arrange the slices on a warmed serving platter. Drape foil over the platter to keep the slices warm.

8 **Serving.** Strain the shell-and-stock mixture into a pan. Boil the stock for a minute or two, until it is syrupy, then take the pan off the heat and whisk in chunks of butter, a few at a time. Garnish the sausage slices with watercress and pour the sauce over them.

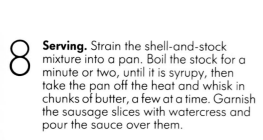

Steamed Mussels Hot and Cold

Brief steaming safeguards the natural flavors of live mussels and tender clams while it cooks their meat through. Because of the abundant juices these shellfish release as they are heated, all can be steamed in a tightly covered pot containing no other liquid. However, adding a layer of flavored liquid about ½ inch [1 cm.] deep will enhance the taste of the shellfish and produce a fragrant broth to use as a simple dipping sauce or as a seasoning for richer sauces.

The liquid used for steaming may be salted water, fish stock or court bouillon *(pages 22-23)*. Clams or the mussels shown in this demonstration also may be steamed *à la marinière*—literally, in the style of the sailor's wife—in white wine blended with finely chopped, sautéed aromatic vegetables, and fresh herbs *(recipe, page 99)*. Onions, shallots, parsley, thyme and bay leaf are shown here; other suitable choices are carrots, celery, chervil, fennel, marjoram and dill.

Before they are steamed, every specimen must be tested so that no dead shellfish are used. The shellfish must then be scrubbed and mussels must be debearded *(pages 16-17)* to yield potable broth; any sand they contain will settle to the bottom of the pot.

To keep the steaming time short, the liquid should be boiling before the shellfish are put in the pot. As they steam, clams and mussels will open and thus increase in volume. For this reason, the pot should be filled no more than halfway.

Steaming is always done over high heat and the pot kept covered so that the moisture rising from the shellfish will be captured by the underside of the lid. During the steaming, the pot should be shaken vigorously at frequent intervals to redistribute the shellfish and ensure that they cook evenly. Time the cooking from the moment steam begins to escape from around the lid. Clams and mussels are ready to eat as soon as their shells open—five to seven minutes.

The steamed shellfish may be eaten hot, accompanied by their own broth or by a complementary white butter sauce *(page 24)*. Alternatively, they may be drained, cooled and presented at room temperature with a cold sauce such as the mayonnaise used for the mussels in the demonstration below.

A Sauce-garnished Display

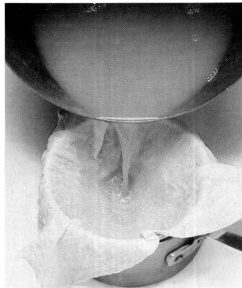

1 **Reducing cooking liquid.** Steam mussels and remove them from the pot, as in Steps 1 to 3 above. Strain the broth through dampened muslin or cheesecloth into a pan. Boil the liquid over high heat until it has reduced to about one quarter of its original volume. Let the liquid cool to room temperature.

2 **Flavoring mayonnaise.** Prepare a mayonnaise *(page 24; recipe, page 165)*. When the reduced cooking liquid has cooled, whisk 1 or 2 tablespoons [15 or 30 ml.] of it into the mayonnaise to achieve the intensity of flavor desired.

3 **Dressing the mussels.** Pull each mussel shell apart, leaving the flesh in the deeper shell. If desired, pull off the dark-colored rim of each mussel. Arrange the mussels on a serving dish. Spoon a little of the mayonnaise into each half shell. Pass the remaining mayonnaise in a separate bowl.

1 **Preparing seasonings.** Clean mussels *(page 16)*. Melt butter in a large pot. In it sauté chopped onions and shallots until they are soft—about five minutes. Add chopped parsley, a bay leaf, a sprig of thyme and ground pepper, and cook the mixture for about two minutes more.

2 **Adding wine.** Pour white wine into the pot and bring the mixture to a boil over high heat. Then gently drop scrubbed and debearded mussels into the liquid and cover the pot. To ensure that all of the mussels cook evenly, hold the lid in place and shake the pot from time to time to redistribute them.

3 **Cooking the mussels.** After five to seven minutes, depending on the size of the mussels and their number, their shells will open. Immediately lift the mussels from the pot with a skimmer or a perforated spoon. Discard any mussels that have not opened—an indication that they were dead.

4 **Serving the mussels.** To serve the mussels *à la marinière,* transfer them to a soup plate. Ladle some of the hot cooking broth over the mussels *(left),* leaving any sandy sediment in the bottom of the pot. To eat the mussels, extract each from its shell with a fork and dip it in the broth *(below).*

A Brace of American Favorites

Among the many approaches to steaming live clams, the two demonstrated here are uniquely American. In one—at top—the steaming is done conventionally, but because the clams used are soft-shells they are served a special way. In the second approach—at bottom—the steaming process itself is modified so that the clams can be cooked together with a medley of vegetables and other shellfish to produce a kind of stove-top version of a shore clambake.

Although the meat of a soft-shell clam may be eaten with a fork and knife, the classic New England strategy is to peel and eat it by hand—using the long siphon, or neck, of the clam as a kind of handle. The clams are served still in their shells, accompanied by mugs of the cooking broth and bowls of melted butter. Diners hold the firm-textured neck while dipping the tender nugget of body meat into broth for cleansing, then into butter for flavoring before eating the clam—neck and all. Afterward, the broth provides a flavorful soup to end the meal.

The stove-top clambake can be made with soft-shell, Pacific littleneck or the hard-shell clams used on these pages. The live clams are layered in a pot with vegetables—corn in its husk, potatoes in their skins and whole onions—and with lobsters, Dungeness crabs or, as shown, blue crabs (recipe, page 94). Lobsters and Dungeness crabs should be freshly killed as demonstrated on pages 18-19 and 20-21 to prevent them from disrupting the layers; smaller blue crabs may be left live. Leaves of spinach interspersed between the layers keep the contents of the pot moist during the steaming.

Because the ingredients must be added in layers, the poaching liquid cannot be brought to a boil ahead of time. Furthermore, this dense arrangement of vegetables and shellfish dictates longer cooking—without shaking—at a somewhat lower temperature than usual. Depending on the amount of food, the process may take from 45 minutes to an hour over medium to medium-high heat.

Once steamed, the shellfish and vegetables are presented together—heaped up attractively in shallow bowls—with melted butter for dipping each bite.

Soft-shell Clams Steamed in Their Own Juices

1 Steaming clams. Pour a shallow layer of salted water into a pot; add sliced onion. Bring to a boil and add cleaned soft-shell clams (page 17). Cover and steam for five to seven minutes, shaking the pot often. When the clams open, use a skimmer to put them into a bowl, discarding unopened specimens.

2 Decanting the broth. Carefully pour the broth from the pot into a bowl, leaving the sandy residue and the onion in the pot. Then pour the decanted broth into mugs. Melt butter and pour it into individual serving bowls.

A Stove-Top Clambake

1 Preparing ingredients. Clean clams—here, hard-shell—and blue crabs (pages 16-17). Wash fresh spinach leaves. Peel onions and scrub potatoes. Prepare fresh corn by stripping the husk from one side of each ear and carefully removing the silk; then wrap the ear back up in its husk.

2 Layering clams and spinach. Pour about ½ inch [1 cm.] of water into a large, heavy pot. Sprinkle in salt. Arrange a layer of clams in the bottom of the pot, choosing the largest ones for this layer. Spread a layer of moist spinach leaves over the clams.

3 **Serving the clams.** Provide each diner with a deep plate of steamed clams, a mug of broth, a bowl of the melted butter and an empty dish for the shells. To shuck a clam, spread the half shells apart and pull out the meat.

4 **Eating the clams.** Grasp the body of the clam at the point where it joins the neck and peel off the membrane-like veil from the body and the attached black hood from the neck *(above, left)*. Holding the clam by the neck, rinse it in the broth. Then dip it in the melted butter *(right)* and eat it—neck and all. After eating the clams, drink the broth.

3 **Cooking.** Add clams, potatoes, onions, corn and a blue crab *(left)*. Cover with spinach. Fill the pot with alternate layers of shellfish and vegetables, and spinach; finish with spinach. Cover, bring to a boil over high heat, reduce the heat and steam for about an hour, until the potatoes are tender. Using tongs and a skimmer, arrange the ingredients in warmed, deep plates and pour melted butter into small bowls. If desired, strain the cooking broth into mugs.

Nuggets of Shellfish in Steamed Custard

Cooked on top of the stove in the enveloping moist heat that steam provides, beaten eggs and liquid form a velvety custard to counterpoint tender nuggets of sweet shellfish. Depending upon the richness desired, the liquid used for the custard may be cream, milk, fish stock *(pages 22-23)* or—as in this demonstration of a Japanese variation—*dashi*, a stock made with dried kelp *(kombu)* and dried, flaked bonito *(katsuobushi),* both obtainable at Asian food markets.

Here, both shucked oysters and shelled shrimp are added to the custard, together with slices of dried Japanese mushrooms *(shiitake)* and thin strips of carrot and spinach *(recipe, page 157)*. Lump crab meat, shucked tender clams, or crayfish or Malaysian prawn tails are equally appropriate shellfish ingredients; asparagus tips, shredded lettuce or watercress leaves, or strips of scallion or celery heart may replace the other vegetables.

As a general rule, custard is made with two eggs for each cup [¼ liter] of liquid. The mixture shown here is more delicate, containing only two eggs to 1¼ cups [300 ml.] of liquid; as a result there will be a thin layer of liquid in the bottom of the container after the custard is cooked. To produce a finished custard of consummate smoothness with either set of proportions, the eggs and liquid must be gently combined: Bubbles in the raw mixture will set in the cooking to make the custard spongy.

Any heatproof container—a charlotte mold or soufflé dish, individual ramekin or cup—is suitable for steaming custard. However, the container must be filled only about three quarters full to allow for the custard to expand as it cooks—and the container must be tightly lidded or covered with foil to prevent condensation within the steamer from dripping into the custard and spoiling its surface.

Because custard is fragile and easily curdled, the container must be placed above—not in—boiling water and the steamer must be covered tightly to maintain an even temperature. The custard shown here is steamed in individual lidded cups arranged in an Asian steamer tray, but perfect results can be achieved by using a wire rack set in a deep saucepan or casserole.

1 Preparing mushrooms. Soak dried Japanese mushrooms in hot water for 30 minutes. Cut off their woody stems. In a small saucepan, simmer the mushroom caps with soy sauce and sugar until they are tender—about eight minutes—turning the caps occasionally with chopsticks or a spoon. Drain the caps, slice them and set them aside.

2 Slicing raw vegetables. With a sharp knife, cut half of a carrot into very thin slices and then into thin strips. Holding the knife blade at a diagonal and using the knuckles of one hand to guide it, slice spinach leaves into similarly thin strips. Set the vegetables aside.

6 Filling the cup bottoms. Shell and devein shrimp *(page 18)*; shuck oysters *(page 16)*. Using tongs or chopsticks, layer the shellfish and vegetables into individual heatproof cups. In each cup first place a shrimp, then an oyster, sliced mushrooms and finally slices of carrot and spinach.

7 Adding the custard mixture. With a ladle, pour in the custard mixture, filling each cup about three quarters full. Skim any bubbles off the surface of the custard. Place lids over the cups or cover their tops tightly with foil.

3 **Preparing stock.** Measure dried, flaked bonito into a small bowl. In a saucepan, bring water to a boil. Rinse a square of dried kelp under cold, running water and place it in the pan. Boil the kelp for three minutes and then remove and discard it.

4 **Straining the stock.** Add the flaked bonito to the kelp-flavored water. As soon as the water returns to a boil, remove the pan from the heat. Let the stock cool until the bonito flakes settle. Then strain the stock through a fine sieve into a bowl. Discard the bonito flakes.

5 **Preparing the custard.** Assemble flavorings—in this case, salt, soy sauce and *sake*. With a whisk or—as here—chopsticks, beat eggs until they are well combined, but not frothy. Stirring the eggs gently, slowly pour in the strained stock and the flavorings. Skim any bubbles off the surface of the mixture.

8 **Cooking and serving.** In a wok or other wide pan, bring a shallow layer of water to a boil over medium heat. Arrange the filled custard cups on an Asian steamer tray, and set the tray in the pan—the bottom should be about 1 inch [2½ cm.] above the water. Cover the tray with its lid (*above*). Cook for 15 to 20 minutes, or until a toothpick inserted in the center of a custard comes out clean. Meanwhile, poach additional shrimp in their shells; peel and devein them. When the custard is done, remove the tray from the pan and lift out the cups. Place a shrimp in each cup (*right*) and serve the custard hot—or chill it and serve it cold.

2
Stewing
A Mingling of Many Flavors

The importance of precise timing
Pounding to tenderize conch
Drawing essences from crustacean shells
How to open live mussels

Stewing elaborates on poaching and, in the process, produces an integral sauce that becomes part of the finished dish. The fundamental approach is the same: Whole or cut-up shellfish of one variety or several are gently cooked in barely bubbling liquid. But there the similarity between the methods ends. In stewing, aromatic vegetables and herbs are incorporated into the liquid to perfume and enrich it, and are simmered with the shellfish. The stew then may be served plain, straight from the pot, to preserve the individual flavors and textures of all its ingredients. Or the shellfish may be removed from the pot and the sauce concentrated and perhaps sieved before the stew is served. Whether the stew is to be rustic or refined, however, the cook's aim always remains the same—to mingle the flavors of the ingredients while keeping the shellfish meat succulent.

For every stew, careful timing is the secret of success. To blend the flavors, the cooking liquid and vegetables generally are simmered together first; the shellfish themselves are then incorporated in the mixture only long enough to cook them through. This group includes the spicy Creole stews of Louisiana, made usually with just one type of shellfish *(recipe, page 149),* as well as cioppino, the wine-flavored fisherman's stew of San Francisco, which includes a variety of shellfish *(pages 46-47).*

More elaborate stews—often called braises—require even more precise monitoring. The highly concentrated sauces that characterize these stews need lengthy simmering, and to achieve the right effect, cooking is done in three stages. First, the shellfish are cooked with flavoring ingredients. Then the shellfish are set aside and the other ingredients—having absorbed taste from the shellfish—are reduced to a sauce. Finally, the sauce is flavored and enriched by ground-up crustacean shells; shellfish roe; or cream, butter or eggs, and poured over the reserved shellfish. Among these stews are the creamy types known in France as *à la bordelaise (pages 48-49)* and those whose sauce is a tart brandy-and-tomato mixture known as *à l'américaine (pages 50-51).*

The shellfish for either type of stew may be chosen to suit the cook's taste, as long as adjustments are made to take into account the preliminary preparations and cooking times described in the guide on page 7. To produce variations in form and texture, even stuffed shellfish such as mussels or squid *(pages 51-52)* are welcome selections.

Shrimp, spiny lobster, Dungeness crab, rockfish fillet and hard-shell clams simmer in a wine-based cioppino. To ensure that each type of shellfish would be perfectly cooked, the different varieties were added in sequence, beginning with the crab and lobster, which require the longest cooking.

Two Basic Stratagems

For simple stews, the flavors of shellfish can be married to those of vegetables and cooking liquids—without overcooking any ingredients—by two different methods. The shellfish and the accompaniments may be cooked separately, then combined for a brief final heating, or the ingredients may be cooked together in sequence, beginning with those that require the longest cooking.

Preliminary preparation of the shellfish is the same in either case. Tough-fleshed abalone, geoduck and razor clams must be sliced and, like whole conch, tenderized by the method used in the top demonstration. Oysters must be removed from their thick shells, but thin-shelled bivalves such as hard-shell clams and mussels need not be shucked. Crustaceans may be left in their shells, provided that large species are cut into pieces (right, bottom) for even cooking.

The choice of cooking liquids and vegetables for a shellfish stew is broad indeed. The liquid may be water, fish stock, wine or a combination of these. The vegetables chosen most often are aromatics—onions, celery, garlic and carrots—and tomatoes. All should be peeled and chopped so that they will render their flavors. Only tomatoes demand special handling: Core them, and plunge them into boiling water for 20 seconds to loosen their skins. Then drain the tomatoes, slip off the skins, halve, and squeeze out the seeds before chopping the flesh.

The method of combining the various ingredients depends on the amount of cooking the shellfish require. If the flesh must be simmered for long periods to tenderize it—as for a conch stew (right, top; recipe, page 91)—the shellfish should be cooked separately from the vegetables to ensure that the vegetables do not overcook. If the shellfish need only brief cooking—as do the varieties in the mixed stew shown at right, bottom (recipe, page 158)—you can first cook the vegetables and liquid together. Add the shellfish—and fish, if you use it—to the stew pot in a sequence determined by the cooking time each requires.

A Lengthy Simmering for Tough Flesh

1 **Tenderizing conch meat.** Place shucked conchs in a bowl, cover them with fresh lime juice and let them marinate at room temperature for two hours. Drain the meat and dry it with paper towels. Using a meat pounder, pound each conch for two or three minutes, or until its firm flesh softens and becomes flexible, but not mushy.

2 **Cooking the meat.** Cut the conch meat into cubes ½ inch [1 cm.] thick. Put the cubes in a heavy saucepan and cover them with water. Put the lid on the pan and simmer the conch meat over medium heat for one hour. Uncover the pan and simmer the contents for half an hour more, until the cooking liquid has reduced by a quarter.

Conserving Natural Tenderness

1 **Cooking flavorings.** Warm olive oil in a heavy pot set over medium heat, then stir in chopped onions, mushrooms, green peppers, garlic and parsley. Sauté the vegetables for five minutes or until they are soft. Add peeled, seeded, chopped tomatoes.

2 **Simmering vegetables.** Stir wine—in this case, red wine—into the vegetable mixture. Cover the pot, reduce the heat to low, and simmer the vegetables and wine for 10 minutes to blend their flavors.

3 **Sautéing flavorings.** Make a sauce: Over medium heat, sauté cubes of salt pork, chopped scallions and crushed garlic in olive oil for five minutes, until the salt pork browns and the scallions soften. Season the mixture with ground cinnamon, salt, pepper and a bouquet garni of parsley sprigs, celery leaves, a bay leaf and a dried hot chili.

4 **Combining ingredients.** Stir the conch meat and its cooking liquid into the skillet, cover the skillet, and simmer the mixture for 15 minutes more, until the conch meat feels tender when you pierce it with a fork. Remove the skillet from the heat, discard the bouquet garni, and season the stew to taste with freshly squeezed lime juice.

5 **Serving the stew.** Over medium heat, sauté diced red and green peppers in olive oil until they are soft—about five minutes. Stir the vegetables into freshly cooked rice. For each serving, place the rice in a bowl and spoon the conch stew over it.

3 **Stewing shellfish.** While the vegetables cook, scrub clams, shell and devein shrimp, and cut fish fillets into chunks; set these aside. Kill, halve and clean a live crab and lobster *(pages 18-19 and 20-21)*—here, a Dungeness crab and a spiny lobster. Chop the shellfish into pieces and crack the crab claws and legs. Add the pieces—still in their shells—to the pot, stir to coat them with liquid, cover the pot and simmer its contents for eight minutes. Stir the clams into the stew, cover and simmer for four minutes more.

4 **Finishing the stew.** Add the shrimp and chunks of fish, and stir the stew well to distribute its ingredients evenly. Cover the pot and cook for two minutes, or until the shrimp become opaque and the clams open. Discard any clams that do not open. Garnish the stew with chopped fresh parsley and serve it from the pot.

A Purée of Crayfish Shells to Transform a Sauce

The most luxuriant shellfish stews are those made by cooking tender shellfish briefly with liquid and flavorings, and then reducing and enriching the braising medium to make a sauce. Among these stews, those based on crustaceans —cut-up lobsters or crabs, whole shrimp, prawns or the crayfish shown here—offer a special benefit: The shells of the crustaceans may be used for coloring and flavoring the sauce *(recipes, page 123)*.

The vegetables chosen for the initial braising of the shellfish can vary, as for any stew. However, for stews made *à la bordelaise,* or in the style of Bordeaux, the usual choice is a mirepoix—a mixture of finely chopped aromatics such as onions and carrots, which are precooked together to form a bed for the seafood. The liquid added is most often white wine; it sometimes is augmented with spirits such as brandy that have been set aflame to burn off excess alcohol.

Once the shellfish have been cooked and set aside, the braising liquid, having absorbed flavors from the shellfish and vegetables, can be turned into a simple sauce. The liquid is strained, then boiled over high heat to reduce it and concentrate flavors. It then is enriched by the addition of egg yolks, cream or butter.

Alternatively—to make a sauce with a particularly delicious taste and slightly grainy texture—the cooking liquid is combined with the shells of the crustaceans, and the mixture is ground to a paste in a mortar or food processor. After the paste is blended with a white sauce or fish velouté *(pages 24-25)* to release the flavor in the shells, the resulting sauce is puréed, then strained to remove any shell fragments, and may be thickened with heavy cream.

Either plain or shell-enhanced sauce can be poured over the shellfish meat and the stew reheated in a hot oven. The sauce-covered shellfish can then be broiled for a minute or so to give the assembly a golden gratin finish.

1 **Braising the crayfish.** Cook finely chopped carrots and onions gently in olive oil or butter until they soften—about 10 minutes. Add live crayfish and cook over high heat until they redden—about one minute. Warm brandy, ignite it and, when the flames die, pour it in the pan. Add white wine. Season, bring to a boil, reduce the heat, cover, and simmer the crayfish for five minutes. Remove the pan from the heat, take out the crayfish and let them cool.

5 **Puréeing the shells.** Pass the sauce and shell mixture through a food mill fitted with a fine disk. Add the mixture a little at a time to avoid forcing the blade of the mill upward and reducing its efficiency. Alternatively, purée the mixture in small batches in a food processor.

6 **Sieving the purée.** Using a pestle with a broad head, press the puréed shells and sauce through a fine-meshed sieve to eliminate any remaining fragments of shell. The texture of the sauce should be slightly grainy.

2 **Peeling the crayfish.** Twist the tail from each crayfish body and peel the shell from the tail. Set aside the shell, body, legs, claws and any eggs attached to the shell. If you have not already deveined the crayfish, tear off and discard the dark, threadlike vein that runs down the top of each crayfish tail. Reserve the tails.

3 **Pounding the shells.** Put the crayfish shells, bodies, legs, claws and any eggs in a mortar with some of the braising liquid. With a pestle, pound them to a coarse, grainy paste. This will take up to 20 minutes. Alternatively, grind the mixture in a food processor.

4 **Adding the paste.** In a saucepan set over medium heat, bring a thin fish velouté sauce to a simmer. Add enough of the shell paste to give the sauce the consistency of thick soup; reserve the leftover paste for shellfish butter *(page 25)*. Simmer the mixture for about 10 minutes to extract flavor from the shells.

7 **Serving.** Arrange the crayfish tails in a buttered dish. Gently heat the sauce; whisk in heavy cream, if you like; adjust the seasonings and ladle the sauce over the shellfish *(left)*. Warm the assembly in a preheated 450° F. [230° C.] oven for 10 minutes, then—if desired—slide it under a preheated broiler for a moment to brown it *(below)*.

A Lobster Classic: Homard à l'Américaine

Among the variations of the shellfish stew, one of the most celebrated is the classic styled *à l'américaine*. Some claim this stew is a Breton invention and its name should be *amoricaine*, after the ancient name of Brittany; others say it was devised by a chef in Provence in honor of an American patron. Whatever the origin of this dish, its assembly is uncomplicated: The shellfish is cooked with garlic, onions, brandy, wine and tomatoes, then set aside so that the cooking medium can be reduced and enriched with butter to make a sauce for the shellfish *(recipe, page 146)*.

Shellfish *à l'américaine* can be made with scallops, squid or any crustacean; however, the traditional choice is lobster, because it provides a bonus. Lobster tomalley and the coral from female specimens can be combined with the butter enrichment added to the sauce at the end of cooking to thicken the sauce and give it a faint, briny tang.

1 Cooking lobster. Cut up a lobster and set aside the tomalley and any coral *(pages 30-31)*. Sauté the lobster in olive oil over high heat, until the shells redden—about three minutes. Discard the oil. In the same pan, gently sauté chopped shallots and garlic in butter until they are soft. Warm brandy and ignite it. When the flame dies, add the brandy to the pan. Add white wine.

2 Stewing. Increase the heat to high and stir in peeled, seeded and chopped tomatoes and cayenne pepper. Bring the mixture to a boil, reduce the heat, cover, and simmer the mixture until the lobster meat is opaque—about 15 minutes. Transfer the lobster to a large, warmed serving platter.

3 Reducing the sauce. Increase the heat and bring the braising liquid to a boil. Boil it for about 30 minutes, until it has reduced to a syrupy consistency *(above)*. Season this sauce to taste with tarragon, chervil, salt and pepper. With a mortar and pestle, mash the reserved tomalley and coral, if any, with softened butter to make a smooth paste *(inset)*.

4 Serving the lobster. Reduce the heat so that the sauce barely simmers, then stir in the butter mixture. Stir the ingredients together until they are thoroughly combined, then ladle the sauce over the lobster pieces and serve.

Spinach-stuffed Mussels in Tomato Sauce

Mussels lend themselves to a delicious variation on basic stewing: The mussels may be left in their shells, stuffed, then cooked with liquid and flavoring ingredients that form a sauce for the finished assembly *(recipe, page 101)*.

Only large mussels—those at least 3 inches [8 cm.] long—can hold stuffing. The mussels must be opened with a knife *(Step 1, right)* and immediately stuffed while raw. The flesh will be split in the process and will line the two half shells; as the flesh contracts during cooking, it will neatly enclose the stuffing. To hold the stuffing in place during stewing, the shells should be tied shut with string.

Appropriate stuffings and sauce ingredients are many; the only rule is that the ingredients must cook through in the same time as the mussels. Here, the stuffing includes chopped steamed mussels, spinach and hard-boiled egg. You could use a sautéed mixture of mushrooms, shallots and bread crumbs. The cooking liquid here is tomato sauce, but fish stock or wine could be substituted.

1 Opening the mussels. Clean mussels *(page 16)* and steam the smallest ones open *(page 39)*, saving their juices for sauce. Hold each of the large, live mussels over a bowl to catch the liquid and force the blade of a sharp knife between the curved edges of the shell. Pry the halves apart but do not completely separate them.

2 Stuffing the mussels. Chop the flesh of the steamed mussels and mix it with parboiled, chopped spinach and a chopped hard-boiled egg. Pack this stuffing into the opened mussels; press the shells together and remove any surplus stuffing that squeezes out.

3 Arranging the mussels. Tie each mussel closed with string. Place the mussels close together in a pan with their hinged edges down, so that the stuffing will stay in place during cooking. Scatter any unused stuffing over the mussels.

4 Adding sauce. In a separate pan, stew chopped onions and peeled, seeded, chopped tomatoes in olive oil until the onions soften—about five minutes. Add the cooked mussels' steaming liquid and the juices from the opened, raw mussels. Ladle just enough of the sauce over the mussels to cover them; cover the pan and simmer the mussels for 15 minutes.

5 Serving the mussels. Arrange the mussels on individual plates, ladling some of the sauce over the mussels. Use a sharp-bladed knife to cut off the string from the mussels before serving them.

Squid Pouches: Ready-made for Stuffing

Stewing provides an opportunity to exploit the spicy sweetness of squid and octopus, which marry well with strong flavorings such as garlic, capers, anchovies, tomatoes and the cephalopods' own ink *(opposite page)*. Most recipes for squid and octopus are interchangeable, with the proviso that octopus requires a longer cooking time.

Both cephalopods are usually cut into pieces for stewing, but because their bodies form natural pouches they can be stuffed *(right; recipe, page 153)* for a more unusual presentation. Squids and octopuses with bodies about 6 to 8 inches [15 to 20 cm.] long are just the right size for individual portions.

For the stuffing, you can complement the cephalopod's chopped tentacles and fins with aromatic vegetables and herbs. Whatever the combination of flavorings, enough eggs and either bread crumbs or cooked rice must be incorporated to bind the mixture and ensure that the stuffed pouches are firm enough to cut into neat slices after cooking. To keep the stuffing in place, the mouth of each pouch should be stitched shut with string.

The stuffed squid shown here are briefly sautéed to soften them and release their flavor, then stewed in a rich blend of brandy and white wine. This braising liquid can be reduced to serve as a sauce.

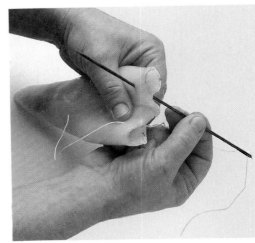

1 **Stuffing squid.** Clean and trim squid *(pages 12-13)*. Chop the trimmings and sauté them with chopped onion until golden—about five minutes. Blend the sautéed mixture with chopped garlic and parsley; peeled, seeded and chopped tomato; bread crumbs and egg yolks. Stuff each pouch loosely with the mixture; the squid will shrink during cooking.

2 **Securing the stuffing.** Thread a trussing needle with kitchen string, and sew up the mouth of each pouch, inserting the needle no closer to the mouth than ½ inch [1 cm.] to avoid tearing the pouch open.

3 **Sautéing.** Gently cook more chopped onion in oil, lay the squid on top of the onion and sauté until the squid turn opaque—about two minutes. Add a generous dash of warmed brandy, and ignite it to burn off the alcohol. Add white wine and a mixture of capers, chopped parsley and filleted and diced anchovies.

4 **Stewing and serving.** Cook the squid, covered, over low heat for 30 minutes to an hour, or until it is tender. Transfer the squid to individual plates *(above)* and cut off the strings. Boil the braising liquid for a minute or two to reduce it to a syrupy sauce, pour it over the squid and serve at once *(inset)*.

Gaining an Added Dimension from Ink

The ink secreted by squids and octopuses to cover their escape from predators can impart a smooth texture and a dark, brownish black color to a stewing liquid *(recipes, pages 151-153)*. The ink is stored in a small internal sac, which must be carefully removed from the body when a squid or octopus is prepared for cooking *(page 13)*. If a squid or octopus is frozen, its ink will coagulate; to liquefy the ink, simply dissolve the granules in a little boiling water.

Octopuses, which are used in this demonstration *(recipe, page 148)*, have smaller ink sacs than squids; some of the smallest sacs contain no more than one drop of ink. However, only a small quantity of octopus ink is needed. To color and enrich the braising liquid here, for example, enough ink was obtained from the sacs of three of the largest of the eight octopuses used in the stew.

1 Parboiling octopuses. Clean and skin octopuses, and remove and reserve their ink sacs. Place the octopuses in a heavy pan. Cover the pan and cook the octopuses for five minutes over medium heat in the liquid they exude. Drain the octopuses, discarding the liquid, and set them aside until they are cool enough to handle.

2 Cutting the octopuses. Lay each octopus on a work surface, aligning the tentacles so that they can be sliced off with one sweep of a knife. Steadying the octopus with one hand, cut the meat into bite-sized pieces.

3 Preparing the braise. Snip open the reserved ink sacs, catching the ink in a bowl *(inset)*. Dilute the ink with water and set it aside. In a skillet, sauté chopped onion and garlic in olive oil until the onion is soft—about five minutes; add the octopus and sauté for five minutes. Pour in red wine and simmer until most of it evaporates. Add peeled, seeded and chopped tomatoes. Pour in the ink.

4 Serving. Gently simmer the octopus for one and one half hours, until it is tender. Add small amounts of water as needed to prevent scorching. Just before serving, stir in chopped parsley and simmer for a minute more. Mix chopped parsley with freshly cooked rice, then pack the rice into a buttered ring mold. Unmold the rice onto a platter. Ladle the octopus into the ring; garnish with parsley.

3
Frying
High Heat Judiciously Applied

The selection of fats and oils
Cutting pieces of equal size
The uses of protective coatings
Sauce made in the pan
Crab presented in the shell

Stir frying turns the shell of a lobster bright red and cooks the flesh through in the classic Chinese dish known as lobster Cantonese. Bean paste and water added to the pan form a sauce that is thickened by cornstarch dissolved in a little water. Chopped scallions will add textural interest and, just before serving, beaten eggs will be stirred into the sauce where they will set as creamy white ribbons (pages 58-59).

Their surfaces golden, their interiors sweet and succulent, properly fried shellfish provide delectable dining. The shellfish may be fried in a shallow layer of oil or butter that has been heated to a moderately high temperature, or in a deep—much hotter—layer of oil alone. In either case, strict precautions must be taken to prevent the flesh from drying out while it is cooking.

In shallow frying (pages 56-57), brevity of cooking is the key. The shellfish pieces are quickly tossed about to sear their surfaces, thereby firming the flesh. Keeping the shellfish in motion as it cooks ensures that contact with the hot oil or butter is brief and that the flesh cooks evenly without drying. This motion explains the names given to the technique in different parts of the world: In the West, shallow frying is known as sautéing, from the French verb sauter—"to jump"; in Asia, the same technique becomes stir frying.

After the shellfish pieces are cooked, the frying medium will have acquired some of the shellfish flavor. To exploit it, the oil or butter can be briefly cooked with additional flavorings and a little liquid to form a light sauce for the shellfish.

The heat of deep frying—the oil temperature is maintained at 375° F. [190° C.]—would appear to make it unsuitable for cooking fragile shellfish. But traditional favorites, ranging from the crusty fried clams of the United States to the mixed-shellfish assemblies known in Italy as fritto misto and in Japan as tempura, depend for effect on this very technique (pages 62-63).

What makes deep frying possible for shellfish is the use of surface protection for its flesh and the careful control of oil temperature. The surface protection is acquired by dipping each shellfish piece into beaten egg or a small bowl of milk to make it sticky, then coating it with seasoned bread crumbs or flour. Or you can use any of a number of interesting batters to coat the delicate flesh. When the pieces are dropped into oil that has been heated to just the right temperature, the coatings almost immediately form a golden crust, sealing in the juices of the shellfish. Only a few moments in the hot oil will then cook the shellfish through without burning its surface, leaving the flesh moist and tender beneath a crisp exterior.

Brief Sojourns in Bubbling Butter

Among frying techniques for shellfish, sautéing is the most straightforward: The shellfish is turned in a little butter or oil over medium heat just long enough to brown the surface and cook the flesh.

Any shellfish may be sautéed. The meat of large univalves such as abalone and conch, once tenderized *(Step 2, opposite),* is delicious when cooked this way, as is the flesh of any crustacean; sautéing is the classic treatment for soft-shell crabs *(bottom demonstration).* Smaller, more fragile shellfish—shucked clams or oysters, or sea urchin roe *(Steps 1 and 2, right)*—also can be sautéed, but because they are easily overcooked, careful timing is critical.

The shellfish need no preparation other than that described in the introduction to this book, but their surfaces must be dry before cooking or they will not brown properly. To encourage browning, you can coat the shellfish lightly with flour. Prepared this way, shellfish dishes are aptly known in France as *à la meunière*—in the style of the miller's wife.

For the frying medium, choose vegetable oil or a butter-and-oil mixture. If you use butter alone, you must first clarify it to remove the milk solids, which burn at high temperatures. To do so, melt over low heat a third more butter than you plan to use. Skim off the foam that rises to the top. Cool the butter for 30 minutes. Carefully pour off the clear liquid, leaving the settled milk solids behind.

For shellfish to brown properly, the frying medium must be properly hot and waiting; you cannot start cooking with cool oil. To test for temperature, drop in a bread cube: The cube should sizzle and brown immediately. And leave plenty of room between the frying shellfish pieces; in a crowded pan, they would stew in their own juices instead of browning.

Flavorings and garnishes for sautéed shellfish should be kept simple to complement their delicate taste. Sauté aromatic vegetables such as garlic, scallions or shallots with the shellfish, if you like. Once the flesh is cooked, you can turn the liquids in the pan into a sauce by deglazing: Add a little liquid—lime or lemon juice, wine or cream—to the pan and boil, stirring and scraping up pan deposits briefly to blend all the flavors.

A Complement of Shallots for Sea Urchin Roe

1 **Marinating the roe.** Extract sea urchin roe *(pages 14-15)* and rinse it. To accentuate its flavor, marinate the roe for 10 minutes in acidulated water: For each cup [¼ liter] of water, allow 1 teaspoon [5 ml.] of salt and the freshly squeezed juice of one lime or lemon. Drain the marinated roe in a strainer. Pat the roe dry with paper towels.

2 **Sautéing.** Warm clarified butter in a skillet over medium heat. When the butter is bubbling, add sliced shallots and sauté them, stirring frequently, for about five minutes, until soft. Add the roe and, with a wooden spatula, turn it gently for about four minutes, until the roe is lightly browned. Place the roe on a warmed serving plate, pour the butter over it, and season with salt, pepper and fresh lime or lemon juice.

A Dusting of Flour to Form a Crisp Crust

1 **Coating the crabs.** Clean and wash soft-shell crabs *(pages 20-21)* and dry them on paper towels. Spread flour mixed with salt and pepper on a plate. Turn each crab in the flour mixture to coat it completely; gently shake the crab to remove excess flour and transfer the crab to a clean plate.

2 **Sautéing.** Heat butter and oil in a skillet over medium heat. When the mixture bubbles, lay the crabs on their backs in the pan; do not crowd them together.

A Preliminary Softening for Abalone Steaks

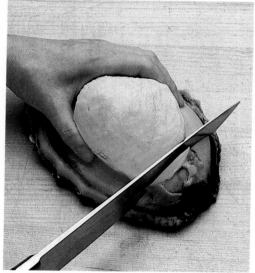

1 Trimming the meat. Shuck abalone *(pages 14-15)*. With a sharp knife, slice off the mouth and the digestive tract, which appears as a dark, veinlike structure at one end of the white meat *(above)*. Cut off the dark mantle that covers one side of the white meat, then slice the meat horizontally into steaks ½ inch [1 cm.] thick.

2 Tenderizing the meat. To break down muscle fibers and prevent toughness, use a heavy kitchen mallet to pound each abalone steak to a thickness of ¼ inch [6 mm.]. If desired, cut slashes ¼ inch deep all around the edges of each steak to help prevent it from curling during cooking.

3 Sautéing. Heat butter and oil in a skillet set over medium heat. When the mixture is bubbling, quickly sauté the abalone steaks for about 30 seconds on each side, just until they color slightly: The steaks should not be brown. Serve the steaks immediately, pouring the butter over them and sprinkling them with salt and pepper.

3 Turning the crabs. Sauté the crabs for two or three minutes, until their shells are crisp and golden brown. Then carefully turn each crab over with tongs to sauté the underside. After two or three minutes more, when the crabs are completely browned, transfer them to a warmed platter.

4 Sautéing almonds. To the butter in the skillet, add sliced almonds that have been toasted for 10 minutes in a preheated 325° F. [160° C.] oven. Stir the almonds over medium heat with a wooden spatula for one or two minutes; pour in freshly squeezed lemon juice.

5 Serving. Increase the heat and let the juice boil for a minute or two as you scrape up the pan deposits with the spatula. Immediately spoon this sauce over the cooked crabs; garnish them, if you like, with lemon slices sprinkled with chopped fresh parsley.

The Chinese Way with Lobster

The stir frying of Asian cookery is akin to Western sautéing, but employs higher heat and is consequently much faster. Stir-frying recipes exist for most kinds of shellfish, but the technique is perhaps displayed at its best in dishes that feature crustaceans fried in their thin shells, which impart additional flavor to the sauce. Shrimp, crabs or the lobster shown here all may be stir fried (recipes, pages 130, 117). The shellfish should be cut into small pieces that will cook through quickly and evenly (Steps 1 to 3).

The flavorings and thickenings called for in stir-fried dishes are frequently exotic and may require a shopping trip to an Asian market. Whatever their nature, these ingredients should be assembled and prepared in advance: Once the cooking begins, no time is left for any other activities.

In the Cantonese lobster dish demonstrated on these pages, for instance (recipe, page 146), the flavorings for the sauce include scallions, fresh ginger and garlic, which require peeling and chopping, and bean paste. The paste must be made by pounding salty fermented black beans (which are available in cans) with crushed garlic cloves. The cornstarch that is used to thicken the sauce must first be dissolved in water, and the egg that provides bland, creamy ribbons in the finished dish must be beaten.

The pan for stir frying should be deep and wide enough for the brisk tossing required to sear the ingredients evenly. Most commonly, the vessel used is a wok, whose sloping sides facilitate the technique, but a large skillet will serve. The frying medium for most Asian dishes is delicate-flavored peanut oil.

1 Halving the claws. Kill a live lobster (page 18, Step 1). Twist off the claws and tail. Divide a claw by placing a large, heavy knife across it at the point where the claw joins its base and by tapping the blade with a mallet to force the blade through the claw.

5 Frying the lobster. Warm a wok over high heat for a few moments, then pour in oil—here, peanut oil—and let the oil heat to sizzling. In the oil, fry chopped ginger and garlic until they begin to brown—about 30 seconds. Add the lobster pieces and toss them in the oil for four to five minutes, until they turn bright red.

6 Adding the bean paste. Transfer the lobster pieces to a bowl. Add the prepared bean paste to the wok and fry it for about one minute, tossing it constantly with chopsticks. Return the lobster pieces to the pan, add hot water and stir well. Cover the wok and let the lobster cook for three minutes. Stir in cornstarch that has been dissolved in a little cold water.

2 **Quartering the claws.** Using the knife and mallet, divide the halved claw lengthwise between its pincers. In the same manner, halve the claw base lengthwise. Quarter the second claw in the same way as the first.

3 **Cutting up the tail.** With the knife and mallet, split the tail lengthwise. Then, with the knife, slice each half into pieces 1 ½ inches [4 cm.] wide. Leave any coral—it will look blackish green—attached to the pieces.

4 **Preparing bean paste.** Place fermented black beans in a strainer and rinse them under cold running water for a few seconds to remove the excess salt. Using a mortar and pestle, pound the beans to a paste with sugar and crushed garlic cloves.

7 **Completing the dish.** Let the mixture cook for about one minute, until the sauce boils and thickens slightly. Then add chopped scallions. Stirring constantly, pour beaten egg into the sauce. Stir for about one minute, until the egg sets in the thin strings called "egg flower" in China.

8 **Serving the lobster.** Arrange the lobster pieces on a warmed serving platter in a shape approximating the lobster's original one. Spoon the sauce from the pan over the lobster. Accompany the dish with boiled rice.

Golden-crusted Shellfish Cakes

Pieces of shellfish meat of any kind can be combined with other ingredients and then formed into patties that brief sautéing will transform into delicious, golden cakes *(recipe, page 120)*. The ingredients can be varied to suit the taste and imagination of the cook.

The meat may be raw or precooked. With tender shellfish such as shrimp, scallops or the crabs used here, the meat can be left in fairly large chunks of ½ inch [1 cm.] or so—or, for a smoother texture, it can be broken or cut into small pieces or shreds. Tougher shellfish meat such as that of razor clams or abalone must be finely chopped or ground.

The shellfish meat is combined with three basic types of ingredients: a starch, which gives body to the cakes; a moistening agent, which ensures that the interiors remain tender; and a binder, which holds the ingredients together.

Suitable starches are bread and cracker crumbs, mashed potatoes, or the kind of thick white sauce used for soufflés *(recipe, page 164)*. Allow about half as much starch as shellfish, measured by volume.

To moisten and enrich the cakes, use milk, cream or melted butter—adding only enough to soften the mixture slightly. Or use eggs, which also serve as the ideal binding agent because they make the raw ingredients cohere for shaping and will set during cooking. You can use whole eggs, as in this demonstration; or you can separate the eggs, stir in the yolks, then beat the whites stiff and fold them in. The air beaten into the whites will expand during cooking, giving the cakes an appealing puffy lightness.

Other ingredients that add interest to shellfish cake mixtures include finely chopped aromatic vegetables such as onions and celery. Chopped fresh herbs—parsley, dill and chives, for example—are well suited to the mild, sweet taste of shellfish. For variety, you can add crushed garlic; however, use it sparingly lest it overwhelm the flavor of the meat.

The cakes can be formed in any shape, but flat patties or sticks are the easiest to turn, ensuring even cooking. The cakes should be no thicker than ½ inch [1 cm.] so that they will cook through quickly.

1 **Preparing crab meat.** Remove the meat from cooked crabs *(pages 32-33)*—blue crabs are used here. Place the meat in a small bowl. Then sift through the meat a few pieces at a time with your fingers, extracting and discarding any bits of shell or cartilage. Place the pieces of crab meat on a large plate.

3 **Shaping the crab cakes.** A small handful at a time, shape the crab mixture into patties about ½ inch [1 cm.] thick. Work quickly and compress the ingredients only enough to make them cohere: The cakes should not be densely packed. Chill the cakes for 30 minutes or so to firm the mixture so that the cakes will hold their shape when cooked.

4 **Sautéing the crab cakes.** Heat clarified butter in a large skillet set over medium heat. When the butter is bubbling, transfer several of the crab cake patties to the pan with a large spatula. Let the patties cook for three or four minutes, then lift one to see if it has formed a golden brown crust on the bottom *(above, left)*. If it has, carefully turn the patty over *(right)* and cook it for three or four minutes more, until golden on the second side.

2 **Adding flavorings.** If you prefer cakes with a fairly even texture, use a fork to break up any large pieces of crab meat *(inset)*. Transfer the crab meat to a large bowl and thoroughly mix it with thickening and binding ingredients and flavorings—in this case, fresh bread crumbs, milk, eggs, Worstershire sauce, chopped fresh parsley and salt.

5 **Serving.** Using the spatula, immediately transfer the cooked crab cakes to paper towels to drain for a moment. Then arrange them on a warmed serving plate and garnish them; lemon wedges and chopped parsley are used for this demonstration. Serve the patties, if you like, with tartar sauce *(page 24)*.

The Secrets of Successful Deep Frying

The heat required for deep frying is so high that shellfish must be given a surface coating to protect its flesh from overcooking or parching. To set the coating as a crisp crust, both the oil temperature and the cooking time have to be carefully monitored. With these provisos, any shellfish—once shucked or shelled or cleaned—can be deep fried. You can fry one type of shellfish or several in combination; for the latter presentation, all pieces fried together should be of about the same thickness so that they will cook through in the same time.

Tender shellfish such as shrimp, softshell crabs, scallops, clams or oysters can be left whole. Tougher varieties such as squid or abalone should be cut into small pieces, after they have been tenderized *(pages 46-47)*.

The range of batter coatings to protect the shellfish surfaces is broad indeed. Most batters start with flour and liquid. The liquid can be water, milk, wine or lemon juice, or the beer used in this demonstration, which imparts a faint, bitter tang and aerates the batter by making it ferment slightly. To enrich the mixture and make it more cohesive, many batters include egg yolks or whole eggs—added when the batter is assembled. For a light, airy texture, you can fold beaten egg whites into the batter just before using it *(recipe, page 167)*.

Whatever batter you use, it should be as thick as heavy cream to provide an even covering. Beat the ingredients only long enough to eliminate lumps, then let the mixture rest before using it. During the resting period, the batter will lose the elasticity caused by beating, and will cling better to the shellfish.

For safety, choose a deep, heavy pan for cooking, and fill it no more than half-full of oil. Otherwise, the oil might bubble over when the shellfish is dropped in.

So that the batter coatings seal immediately, the oil must be preheated; and for them to crisp perfectly, the temperature must be kept at 375° F. [190° C.]. The batters may burn in overly hot oil; they will absorb oil that is too cool, thus becoming unappetizingly soggy. Use a deep-frying thermometer to check the oil temperature, or test it as shown in Step 5.

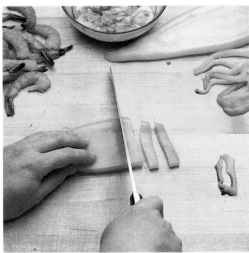

1 Preparing shellfish. Shuck oysters *(page 16)* and set aside in a bowl. Shell and devein shrimp *(page 18)*, leaving the tails intact. Clean small squid *(pages 12-13)*. Cut off and discard the irregular open end of each squid pouch; slice across the pouch at ¼-inch [6-mm.] intervals to divide it into rings.

2 Opening the squid rings. Leave the squid tentacles intact; cut the fins into bite-sized pieces. To prevent the squid rings from collapsing during cooking, turn them inside out. Refrigerate the shellfish until you are ready to cook them.

6 Coating with batter. Pat the shellfish dry with paper towels; to ensure that the surfaces are completely dry, dust them with flour, shaking off any excess. With tongs, grasp each piece of shellfish by one edge—here, a shrimp is held by its tail—and immerse it in the batter; then raise the piece and shake excess batter back into the bowl.

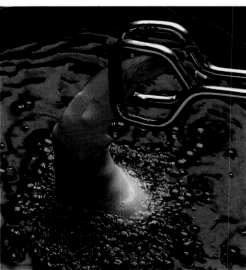

7 Frying. Still using the tongs, immediately lower the batter-coated piece of shellfish into the hot oil. Repeat this step with several more pieces, but do not crowd the pan: You must cook the shellfish in small batches to keep from lowering the oil temperature.

3 **Mixing batter.** Sift flour into a bowl, season it with salt and pepper, and add a little vegetable oil. Whisking continuously, pour in beer; whisk just until the batter is smooth. Cover the bowl and set the batter aside at room temperature for about one hour.

4 **Lightening the batter.** Separate eggs. Whisk the whites until they form stiff peaks and fold them gently into the batter. Reserve the yolks for another use.

5 **Testing oil temperature.** Pour vegetable oil to a depth of 3 inches [8 cm.] in a deep, heavy pot. Heat the oil to a temperature of 375° F. [190° C.]. If you have no deep-frying thermometer, test the oil temperature by dropping in a spoonful of batter; it should sizzle and brown immediately *(above)*.

8 **Draining and serving.** The shellfish will be cooked after one or two minutes, when they are crisp and golden brown on all sides. Lift them out of the oil with a wire skimmer *(left)* and drain them briefly on paper towels. Keep each batch warm in a preheated 175° F. [80° C.] oven until all are cooked. Serve the shellfish on a napkin *(inset)*, garnishing them with lemon wedges.

A Soufflé Topping for Crab Meat

With some modifications, deep frying can be used to produce an appealing version of individual soufflés. To make the soufflés *(recipe, page 116)*, pieces of shellfish meat are mixed with vegetables and seasonings, then stuffed into shells and covered with beaten egg. Frying transforms the toppings into golden domes.

To contain the stuffing, you will need clean shells of the appropriate size for individual servings. Crab shells are used here, but large scallop half shells would also be suitable. Empty shells should be thoroughly washed under cold running water—use a vegetable brush to remove debris, if necessary—and dried with towels. If you do not plan to use the shells the same day you clean them, dry them completely by baking them in a preheated 250° F. [120° C.] oven for 10 minutes before storing them.

The filling can include any kind of shellfish meat. You can use the meat from the cleaned shell containers, as in this demonstration; although meatiness will vary, the amount of flesh crabs yield will probably produce enough stuffing for about two thirds of the shells. Or you can use a mixture of shellfish—shrimp, crabs and scallops, for instance. The meat should be enriched with aromatic ingredients such as scallions and garlic that have been briefly sautéed to bring out their flavors. Moisture helps keep the filling tender; it is supplied here by stewed tomatoes, but heavy cream could serve the same purpose.

Eggs provide the soufflé-like topping for dishes of this type. The eggs are separated and the whites beaten stiff, then combined with the yolks and spread over the stuffed shells. The topping is too delicate to be immersed in hot oil; instead, the shells are only partly submerged during cooking and hot oil is spooned over the tops. The heat thus provided will be enough to expand the air beaten into the egg whites, puffing the topping up.

1 **Extracting crab meat.** Poach crabs—here, blue crabs—and remove the meat *(pages 32-33)*; use a sharp-pointed instrument such as the nut pick shown to extract all of the back-fin meat from its chamber. Wash the shells under cold water, dry them and set them aside.

4 **Mixing the topping.** Separate eggs. Beat the whites, adding a little salt, until they form stiff peaks. Beat the yolks until they are creamy. With a rubber spatula, fold the yolks into the whites.

5 **Adding the topping.** With a narrow-bladed metal spatula, gently spread the egg topping over each filled crab shell. The topping layer should be smooth and about 1 inch [2½ cm.] thick. In a large skillet, heat a ½-inch [1-cm.] layer of oil until a bread cube dropped in it browns in about one minute.

2 **Forming a stuffing.** Warm a little vegetable oil in a skillet set over medium heat, and in it sauté thinly sliced scallions and finely chopped garlic for about three minutes, until the scallions are soft but not brown. Add chopped tomato and cook for five minutes more, until most of the liquid in the pan has evaporated. Stir in the crab meat and season the mixture with salt and pepper.

3 **Filling the crab shells.** Cook the stuffing mixture only for a minute or two, until it is heated through. Remove the pan from the heat. With a large spoon, pack the stuffing into each crab shell, mounding it slightly in the center.

6 **Frying the shells.** With a skimmer, lower a few stuffed crabs into the hot oil one at a time, keeping the topping side up. Cook the crabs for about two minutes, using a large metal spoon to dribble hot oil gently over the toppings. Serve the crabs as soon as the toppings are puffed and golden; garnish them, if desired, with scallions and lime wedges.

4
Baking and Broiling
Safeguards for Succulence

The dry heat of baking and broiling would render delicate shellfish flesh unappetizingly tough were it not for two basic rules: The cooking time must always be brief, and the shellfish must always be baked or broiled in the company of moistening ingredients that will keep the flesh succulent. The need for moisture is actually a boon, for it has inspired an array of marinades, coatings, toppings and sauces that not only protect the shellfish but also enhance its flavor.

The most straightforward way to bake such shellfish as oysters and tender clams is in their unopened shells with their own liquor for moisture. But this is only one of the many possible presentations for these bivalves. Opened and left on their half shells, they may be covered with vegetables for flavor and with oil, fat or sauce for moisture, then baked to produce delectable miniature assemblies. Among the most popular of these dishes are the spinach-covered oysters, dubbed oysters Rockefeller—because of their richness—by the New Orleans chef who invented them *(recipe, page 105),* and the bacon-covered clams shown at left.

This simple formula—shellfish flesh, flavoring ingredients and moistening agents—lends itself to a wide variety of elaborations. The mixtures may be covered by a pastry to produce individual pies such as turnovers or large pies such as those demonstrated on pages 70-71. Instead of serving as a pastry filling, the shellfish mixtures can become stuffings for other shellfish or for whole fish *(pages 74-75);* baking melds the various ingredients into a harmonious whole. And that airiest of baked shellfish dishes, a soufflé, is really nothing more than a mixture of shellfish and enriched white sauce that is lightened with beaten egg whites *(pages 72-73).* Air in the whites expands during baking to give the soufflé its ethereal puff.

Broiled shellfish dishes tend to be simpler than those that are baked because, in the high, direct heat of a broiler, extreme brevity of cooking is crucial: The object is to firm the surfaces of the shellfish lightly without drying out the interiors. Most broiled shellfish dishes consist of shellfish flesh lightly coated with butter or oil and quickly seared. For additional flavor, you can marinate the shellfish before cooking them *(pages 76-77);* for variety, you can string shellfish with vegetables and other ingredients on skewers for broiling.

A colorful layer of chopped sweet green and red peppers shields the flesh of clams on their half shells during baking. Moisture for the bivalves is provided by the fat rendered from partially cooked bacon. The entire assembly is known as clams Casino *(page 69).*

A Trio of Tactics for Bivalves

Many shellfish provide a bonus for baking: Their shells can be used as ovenproof cooking and serving vessels. Presentations of this type can be as plain or as elaborate as you please, as long as you take steps to protect the shellfish flesh from drying in the oven's heat.

For the simplest presentations, live bivalves such as tender clams, mussels or the oysters shown at right are baked in their shells with no preparation other than cleaning: The shells protect the flesh and preserve its juices. To steady the shells in the baking pan, place them on a layer of salt—rock salt or any coarse kitchen salt. To speed the cooking, preheat the salt. Once baked, the bivalves should be served immediately on their half shells; the only garnish they need is a sprinkling of lemon juice.

For a more complex blend of flavors, you can bake opened bivalves on their half shells. The flesh should be covered beforehand with a coating that includes fat—butter, oil, or the bacon used in the demonstration opposite, top—and bread crumbs or chopped vegetables such as tomatoes, mushrooms, peppers or spinach.

The most elaborate version of shellfish baked on the half shell is demonstrated at right, bottom. For dishes of this type, the shellfish is precooked, then mixed with flavoring ingredients and a moistening sauce, placed on half shells, and baked just long enough to heat the shellfish through and form a crisp gratin finish atop the assembly. Poached scallops layered with mushrooms and fish velouté sauce and topped with bread crumbs are used in this demonstration (recipe, page 114). The meat of other shellfish—mussels, lobsters or crabs, for instance—could be combined with the scallops or substituted for them; onions, tomatoes or green peppers could replace the mushrooms, and the moisture could be provided by white sauce—enriched, if you like, with grated cheese (page 24).

Oysters Cooked in Their Own Juices

1 **Preparing oysters.** Scrub live oysters with a vegetable brush under cold running water. Spread a layer of coarse salt 1 inch [2½ cm.] deep in a baking pan; set the pan in a preheated 450° F. [230° C.] oven to heat for five minutes. Set the oysters flat side up in the hot salt, being careful not to touch the salt with your fingers.

2 **Serving.** Bake the oysters for eight to 10 minutes, until the shells open. Then, protecting your hand with a cloth and using an oyster knife, open each shell completely, cut the meat loose and remove the top shell (page 16). Serve the oysters on their half shells, garnished, if you like, with peeled lemon slices dipped in chopped parsley.

Scallops and Mushrooms Layered in a Creamy Sauce

1 **Poaching the scallops.** Shell fresh sea scallops (page 17) and scrub the shells, or drain shucked scallops and rinse separately purchased shells. Simmer the scallops' white muscle—and coral, if you have shelled your own scallops—in a white-wine court bouillon (pages 22-23) for two to four minutes, or until the meat is opaque.

2 **Slicing the scallops.** With a slotted spoon, lift the scallops out of the liquid. Slice them thin. Make a velouté sauce (page 25) using the scallops' cooking liquid instead of fish stock, and keep it warm over low heat while you prepare the mushrooms.

A Garlicky Topping for Clams

1 **Preparing the topping.** Melt butter in a skillet set over medium heat and sauté chopped garlic and red and green peppers until the vegetables are soft—about five minutes. Cut thickly sliced bacon into ¼-inch [6-mm.] squares and sauté it in another pan until the bacon is not quite crisp —about five minutes.

2 **Cooking the clams.** Open live clams, leaving them on their half shells (pages 16-17). Spread a layer of coarse salt in a baking pan; preheat the salt for five minutes in a 425° F. [220° C.] oven. Set the clams in the salt. Spoon a little of the garlic-and-pepper mixture over each clam.

3 **Serving.** Place a few bacon pieces on top of the garlic-and-pepper mixture on each clam, and bake the clams for seven minutes, until the bacon is crisp. Serve the clams immediately.

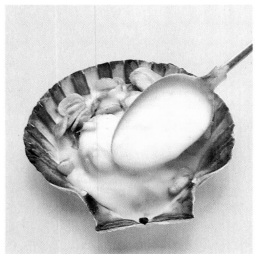

3 **Cooking mushrooms.** Wipe small mushrooms clean and slice them thin. Gently stew them in butter for about three minutes to release their juices, then add the scallops. Cover the pan and set it aside while you complete the sauce.

4 **Preparing the gratin.** Mix egg yolks with court bouillon or cream, and stir them into the velouté sauce. Heat the sauce gently; do not let it boil, lest the mixture curdle. Spoon some sauce into each scallop shell. Add scallop pieces, more sauce, mushrooms and a final spoonful of sauce. Cover with bread crumbs and melted butter.

5 **Browning the surface.** Set the scallop shells in a shallow baking pan and bake them in a preheated 475° F. [250° C.] oven for five or six minutes. If the bread-crumb topping has not browned after this time, complete the gratin by putting the shells under a preheated broiler for a minute.

Pastry Dough: A Versatile Ally

Innumerable baked shellfish dishes feature pastry, and with good reason: Properly handled, pastry not only provides a crisp, golden cover or casing—a pleasant contrast to the tender shellfish meat—but also serves to shield the shellfish from the oven's heat during baking. Depending on the time available for preparing the dough, either short-crust or puff-pastry dough *(pages 26-27)* may be used for the traditional shellfish pie and individual turnovers shown here.

The pie *(right, top)* is the simpler composition, made up only of a richly sauced filling that is placed in a baking dish and covered with a lid of dough *(recipe, page 96)*. There is no bottom crust to the pie: The moist filling would penetrate during cooking and make the crust soggy unless it was prebaked *(recipe, page 95)*.

Almost any combination of ingredients can form the filling; clams and mushrooms in velouté sauce are used here, but oysters, scallops and crustacean flesh swathed in white or Bercy sauce *(recipes, pages 163-164)* could be used instead.

Turnovers are fashioned by wrapping squares or disks of dough around a filling, and demand only careful cutting and folding to keep their shapes neat and their edges tightly sealed. The filling can consist of any shellfish combined with any sauce; in this demonstration, the filling includes prawn tails and white sauce that has been flavored with the crustaceans' shells *(recipe, page 137)*. To keep the shellfish moist without making the pastry soggy, spoon only a small amount of sauce into each turnover before baking. Additional sauce can be served with the completed dish.

Short-crust or puff-pastry dough can be shaped easily as long as it is kept cold to prevent stickiness, and is rolled out lightly and briskly to prevent overworking, which could toughen it. For the pie, the rolled dough is cut to fit the top of the pan or dish and the upturned vessel provides the template. For the turnovers, the dough is cut with the aid of a ruler or—to make disks—an inverted saucer or small round pan. In either case, a sharp knife is necessary for perfectly smooth edges—a precision particularly important for puff pastry, which will not rise evenly with crushed or jagged edges.

Short Crust to Cover a Deep-dish Pie

1 **Preparing clams.** Steam clams—in this case, hard-shell clams—for five minutes in white wine *(page 39)*. With a slotted spoon, transfer the clams to a bowl; strain the cooking liquid and use it to make a velouté sauce *(page 25)*. Shuck the clams.

2 **Making a filling.** Melt butter in a skillet set over medium heat and in it sauté sliced mushrooms until they release their juices—about five minutes. Turn off the heat and stir in the shucked clams, the velouté sauce, chopped parsley, salt, pepper and dry sherry.

Puff-Pastry Packages

1 **Preparing the filling.** Poach Malaysian prawns in court bouillon *(page 10)* for one or two minutes. Drain the prawns, twist off the heads, claws and legs, and shell the tails *(page 19)*. With the prawn debris, make shellfish butter *(page 25)*. Prepare white sauce *(page 24)* and stir in the shellfish butter.

2 **Forming shells.** Roll puff-pastry dough into a sheet ⅛ inch [3 mm.] thick. Using a ruler and a sharp knife, trim the sheet into a perfectly even rectangle. Still using the ruler and knife, cut the rectangle into 4-inch [10-cm.] squares.

3 **Filling the pie dish.** Roll out chilled short-crust dough. Invert a pie dish over the dough for a template, and cut a disk of dough to fit the pie. If desired, cut leaf-shaped decorations. Slide a baking sheet under the dough; refrigerate the dough to firm it. Meanwhile, spoon the filling into the pie dish and let it cool.

4 **Covering the pie.** Roll the disk of dough around the rolling pin, then unroll it to fit over the filled pie dish. Brush the dough with a glaze made by beating an egg yolk with a little water. Arrange the decorations on the top of the pie and brush them with glaze.

5 **Baking the pie.** Place the pie in a preheated 450° F. [230° C.] oven for 15 minutes. Reduce the heat to 350° F. [180° C.] and bake for 20 minutes more, until the pastry is golden brown. Serve the pie in wedges.

3 **Filling the turnovers.** Brush the edges of each square of pastry with beaten egg yolk. Place prawn tail flesh on one side of each square, and spoon on a little flavored white sauce.

4 **Sealing the pastry.** With the help of a pastry scraper, lift the uncovered edge of each square of dough and fold it over the filling. Press the cut edges gently together with the side of your hand to seal them. Brush each turnover with a glaze made by beating an egg yolk with a little heavy cream.

5 **Baking.** Set the turnovers on a baking sheet lined with parchment paper and bake them for 10 minutes in a preheated 425° F. [220° C.] oven. Reduce the heat to 375° F. [190° C.] and bake for 15 minutes more, until the turnovers are puffed and golden. Transfer them to a warmed serving platter; pass the remaining sauce separately.

Soufflés: Airy Mediums for Delicate Meat

Of all baked shellfish dishes, perhaps the most spectacular is a soufflé, formed by combining cooked shellfish meat with a thick base of white sauce and egg yolks, then adding stiffly beaten egg whites. The air in the egg whites gives the soufflé its lightness and puffy golden top.

Any shellfish—either leftover or prepared just for the purpose—may be used in a soufflé base, but the best choices are tender crustaceans or scallops. The meat may be puréed for a homogeneous texture or, as here, part of the meat may be puréed and part chopped for textural variety. The white sauce that binds the meat and gives body to the soufflé is made as shown on page 24, but using only half the standard amount of milk.

The amount of egg white added to the soufflé base is critical: If you use too few whites, the soufflé will not rise, but too many produce a soufflé of such lightness that it will not hold its shape. As a rule, a soufflé containing 1 cup [¼ liter] of sauce and 1 cup of shellfish meat requires four large egg yolks to yield a firm base and should be lightened with at least four—but no more than six—large whites.

It is important to incorporate as much air as possible into the whites before adding them to the soufflé base. Have the whites at room temperature: They will be more elastic and able to hold more air. A large wire whisk is the best utensil for beating. The ideal bowl is of unlined copper; the metal interacts with the whites, helping them hold their puff. All utensils should be clean; even a speck of oil or fat could prevent the whites from rising. The beaten whites should be folded—gently, to prevent deflating—into the soufflé base, and the soufflé should be baked immediately so that the whites lose as little air as possible.

Soufflés rise to great heights when they are baked in deep, straight-sided dishes. However, for an unusual presentation, the cleaned body shells of lobsters or crabs can become baking and serving vessels, as here (recipe, page 144).

A soufflé must be served as soon as it is done, or it will collapse. Complements to soufflés are such flour-thickened sauces as the wine-flavored velouté shown (recipe, page 163), or white sauce enhanced with shellfish butter (recipe, page 164).

1 Preparing the shells. Poach lobsters—American lobsters are used here—until they are half-done (pages 30-31), and drain them. Lay each lobster on its back and, with a sharp knife, split it in half lengthwise. Twist off the claws; cut off the legs. Remove the meat from the claws and body. Then rinse and dry the body shell halves and reserve them.

2 Puréeing the meat. Divide the lobster meat in half. Cut half of the meat into small chunks and set aside. With a mortar and pestle or a food processor purée the remaining meat. Season the purée with salt, freshly ground black pepper, freshly grated nutmeg and a pinch of cayenne pepper.

4 Flavoring the sauce. Stir the puréed lobster meat into the white sauce. In a large bowl—preferably copper, such as the one shown here—whisk egg whites until they form stiff peaks.

5 Lightening with egg whites. Stir about a quarter of the beaten egg whites into the flavored sauce to lighten it. Then gently fold the remaining whites into the sauce.

3 **Smoothing the mixture.** With a plastic scraper, press the puréed lobster meat through a fine-meshed sieve into a bowl and set it aside. Prepare white sauce and enrich it with beaten egg yolks.

6 **Filling the shells.** Place the lobster shells, cavities upward, in a shallow baking dish. Line each shell with a thin coat of soufflé mixture. Add a shallow layer of the chopped lobster meat and cover the meat with soufflé mixture. Bake the soufflés in a preheated 400° F. [200° C.] oven for 15 to 20 minutes, until they are puffed and golden.

7 **Serving.** While the soufflés bake, boil a little white wine and fish stock with chopped shallots until the mixture is reduced to a few spoonfuls. Stir in fish velouté *(page 25)*; enrich the sauce with butter and chopped fresh parsley. Serve the lobster soufflés as soon as they are ready; pass the sauce separately.

Stuffings Based on Shellfish Morsels

Mixed with flavoring ingredients, bread crumbs, and melted butter or cream, raw shellfish flesh makes a delicious stuffing for baked assemblies. Any shellfish may be used as part of a stuffing, and the range of bases is extensive.

You can, for instance, use shellfish stuffings to top other shellfish. Clams or oysters on the half shell and split lobsters form naturally broad foundations. Prawns or shrimp can be butterflied as demonstrated at right to provide flat surfaces that will support a filling (recipe, page 136).

For more elaborate effects, you can fill a whole fish with stuffing (below; recipe, page 120). The fish should be a very fresh one that has been cleaned and gutted; trout is used here, but any round fish— sea bass or snapper, for example—can be stuffed similarly. To prepare the fish, clip out its gills with scissors, then, for ease in serving, bone the fish as shown in the box opposite.

Butterflied Shrimp Heaped with Scallops

1 **Butterflying shrimp.** Peel and devein large shrimp (page 18), leaving the tail shells intact. Deepen the cut in each shrimp almost all of the way through the flesh. Open the shrimp. Place the flat of a knife blade across the cut side of the shrimp and pound it to flatten the shrimp; the tail shell will rise. Chop bay scallops fine.

2 **Filling the shrimp.** Mound a spoonful of scallops on each flattened shrimp. Combine fresh bread crumbs with grated Parmesan cheese and press some of the mixture onto the scallops. Place the shrimp in a buttered shallow baking dish and sprinkle on paprika. Drizzle melted butter mixed with crushed garlic over the shrimp.

A Crab-filled Trout

1 **Extracting crab meat.** Twist off the large joints from the ends of king crab legs. With kitchen shears, slice the shell of each leg open lengthwise, breaking the leg apart at each joint. Pull out the meat. Remove the meat from king crab claws (page 33, Step 6). Chop all of the crab meat.

2 **Cooking the filling.** Melt butter in a skillet set over medium heat, and in it sauté chopped carrots, scallions and celery until they are soft—about five minutes. Add the crab meat, salt, pepper, grated nutmeg and chopped parsley. Stir in heavy cream and simmer for 10 minutes, until thick.

3 **Filling the fish.** Lay a whole boned fish—in this case, a trout—on its back. Spoon the filling into the belly cavity. Do not pack the cavity too tight: The stuffing will expand during baking. Slide small metal skewers through both flaps of the belly at 1-inch [2½-cm.] intervals to pull the edges together.

Boning a Fish

Removing the backbone. With a sharp knife, extend the belly opening of a whole, cleaned fish—here, a trout—to the tail. Open the fish and slice just under the ribs and backbone on either side *(above, left)*. Lift the backbone free and use kitchen shears to sever it behind the head and at the tail end *(right)*. Remove the backbone and ribs.

3 **Serving.** Bake the shrimp in a preheated 350° F. [180° C.] oven, basting them with white wine, if desired. After 15 minutes, when the stuffing is golden, squeeze fresh lemon juice over the shrimp and serve.

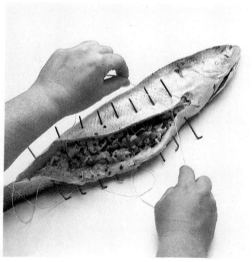

4 **Securing the stuffing.** Cut a piece of cotton string about 4 feet [1¼ meters] long. Loop the midsection of the string around both of the skewers closest to the head. Cross the string ends and wind them around the next pair of skewers. Lace up the fish in this crisscross fashion. Tie the string.

5 **Cooking.** Place the fish in a buttered shallow baking dish and bake it in a preheated 425° F. [220° C.] oven, allowing 10 minutes for each 1 inch [2½ cm.] of the stuffed fish's greatest thickness. To serve the fish, remove the string and skewers, and garnish it with lemon wedges and chopped parsley.

Easy Ways to Enhance Flavor

Broiling is among the simplest of cooking methods, but its simplicity does not preclude dishes with complex blends of flavors. For a range of tastes in a single assembly, one or more types of tender shellfish may be broiled with other ingredients by stringing them all on skewers. Or the shellfish may be marinated before cooking to imbue its flesh with the scents of herbs and spices.

When broiling skewer assemblies, you must take care to ensure that all of the ingredients will cook in the same brief period. Bivalves such as tender clams, oysters and scallops must be shucked before broiling; mussels, used in the demonstration at top right *(recipe, page 101)*, generally are steamed first—the easiest way to remove them from their shells. Shrimp, Malaysian prawns and crayfish may simply be shelled; lobster tails may be shelled and cut into pieces; crabs are not suitable for skewering.

Complementary ingredients may require precooking so that they will be done at the same time as the shellfish. The bacon pieces used here, for instance, require longer cooking than the mussels they complement, and are sautéed ahead of time until their fat is transparent. If you include firm vegetables—green pepper squares or small whole onions are the usual choices—parboil them for two or three minutes to soften them slightly and shorten their final cooking. Softer vegetables such as cherry tomatoes or mushrooms need no preliminary cooking.

To prevent drying, the skewered ingredients should, of course, be coated with fat or oil: butter, bland vegetable oil or fruity olive oil—even lightly beaten egg yolks, which provide rich flavor as well as fat. Fine bread crumbs, held in place by the fat or oil, will give a crisp finish.

Shellfish marinated before broiling—such as the rock shrimp shown at bottom right—needs no additional coating for cooking: Marinades combine tangy acidic liquids such as wine or citrus juice with oil, and serve both to flavor shellfish and to moisten its flesh. This basic mixture can be enhanced by chopped aromatics—garlic and shallots, for example—and by herbs and spices *(recipe, page 138)*. Reserved marinade is used to baste and moisten the shellfish during broiling.

Skewered Mussels Interleaved with Bacon

1 **Assembling skewers.** Cut slices of slab bacon into thin strips and sauté the strips in butter for about five minutes. Steam cleaned mussels open *(page 39)*. Shuck them, place in a bowl and moisten with their cooking liquid. Alternate the strips of bacon and the mussels on long metal skewers.

Rock Shrimp Marinated in Scented Oil

1 **Splitting rock shrimp.** Place each rock shrimp on its back. With a sharp knife, cut down between the legs to split the top shell and flesh along its length; leave the shell beneath the flesh uncut. Open the shrimp like a book, until it lies flat. Rinse the shrimp thoroughly under cold running water to flush out the intestinal vein.

2 **Marinating.** Mix marinade ingredients—in this case, lemon juice, olive oil, saffron, and chopped shallots, garlic and thyme. Place the shrimp in a deep dish and pour the marinade over them. Cover, and refrigerate for one to two hours; turn the shrimp occasionally if the marinade does not cover them.

2 **Coating.** Brush melted butter—as here—or beaten egg onto the mussels and bacon. Spread dry bread crumbs on a shallow tray. Roll each assembly in the crumbs and sprinkle more crumbs over the top. Lay the skewers across a shallow baking pan to suspend the mussels and bacon.

3 **Cooking.** Slide the pan under a preheated broiler, placing it 4 inches [10 cm.] from the heat source. Let the mussels and bacon cook for two minutes, until one side has browned. Turn the skewers and cook for two minutes more. Slide the mussels and bacon onto a warmed plate. Garnish with watercress, if desired.

3 **Broiling.** Drain the shrimp, reserving the marinade. Spread the shrimp, flesh side up, in a shallow baking pan. Brush a little marinade on each shrimp. Place the pan 4 inches [10 cm.] from the heat source of a preheated broiler; cook the shrimp for two minutes—until their tails curl.

4 **Serving.** Arrange the shrimp on a warmed serving platter. To make a sauce, stir melted butter into the remaining marinade. To eat a shrimp, grasp it by the tail and dip the meat into the sauce before taking each bite.

Special Techniques to Ensure Even Cooking

The aim of broiling lobsters, clams or oysters is to produce shellfish that are firm, but still moist. In every case, success is achieved by coating the shellfish with ingredients that moisten and enrich the flesh, and by ensuring that the cooking is both swift and even. The nature of the shellfish determines how to handle it.

Lobsters are generally split in half and broiled in their shells. But even when split, the body of a lobster is too thick to cook evenly in high heat coming from just one direction: The surfaces that are closest to the heat will overcook and dry out before the interior flesh is done. To produce succulent and fully cooked lobster halves, first heat them—shell sides down—on the top of the stove, as demonstrated at right. Brief broiling will then brown the cut surfaces of the lobster halves and cook them through.

With its delicate sweetness, lobster meat demands the most unobtrusively flavored of moisteners. The best choice is melted butter, which has been brightened with a little lemon juice or dry white wine, if desired.

For oysters and tender clams, which cook through quickly whatever the heat source, broiling is a method for providing an appealing finish *(bottom)*. The bivalves are shucked and their deeper shells preheated on a bed of salt, while the flesh is briefly warmed. After the oysters or clams are returned to their shells, moistened and garnished, they can be broiled in less than a minute.

The abundant, flavorful juices of these bivalves should form part of the moistening ingredients in the assemblies. The juices may be supplemented by butter or, as here, white butter sauce, and the flesh may be covered with any of the gratin coatings demonstrated on pages 68-69.

Starting Lobster in a Pan

1 **Starting the cooking.** Split lobsters—here, American lobsters—in half and remove the stomach sacs and intestinal veins *(page 18)*. Set a large skillet over high heat; in it place the lobster halves, shell sides down. Cook the lobsters for about five minutes, until the shells begin to redden.

Preheating Oysters in Their Own Liquor

1 **Preparing shellfish.** Shuck oysters *(page 16)*, reserving their liquor and the deeper half shells. Poach periwinkles in court bouillon *(page 23)* for three minutes, until their operculums (the dark disks that seal in the meat) open. Drain the periwinkles, reserving some liquid. Pull off the operculums; with a skewer, pry out the flesh.

2 **Making white butter sauce.** Mix the reserved periwinkle cooking liquid with lemon juice and white pepper, and boil over high heat until the mixture is reduced by half. Reduce the heat under the pan and whisk in chunks of cold butter; when this sauce is thick *(page 24)* remove the pan from the heat.

3 **Warming the oysters.** Heat the reserved half shells on a bed of salt *(pages 68-69)* for five minutes under a preheated broiler. Warm the oysters and liquor over medium heat for about two minutes; monitor the temperature of the liquid with a deep-frying or instant reading thermometer to ensure that it does not exceed 140° F. [60° C.].

2 **Basting the lobsters.** Melt butter and stir in lemon juice for flavor. Drizzle this mixture over the lobster flesh to coat the cut surface uniformly and keep it juicy during broiling.

3 **Broiling.** Slide the skillet under a preheated broiler, placing it on a shelf so positioned that the tops of the lobsters are 4 inches [10 cm.] from the heat source. Cook the lobster halves for seven minutes, or until their flesh is opaque and lightly browned.

4 **Serving.** Transfer two of the lobster halves to each warmed individual serving platter. Garnish each platter with lemon wedges and a bowl of melted butter. To eat the lobsters, follow the technique that is shown in the top demonstration on pages 30-31.

4 **Broiling.** Spoon a little white butter sauce into each oyster shell. Drain the oysters and place one in each shell, smooth side up (*above*). Spoon on a little more sauce, and top each oyster with periwinkles. Broil the assembly 4 inches [10 cm.] from the heat source for about one half minute, until the sauce bubbles. Serve immediately, garnished with chopped fresh parsley (*right*).

Special Presentations
Elaborating
on Basic Techniques

Applying layered aspic coatings
Incorporating cream in a mousseline mixture
Templates to aid the cutting of pastry
Supporting a vol-au-vent as it rises

Delicacies that they are, shellfish are a natural choice for elaborate presentation, and in fact, shellfish assemblies were given careful attention by the famous chefs of 19th Century France, who delighted in formality. Gracing these chefs' repertoire were magnificent molded shellfish dishes glittering with aspic and gleaming with cream, wonderfully airy concoctions based on shellfish purées, and any number of fanciful pastry containers that concealed rich mixtures of shellfish and sauce. Dishes in this tradition still can be made for special occasions—and all are composed with the aid of familiar cooking techniques.

Aspic, for instance, is simply fish stock reinforced with gelatin that sets as it chills to a firm, transparent jelly. Aspic often is used as surface decoration, as shown opposite. The complex-looking assembly is nothing more than a lobster salad presented in a spiny lobster shell; its shining aspic surface adds a touch of elegance. Liquid aspic also is a molding medium *par excellence*. When cool and syrupy, it can be used to line and fill molds containing layers of shellfish meat and—for color—vegetables such as tomatoes, cucumbers or avocados. Chilled until firm, the aspic can be turned out to stand free, the shimmering jelly displaying the bright layers of ingredients trapped within.

Mousseline, another classic preparation, is an ethereally light purée of delicate meat—chicken breast, firm fish or tender shellfish flesh—bound with egg white and enriched and lightened with whipped cream. The shellfish version of mousseline is displayed at its best in feathery quenelles, which are small, egg-shaped dumplings (the word "quenelle" derives from *knödel,* the Alsatian word for dumpling), swathed in sumptuous sauces *(pages 84-85).*

Elaborate pastry presentations are most artfully made with the puff pastry demonstrated on pages 26-27. The pastry dough is time-consuming to prepare, but not at all difficult to shape into the containers known as vol-au-vent. The fish-shaped pastry case filled with shrimp, lobster, scallops and creamy sauce shown on pages 86-88 is a prime example of the technique. Puff pastry's buttery lightness gives containers of this type both their distinction and their name. It is said that the great chef Antoine Carême constructed a tower of the pastry that pleased him so much he cried *"Elle vole au vent"*—"It flies with the wind."

A paint brush that has been dipped in syrupy aspic is used to apply the finishing touches to a cold lobster presentation *(page 83).* The shell of a spiny lobster was first filled with lobster salad and crowned with medallions of tail meat; the assembly was then glazed with aspic, which unifies these elements and gives them a satiny sheen.

Glistening Assemblies Created with Aspic

Tiers of Shrimp in a Freestanding Mold

Smooth and shining aspic is the source of a range of cold shellfish preparations. It can simply be a coating for shellfish meat or—used more lavishly—it can be transformed into a freestanding mold encasing a rich array of shellfish and vegetables. Though details of preparation vary, depending on the dish, the basic rules of handling the aspic do not.

Aspic starts as gelatinous stock—for shellfish dishes, usually fish stock that has been clarified and reinforced with gelatin (pages 22-23). The stock sets to firm aspic when it is completely chilled. But while you are composing aspic dishes it should be only partially set: The stock must be thick enough to adhere to molds and food surfaces, but liquid enough for pouring and dipping.

To achieve this consistency set a metal bowl filled with stock—metal conducts cold well—in a bowl of ice. Stir the stock often until it is syrupy, at which point it is ready for use. Leave the stock in the ice as you work; if it becomes too thick to pour, warm it over low heat until it melts and chill it again. Refrigerate finished assemblies to set the stock completely.

The soft and silky texture of chilled aspic best complements the firm flesh of cooked scallops or crustaceans such as crabs, prawns, or the shrimp and lobster used in these demonstrations. For extra flavor, the shellfish can be cooked in the stock used for the aspic. The shellfish meat and any other ingredients included in aspic assemblies should be chilled before use to help the stock set quickly.

To achieve the tiered effect that distinguishes molded dishes (right) you must mold the aspic and filling ingredients in layers, allowing each layer to set before the next is added; otherwise the filling ingredients will float to the top of the mold before the aspic sets completely. Use a metal mold for the process, and dampen it before use to aid unmolding.

Individual shellfish pieces to be coated with aspic (opposite, below) also should be chilled beforehand. To produce smooth surfaces, you will need at least two thin coats of gelatinous stock. The coats are most easily formed by pouring stock over shellfish that are resting on a rack set over a pan to catch drips. Stock that hardens in the pan can be warmed and reused.

1 **Coating a mold.** Bury a dampened metal mold to its rim in an ice-filled bowl. Ladle in cooled but liquid gelatinous stock and rotate the mold slowly in the ice for about five minutes, until the stock coats the mold sides in an aspic layer about ¼ inch [6 mm.] thick. Place the container of unused stock in a second ice-filled bowl; stir it until it is syrupy.

2 **Adding tomatoes.** Peel, seed and quarter chilled tomatoes. Chill cooked, cleaned shrimp. Pour some unused aspic into a bowl. Into it, dip each tomato quarter; arrange the quarters in the mold. The dipping aspic will be cloudy. Ladle clear aspic over the tomatoes and let it chill for 10 minutes, until firm.

6 **Serving.** Garnish the aspic. In the demonstration shown here, the hollow of the molded aspic ring was lined with sorrel leaves, then filled with mayonnaise flavored with chopped spinach, parsley, chives, tarragon and chervil.

3 **Adding shrimp.** Spear each shrimp with a skewer, coat it with the dipping aspic and lay it in the mold, curved side out but not touching the mold sides. When you have formed a layer of shrimp, pour on a layer of clear aspic and let it set. Continue layering shrimp and aspic in this manner until the mold is filled. Discard the dipping aspic.

4 **Loosening the aspic.** Cover the molded aspic with plastic wrap and refrigerate it for at least four hours, until the assembly has set. When you are ready to serve the aspic, run a knife blade around its edge to a depth of ¼ inch [6 mm.] to loosen it.

5 **Unmolding.** Dip the mold for a second into a bowl of hot tap water. Immediately invert a plate over the mold, then turn plate and mold over together and shake them sharply to loosen the aspic. Lift off the mold.

Lobster Medallions with a Shining Glaze

1 **Preparing a shell.** Twist apart the tail and body shells of each of two poached spiny lobsters (page 30, Step 1, bottom demonstration). With shears, cut around the tail edges to remove the membrane covering the meat; lift out the meat. Clean the tail and body shells of one lobster; discard the other shells. Chill the meat and shells.

2 **Coating.** Slice the tail meat into medallions. Mix imperfect pieces and other scraps with tartar sauce (page 24). Place the medallions on a rack set over a pan. Ladle chilled aspic over them. Dip briefly blanched scallion leaves in the aspic, place them on the medallions and chill until the aspic sets. Coat and chill again.

3 **Assembling.** Lay the shell sections on a rack set over a pan, with the back of the body shell and the cavity of the tail shell upward. Use a wooden pick to join them. Fill the tail with the sauce-coated lobster and ladle on aspic. Arrange the medallions on top. Ladle aspic over them and refrigerate until the aspic sets.

Enriching and Shaping Shellfish Purées

Airy warm mousselines and creamy cold mousses can both be based on smoothly puréed shellfish meat. Crabs, crayfish, lobsters, prawns, scallops and shrimp are all suitable, but must be absolutely fresh to produce a fine-textured purée. Both mousses and mousselines are enriched and lightened with whipped cream (recipes, pages 166 and 140); however, the finished dishes are considerably different in character.

A cold mousse is essentially an enhanced aspic. Cooked shellfish meat is puréed in a food processor or with a mortar and pestle and then, for perfect smoothness, pressed through a sieve. The purée is combined with fish velouté sauce (page 25) and whipped cream, and bound with liquid aspic (pages 22-23). The mixture is molded and chilled to set the mousse firm, after which it is ready to serve.

Mousseline can be steamed like custard in a ring mold or individual cups or ramekins (pages 42-43) or, as here, turned into poached dumplings of unique delicacy. The shellfish meat that serves as the basis for the mousseline must be puréed raw and can be augmented with raw fish. The purée is bound with egg whites and lightened with cream, and is then formed into small, egg-shaped dumplings and poached.

If it is to absorb the cream, the shellfish purée has to be very firm; this is achieved by keeping the purée well chilled. A classic mousseline is formed by beating the cream into the purée in very small increments, chilling the mixture after each addition. However, you can add the cream in one step, as in this demonstration, if you keep both cream and purée very cold during the process.

The liquid for poaching may be fish stock (pages 22-23) or simply salted water, but it must never be allowed to heat above a gentle simmer. If the liquid boils, the delicate dumplings will fall apart.

Quenelles are usually served with an elegant coating—Nantua sauce, for instance, or the fish velouté used in this demonstration (recipes, pages 165 and 163). A dish that is coated with a milk-based sauce can be placed under a hot broiler for a few moments to achieve a rich golden crust.

A Chilled Amalgam of Crab Meat and Aspic

1 **Flavoring crab meat.** Over low heat, sauté chopped onion, carrot and celery in butter until they soften—about 10 minutes. Add white wine; ignite warmed brandy and, when the flame dies, stir it into the mixture. Add seasonings and crab meat. Heat the mixture, then purée it with a food processor or mortar and pestle.

2 **Refining the purée.** Force the purée through a fine-meshed sieve into a metal bowl; discard any cartilage left on the mesh and chill the purée. Make fish aspic and chill it until it is syrupy—about two hours in the refrigerator.

Shrimp Quenelles Gently Poached

1 **Lightening the purée.** Use a food processor or mortar and pestle to purée cleaned shrimp and skinned fish fillets; sieve the purée into a metal bowl (Step 2, above). Set the bowl in a larger, ice-filled bowl and use a wooden spoon to beat in egg white by small spoonfuls, making sure each spoonful is completely incorporated before adding the next.

2 **Adding cream.** Whisk chilled heavy cream until soft peaks form. Still working over ice, beat the cream into the mousseline mixture by spoonfuls until the ingredients are thoroughly combined. Then season the mousseline with salt and pepper.

3 **Forming the mousse.** Prepare and chill fish velouté *(recipe, page 163)*. Whip chilled heavy cream until it forms soft peaks. Put the bowl of crab meat purée in a larger, ice-filled bowl. Gently fold in the chilled velouté, the whipped cream and finally the chilled aspic.

4 **Molding.** Spoon some of the mousse mixture into the bottom of a chilled metal mold; shake the mold so that the mixture settles evenly. Then fill the mold with the mousse mixture, pressing it into crevices with a rubber spatula. Press plastic wrap onto the surface of the mousse, and refrigerate it for at least six hours, until firm.

5 **Serving.** Uncover the mousse and run a knife tip around the edge to loosen it. Dip the bottom of the mold for a second into hot water; invert a plate over it, then turn mold and plate upside down. Lift away the mold. Garnish the mousse, if you like, with chilled and chopped aspic *(pages 22-23)* and with poached, cracked stone-crab claws.

3 **Shaping quenelles.** Dip a tablespoon in hot water to prevent sticking, and scoop up a little mousseline. With a second dampened spoon, smooth the mousseline into an egg shape. Transfer this quenelle to a shallow, buttered pan. Form other quenelles; do not crowd the pan.

4 **Cooking the quenelles.** Pour into the pan enough simmering water or fish stock to cover the quenelles. Cover the pan and simmer the quenelles gently for about three minutes on each side; they are done when they float to the surface. With a slotted spoon, transfer the quenelles to paper towels and let them drain briefly.

5 **Serving.** Arrange the quenelles on a warmed serving platter. Decorate the quenelles, if you like, with small shrimp that have been poached and peeled, and coat the quenelles with a sauce. Here, the sauce is a fish velouté flavored with lemon juice, grated lemon peel and chopped fresh parsley. Serve the quenelles immediately.

A Pastry Maker's Tour de Force

Among the richest and prettiest of classic shellfish presentations are the golden pastry cases called vol-au-vent that enclose creamy mixtures of shellfish and sauce. Properly made, the cases are characterized by an incomparable lightness.

Hollow vol-au-vent cases are fashioned from puff-pastry dough (pages 26-27), whose buttery layers puff during baking to give the pastry its lightness. The basic rules for handling the dough are the same no matter what shape you choose. The dough must be rolled with a light hand and cut with a sharp knife: If you stretch the dough during shaping or cutting, you will distort the butter layers, causing uneven rising. And the dough must be kept very cold; otherwise, the butter layers will melt into the dough layers and the dough will not puff. Work only with small portions of dough, keeping any dough that you are not using in the refrigerator.

To fashion a large case, such as that demonstrated here, you will need about 4 pounds [2 kg.] of puff-pastry dough, templates for cutting a dough base and lid, and a means of supporting the sides during baking so that a hollow is left for filling. Cake pans can be used as guides for cutting round or rectangular cases. For more elaborate shapes, cut templates from cardboard. Coiled linen towels enclosed in the dough will support the sides of the case as it bakes.

Fillings for the crisp, baked pastry— you will need approximately 4 cups [1 liter] for the case shown—should be light and moist. You can use seafood Newburg, as in this demonstration (recipe, page 141) or such preparations as curried oysters (recipe, page 110) or scallops with saffron (recipe, page 111). Fill the baked case just before serving it to prevent the filling from seeping into the pastry and making it soggy.

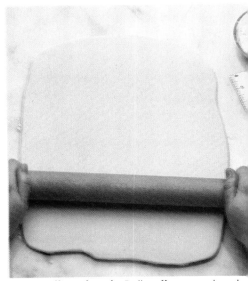

1 Rolling dough. Roll puff-pastry dough into a rectangle ½ inch [1 cm.] thick an several inches larger all around than th base template for the vol-au-vent. In th case, the base template is an oval fish shape 15 inches [38 cm.] long and 8 inches [20 cm.] wide drawn freehand c cardboard; it requires 2 pounds [1 kg. of puff-pastry dough.

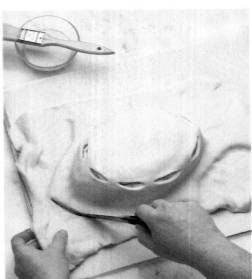

5 Trimming the pastry case. Using a sharp knife, and following the raised outline of the pastry base, trim the sheet of dough to the exact size of the base. Beat egg yolk and cream together to use as a glaze.

6 Sealing the case. Lifting the edge of the dough top a small section at a time, brush all around the inside edge of the dough base with the egg glaze. Gently press down the edge of the dough top to seal the case. Make several lengthwise slashes through the tail.

7 Baking. With the plain decorating tube, stamp circles on the pastry case represent scales. Glaze the disk of dough and press it onto the head of t fish as an eye. Fold the fin lengthwise and use glaze to secure it to the lid of t case. Glaze the surfaces of the case. Bake the case at 425° F. [220° C.] for minutes; reduce the heat to 375° F. [190° C.] and bake for one hour more

2 **Cutting the base.** Hold the base template on the dough and cut around its edge with a sharp knife. Use a plain pastry-decorating tube to stamp out a disk-shaped eye; use a knife to cut a triangular fin. Remove excess dough, stack and wrap it and refrigerate, reserving it for another use.

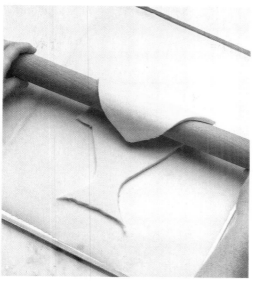

3 **Moving the base.** Roll the base onto the rolling pin; unroll it on a baking sheet lined with parchment paper, and chill it. Roll more dough—in this case, 2 pounds—into a rectangle several inches larger than the base. Score the shape of a lid template—here, an oval 1 ½ inches [4 cm.] smaller than the base—in the center of the rectangle.

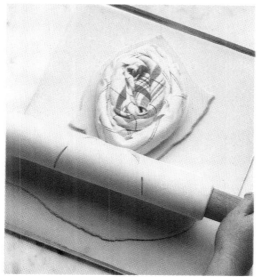

4 **Making the top.** Roll up linen towels; coil them into an oval the size of the lid template. Center the towels on the dough base. Using the pin, unroll the scored sheet of dough over the base, centering the oval section on top of the towels. Press the sides of the dough sheet around the towels. Refrigerate the assembly for half an hour.

8 **Cooking filling.** Poach a spiny lobster, shrimp and scallops (chart, page 7). Shell the lobster tail (page 30, Steps 1 and 2, bottom demonstration) and the shrimp (page 18). Slice the lobster tail crosswise into medallions. Stew the shellfish in butter over medium heat for three minutes; season with salt, cayenne, grated nutmeg, sherry and brandy. Simmer for one minute; stir in heavy cream. Let the mixture come to a simmer, reduce the heat and stir in beaten egg yolks. Set the filling aside. ▶

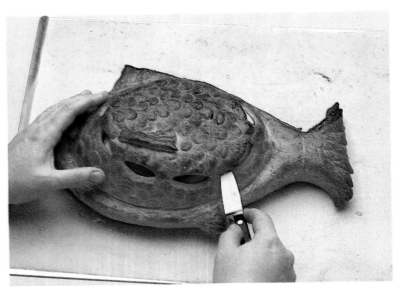

9 **Cutting out the lid.** As soon as the pastry case is golden brown, remove it from the oven. When it is cool enough to handle, use a sharp knife held horizontal to the work surface to slice off the pastry case lid along the scored lines. With a spoon, scrape any damp pastry from the underside of the lid. Set the lid aside.

10 **Removing the towels.** Beginning with the innermost towel, gently lift the towels straight up and out of the pastry case. Scrape any damp pastry from inside the case. With the aid of a large spatula, transfer the case to a serving platter.

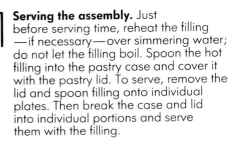

11 **Serving the assembly.** Just before serving time, reheat the filling —if necessary—over simmering water; do not let the filling boil. Spoon the hot filling into the pastry case and cover it with the pastry lid. To serve, remove the lid and spoon filling onto individual plates. Then break the case and lid into individual portions and serve them with the filling.

Anthology of Recipes

Drawing upon the cooking literature of more than 15 countries, the editors and consultants for this volume have selected 204 published recipes for the Anthology that follows. The selections range from three variations of American clam fritters to a Japanese recipe for deep-fried shrimp balls filled with candied chestnuts and studded with noodle "thorns."

Many of the recipes were written by world-renowned exponents of the culinary art, but the Anthology also includes selections from rare and out-of-print books and from works that have never been published in English. Whatever the sources, the emphasis is always on fresh ingredients that blend harmoniously and on techniques that are practical for the home cook.

Since many early recipe writers did not specify amounts of ingredients, sizes of pans or even cooking times and temperatures, the missing information has been judiciously added. In some cases, clarifying introductory notes have also been supplied; they are printed in italics. Modern recipe terms have been substituted for archaic language and some instructions have been expanded; but to preserve the character of the original recipes and to create a true anthology, the authors' texts have been changed as little as possible. For this reason, cooking times, especially in older recipes, may seem overlong by today's standards—and you may want to shorten them, following the guidelines in the chart on page 7.

In keeping with the organization of the first half of the book, most of the recipes are categorized according to the technique and the ingredients. Recipes for standard preparations—pastry dough, stocks and sauces among them—appear at the end of the Anthology. Unfamiliar cooking terms and uncommon ingredients, such as Indian spices and Japanese wines, are explained in the combined General Index and Glossary.

Apart from the primary components, all ingredients are listed within each recipe in order of use, with the customary U.S. measurements and the metric measurements provided in separate columns. All quantities reflect the American practice of measuring such solid ingredients as flour by volume rather than by weight, as is done in Europe.

To make the quantities simpler to measure, many of the figures have been rounded off to correspond to the gradations on U.S. metric spoons and cups. (One cup, for example, equals 237 milliliters; however, wherever practicable in these recipes, the metric equivalent of 1 cup appears as a more readily measured 250 milliliters—¼ liter.) Similarly, the weight, temperature and linear metric equivalents have been rounded off slightly. Thus the American and metric figures do not exactly match, but using one set or the other will produce the same good results.

Abalone and Conch

Japanese Sweet Abalone

To serve 2

1 lb.	abalone meat, pounded	½ kg.
1 cup	water	¼ liter
3 tbsp.	dry white wine	45 ml.
2 tbsp.	sugar	30 ml.
1 tbsp.	soy sauce	15 ml.

Place the abalone meat in a large saucepan and add the water. Bring to a boil, then reduce the heat and simmer uncovered for 10 minutes. Add the wine and sugar and cook for five minutes; then stir in the soy sauce and cook for three minutes more. Cool, then drain the abalone and cut it into slices ½ inch [1 cm.] thick.

PHILLIP MASON
SHELLFISH COOKBOOK

Stewed Abalone

The original version of this old recipe calls for ormers, the European species of abalone found in the English Channel, and recommends cooking them for eight hours — an excessive time by modern standards.

The meat should be as tender as veal but more delicious.

To serve 6

2 lb.	abalone meat, pounded and cut into cubes	1 kg.
2 tbsp.	butter	30 ml.
1½ tbsp.	flour	22½ ml.
1	large onion, sliced	1
1 tbsp.	chopped mixed fresh herbs	15 ml.
	salt and pepper	
2 cups	fish stock *(recipe, page 163)*	½ liter

Heat the butter in a skillet and brown the abalone cubes on all sides. Remove them to a large pot with the onion, herbs and seasoning. Add the flour to the skillet and cook, stirring until lightly browned. Gradually stir in the stock. When the stock has thickened, pour it over the abalone in the pot. Cover and simmer very gently for one hour.

J. STEVENS COX (EDITOR)
GUERNSEY DISHES OF BYGONE DAYS

Abalone with Grape Sauce

To serve 12

12	abalone steaks, pounded thin and patted dry	12
½ cup	sugar	125 ml.
1½ cups	boiling water	375 ml.
½ lb.	green seedless grapes	¼ kg.
2	navel oranges, tops and bottoms cut off, each orange cut into 6 slices	2
1 cup	milk	¼ liter
½ cup	flour	125 ml.
3	eggs, beaten	3
8 tbsp.	salted butter	120 ml.
	salt and freshly ground pepper	

Grape sauce

1 tsp.	chopped shallots	5 ml.
1 cup	red wine	¼ liter
1 cup	grape juice, extracted from 1 to 2 lb. [½ to 1 kg.] fresh grapes	¼ liter
1 tsp.	Cognac	5 ml.
1 tbsp.	heavy cream	15 ml.

For the sauce, combine the shallots, wine and grape juice in a saucepan. Over low heat, reduce the liquid by half. Stir in the Cognac and the cream. Keep the sauce warm.

In a saucepan, dissolve the sugar in the boiling water to make a sugar syrup. Gently poach the grapes in the syrup for five minutes, or until tender; set aside.

Moisten the abalone steaks in the milk, dust with the flour, then dip them in the beaten eggs. In a large, heavy skillet, melt the butter and sauté the steaks over high heat to a golden-yellow color — about 30 seconds on each side. Season with salt and pepper. Arrange the steaks, alternating with the orange slices, overlapping in a row on a warmed serving platter. Sprinkle the poached grapes over the assembly and cover it with the sauce.

A. J. MC CLANE
MC CLANE'S NORTH AMERICAN FISH COOKERY

Abalone Sesame Steaks

To serve 4

4	abalone steaks (about ¼ lb. [125 g.] each), pounded thin and patted dry	4
¼ cup	sesame seeds	50 ml.
1 cup	dry bread crumbs	¼ liter
⅛ tsp.	cayenne pepper	½ ml.
	flour, seasoned with salt and freshly ground pepper	
2	eggs, beaten with 2 tbsp. [30 ml.] milk	2
8 tbsp.	butter	120 ml.
2 tsp.	fresh lemon juice	10 ml.
1	lemon, cut into 4 wedges	1

In a heavy skillet, toast the sesame seeds over medium heat—shaking the skillet often to prevent burning—for 30 seconds, or until the seeds are evenly browned. In a wide shallow bowl, combine the toasted sesame seeds, bread crumbs and cayenne pepper. Put the seasoned flour in another shallow bowl. Dredge the abalone steaks first in the seasoned flour, then in the beaten egg mixture, then in the sesame-crumb mixture.

In a large skillet, heat the butter and lemon juice over medium heat until frothy. Immediately add the steaks and sauté them for about two minutes on each side, or until browned. Do not overcook, lest the abalone toughen. Serve the steaks accompanied by lemon wedges.

ALICE WATSON HOUSTON
THE AMERICAN HERITAGE BOOK OF FISH COOKERY

Abalone Fritters

To serve 4

2 cups	ground abalone meat	½ liter
2	eggs, beaten	2
½ cup	milk	125 ml.
1 cup	flour	¼ liter
1 tsp.	baking powder	5 ml.
1 tsp.	salt	5 ml.
	Worcestershire sauce	
	grated nutmeg	
	fat for deep frying	
	lemon wedges	

Mix together the abalone, eggs, milk, baking powder, salt, a dash of Worcestershire sauce and a grating of nutmeg. Heat the fat to 375° F. [190° C.] and drop the mixture into it by spoonfuls. Cook the fritters until lightly browned—about two minutes. Serve with lemon wedges.

HELEN EVANS BROWN
SHRIMP AND OTHER SHELLFISH RECIPES

Conch Stew

Daube de Lambis

In Guadeloupe the stew may be thickened with a roux made of 1 tablespoon [15 ml.] of flour mixed with 1 tablespoon of butter. The dish also may be turned into conch with rice—*lambi au riz*—by adding enough water to the conch cooking liquid to make 2 cups [½ liter], and adding 1 cup [¼ liter] of white rice to the casserole with the conch. Cook, covered, for 20 to 30 minutes, or until the rice is tender.

To serve 4

10	conchs, meat extracted and cleaned (about 2 lb. [1 kg.])	10
¾ cup	fresh lime or lemon juice	175 ml.
3 tbsp.	olive oil	45 ml.
2 oz.	salt pork with the rind removed, cut into ½-inch [1-cm.] dice	60 g.
1	bouquet garni, made of 4 sprigs parsley, 1 sprig thyme, 1 sprig celery leaves, 2 or 3 basil leaves, 1 whole fresh chili and 1 bay leaf, tied together in a square of cheesecloth	1
2	garlic cloves	2
2	scallions, chopped, including 2 inches [5 cm.] of the green tops	2
⅛ tsp.	ground cinnamon (optional)	½ ml.
	salt and freshly ground pepper	
	cooked white rice	

Put the conchs to marinate for several hours in ½ cup [125 ml.] of the lime or lemon juice. Drain the conchs, rinse them and beat them thoroughly with a mallet to tenderize them. Cut the conchs into ½-inch [1-cm.] pieces and put them in a heavy saucepan. Cover the pieces with water, bring to a boil, reduce the heat, cover the pot with a lid, and simmer the conch until tender—about one and one half hours. During the last half hour, set the lid ajar to reduce the liquid.

Heat the olive oil in a heavy casserole. Add the salt pork, garlic, scallions, cinnamon—if using—and salt and pepper to taste. Stew gently for five minutes, then add the conch pieces and their cooking liquid, and the bouquet garni. Cover and simmer for 15 minutes. Remove and discard the bouquet garni, add the remaining lime or lemon juice and serve the stew accompanied by cooked white rice.

ELISABETH LAMBERT ORTIZ
THE COMPLETE BOOK OF CARIBBEAN COOKING

Conch Fritters

To serve 4 to 6

12	conchs, meat extracted and cleaned (about 2 lb. [1 kg.] conch meat) and ground in a food grinder	12
3	eggs, the yolks separated from the whites, and the whites stiffly beaten	3
½ cup	finely chopped onion	125 ml.
1	large tomato, peeled, seeded and chopped	1
2 tbsp.	finely chopped fresh parsley	30 ml.
1	garlic clove, finely chopped	1
1 tsp.	salt	5 ml.
½ tsp.	black pepper	2 ml.
1 cup	fine cracker crumbs	¼ liter
1 tbsp.	cream (optional)	15 ml.

Combine the conch meat, egg yolks, onion, tomato, parsley, garlic, salt and pepper, and crumbs. Blend thoroughly. If the mixture is too stiff to drop from a spoon, blend in the cream. Fold the egg whites into the mixture. Heat a well-oiled cast-iron skillet or griddle to sizzling. Drop the mixture by table-spoonfuls onto the hot pan. Cook until browned on one side—about two minutes—then brown the other side.

FRANCES MAC ILQUHAM
FISH COOKERY OF NORTH AMERICA

Spicy Conch Fritters

The volatile oils in chilies may irritate your skin. Wear rubber gloves when handling them.

To serve 4

1 lb.	conch meat	½ kg.
1	egg	1
⅓ cup	milk	75 ml.
1⅓ cups	sifted flour	325 ml.
2 tsp.	baking powder	10 ml.
½ tsp.	salt	2 ml.
½ tsp.	celery seeds or 1 tbsp. [15 ml.] finely chopped onion	2 ml.
2	small fresh hot chilies, stemmed, seeded and finely chopped, or ¼ tsp. [1 ml.] hot pepper sauce	2
	peanut oil for deep frying	

Put the conch meat through a food grinder, using the coarse disk, or pound the meat with a mallet and cut it into very small pieces. Beat the egg and add the milk. Sift the flour with the baking powder and salt, and add to the egg mixture. Add the conch, celery seeds or onion, and chopped peppers or hot pepper sauce. Heat the oil to 375° F. [190° C.]. Drop the conch mixture by the tablespoonful into the oil. Deep fry the fritters until they brown on all sides—three to five minutes. Drain the fritters on absorbent paper. Serve the fritters hot, accompanied by tartar sauce or cocktail sauce if desired.

A. J. MC CLANE
THE ENCYCLOPEDIA OF FISH COOKERY

Arthur Lem's Conch with Green Beans and Scallions
Dow Jai Chow Heung Lor

Oyster sauce is a pungent condiment made from oyster liquor, soy sauce and brine. It is obtainable at Asian food stores.

To serve 4 to 6

4	conchs, meat extracted, cleaned and pounded	4
1 cup	chicken stock (recipe, page 166)	¼ liter
½ cup	sliced fresh mushrooms	125 ml.
½ cup	sliced water chestnuts	125 ml.
¾ tsp.	salt	4 ml.
1 tsp.	sugar	5 ml.
	freshly ground black pepper	
¼ tsp.	sesame-seed oil	1 ml.
2 tbsp.	oyster sauce	30 ml.
2 tbsp.	cornstarch	30 ml.
4 tbsp.	cooking oil	60 ml.
2	thin slices peeled fresh ginger	2
2 tbsp.	sherry	30 ml.
¾ lb.	green beans, trimmed, cut diagonally into thin slices, blanched for 2 minutes, drained, refreshed and drained again	175 kg.
2	scallions, chopped	2

Heat the chicken stock, add the mushrooms and sliced water chestnuts, cover, and simmer for three or four minutes. Drain the vegetables and set them aside, reserving the stock. When the stock cools, add the salt, sugar, pepper, sesame-seed oil, oyster sauce and cornstarch. Stir until the cornstarch is dissolved and the mixture is smooth. Set aside.

Heat a wok or large skillet, add 2 tablespoons [30 ml.] of the oil and, when the oil is hot, add the ginger and sliced conch. Stir fry for no more than two minutes. Add the sherry, stir and cook for another minute. Pour the conch and ginger into a colander, drain and set them aside.

Thoroughly wash and dry the wok or skillet, add the remaining oil, heat, then add the green beans, mushrooms and water chestnuts, and stir fry for two minutes. Stir in the reserved sauce and cook over medium heat, stirring constantly, until the sauce is slightly thickened. Add the conch and stir to coat the slices evenly with the sauce, then pour the mixture into a serving dish, garnish with the chopped scallions and serve.

DAN AND INEZ MORRIS
THE COMPLETE FISH COOKBOOK

Clams, Mussels, Oysters and Scallops

Clams in Green Sauce
Almejas en Salsa Verde (Basconia)

To serve 4

18 to 20	hard-shell clams, scrubbed, steamed open, and the cooking liquid strained and reserved	18 to 20
2	chopped garlic cloves	2
1 tbsp.	olive oil	15 ml.
1 tbsp.	flour	15 ml.
¼ cup	freshly shelled peas	50 ml.
1 tbsp.	finely chopped fresh parsley	15 ml.
	salt and pepper	
2	lemons, quartered	2

In a deep skillet, sauté the garlic in the oil until it is golden brown. Stir in the flour, then add the reserved clam cooking liquid, the peas, parsley, and salt and pepper to taste. Bring the mixture to a boil, reduce the heat, add the clams and simmer for five minutes. Serve the clams hot, accompanied by the quartered lemons.

D. E. POHREN
ADVENTURES IN TASTE: THE WINES AND FOLK FOOD OF SPAIN

Pork and Clams Alentejo
Carne de Porco com Ameijoas a Alentejo

This is a typical dish from Alentejo in the south of Portugal. It may be served over boiled potatoes, or over toasted bread slices arranged in the bottom of generous-sized soup plates.

To serve 4 to 6

30	littleneck clams, scrubbed	30
2 lb.	boneless pork butt, cut into ½-inch [1-cm.] cubes	1 kg.
2	medium-sized onions, thinly sliced	2
2	garlic cloves	2
4	tomatoes, peeled, seeded and chopped	4
4 tbsp.	lard	60 ml.
½ tsp.	salt	2 ml.
¼ tsp.	pepper	1 ml.
	Tabasco sauce	
1	sprig fresh coriander or flat-leafed parsley, chopped	1
	lemon wedges	

Wine-garlic marinade

2 cups	dry white wine	½ liter
4	garlic cloves, chopped	4
1 tbsp.	paprika, dissolved in ⅓ cup [75 ml.] water	15 ml.
2	bay leaves, broken	2
2	whole cloves	2
1 tsp.	salt	5 ml.
¼ tsp.	pepper	1 ml.

Combine the pork with the wine-garlic marinade. Marinate the pork overnight, covered, in the refrigerator, turning the cubes occasionally, if possible. Discard the bay leaves. Drain the cubes, reserving the marinade, and pat the pork dry.

In a heavy casserole or pot, simmer the onions, garlic and tomatoes in 2 tablespoons [30 ml.] of the lard until tender. Add the salt, pepper and clams; cover, increase the heat, and cook until the clams open—about five minutes.

In a heavy skillet, heat the remaining 2 tablespoons of lard until very hot. Brown the pork over medium heat, stirring frequently. Add the reserved marinade, bring the mixture to a boil, and cook for five minutes. Combine the pork and clam mixtures; add a dash of Tabasco sauce. Stir and simmer for a few minutes, add the chopped coriander or parsley, and serve over bread or boiled potatoes, accompanied by lemon wedges.

JANE CHEKENIAN AND MONICA MEYER
SHELLFISH COOKERY

Clam Fritters

To serve 6

1 pint	shucked clams, drained and chopped	½ liter
1¾ cups	flour	425 ml.
1 tbsp.	baking powder	15 ml.
¼ tsp.	grated nutmeg	2 ml.
1 tsp.	salt	5 ml.
2	eggs, beaten lightly	2
1 cup	half-and-half cream	¼ liter
1 tbsp.	butter, melted	15 ml.
1 tsp.	grated onion	5 ml.
	fat or oil for deep frying	

Sift the dry ingredients together. Combine the eggs, onion, half-and-half cream and clams, and stir the mixture into the dry ingredients. Drop the batter by teaspoonfuls into a deep layer of fat or oil heated to 375° F. [190° C.]. Cook the fritters until brown—about three minutes. Drain the fritters on paper towels. Salt lightly just before serving.

MIKE LINZ AND STAN FUCHS
THE LOBSTER'S FINE KETTLE OF FISH

Maine Coast Clam Fritters

To serve 4

about 30	medium-sized hard-shell clams, scrubbed, shucked and very finely chopped (about 2 cups [½ liter])	about 30
2	large eggs	2
1 cup	flour	¼ liter
1 cup	milk	¼ liter
½ tsp.	salt	2 ml.
¼ tsp.	pepper	1 ml.
	oil or fat for deep frying	

Make the batter by beating the eggs and adding the flour gradually. Add the milk slowly, then the salt and pepper. Add the chopped clams and stir all together. Heat the fat or oil until it registers 375° F. [190° C.] on a deep-frying thermometer, or until it turns a 1-inch [2½-cm.] cube of bread golden brown in 30 seconds. Drop the clam mixture by spoonfuls into the fat. When the fritters are brown on one side— about one minute—turn them and brown the reverse side. Serve them piping hot.

A MAINE COOKBOOK

Clambake without Sand

An alternative method of layering the shellfish with vegetables is demonstrated on pages 40-41.

The amounts of ingredients are flexible, and mussels, lobsters, lobster tails or crabs can be substituted for the small clams. Cheesecloth can be used to hold each of the various layers so that the food can be lifted out easily.

To serve 4

1 dozen	large hard-shell clams, scrubbed	1 dozen
1 dozen	small hard-shell clams, scrubbed	1 dozen
1 lb.	spinach, leaves washed and separated	½ kg.
4	potatoes (either white or sweet), washed but not peeled	4
4	onions, peeled	4
4	ears of corn, silk removed	4
1	chicken, cut into serving pieces (optional)	1

Put about 1 inch [2½ cm.] of water in the bottom of a large pot, add the large clams—they should cover the bottom of the pot—and then the small clams. Bring the water to a boil, then reduce the heat so that the water barely simmers. Lay about one quarter of the spinach leaves in a layer over the clams, and place the potatoes, onions and corn on top of the leaves. Place another layer of leaves over the potatoes, onions and corn. Add the chicken, if using, then another layer of leaves. Cover the pot tightly and steam for 50 to 60 minutes, or until the vegetables are done.

ROBERT H. ROBINSON AND DANIEL G. COSTON JR.
THE CRAFT OF DISMANTLING A CRAB

Fried Clams

To serve 2

2 dozen	clams, scrubbed and shucked	2 dozen
1	egg, the yolk separated from the white, and the white stiffly beaten	1
½ cup	milk	125 ml.
1 tbsp.	butter, melted	15 ml.
½ tsp.	salt	2 ml.
½ cup	flour	125 ml.
	fat or oil for deep frying	

Beat the egg yolk and add to it half of the milk and all of the melted butter. Mix the salt with the flour and sift. Then stir the dry ingredients into the first mixture until smooth. Add the remaining ¼ cup [50 ml.] milk and fold in the stiffly beaten egg white; stir well, and your batter is ready.

Drain the clams and dip each one into the batter. In fat or oil heated to 375° F. [190° C.], deep fry the clams until they turn a golden brown—about 1 minute. Drain the clams on paper towels. Serve plain or with tartar sauce.

PHILLIP MASON
SHELLFISH COOKBOOK

Cape Cod Clam Pie

To serve 4 to 6

2 dozen	large clams, scrubbed, shucked, the liquor reserved and the meat finely chopped	2 dozen
1	slice slab bacon, cut 1½ inches [4 cm.] thick, the rind removed, and the fat and meat diced	1
4 tbsp.	butter	60 ml.
1	large onion, finely chopped	1
1	celery rib, finely chopped	1
1	large baking potato, peeled and diced	1
1	medium-sized carrot, diced	1
1 tbsp.	finely chopped fresh parsley	15 ml.
3 tbsp.	flour	45 ml.
½ cup	clam liquor, hot	125 ml.
1 tbsp.	dry vermouth	15 ml.
⅓ cup	heavy cream	75 ml.
	Tabasco sauce	
	grated nutmeg	
	salt and freshly ground pepper	
Rich pastry dough		
1½ cups	flour	375 ml.
¼ tsp.	salt	1 ml.
	sugar	
6 tbsp.	cold butter, cut into pieces	90 ml.
2¼ tbsp.	cold vegetable shortening, cut into pieces	33½ ml.
4 to 4½ tbsp.	cold water	60 to 65 ml.

For the dough, first place the flour, salt, a pinch of sugar, the butter and shortening in a large mixing bowl. Blend, using a pastry blender, until the mixture has the texture of coarse crumbs. Add the water and continue blending until the dough is smooth. Knead the dough briefly on a floured surface. Refrigerate it for one hour.

Roll out half of the dough to a thickness of ⅛ inch [3 mm.] (keep the remaining dough refrigerated). Line a 9-inch [23-cm.] pie plate with the dough; trim the edges. Line the pastry with aluminum foil or wax paper; weight it with dried rice or beans. Bake the filled pastry shell in a preheated 400° F. [200° C.] oven for 12 minutes.

Fry the bacon in a skillet until it is crisp. Drain it on a paper towel; crumble the bacon. Discard the bacon drippings from the skillet. Add 2 tablespoons [30 ml.] of the butter to the skillet; sauté the onion until golden. Add the celery, potato, carrot, parsley, clams and bacon; cook and stir over medium heat for five minutes. Remove the mixture to a bowl; reserve.

Melt the remaining butter in a small saucepan. Whisk in the flour; cook and stir for two minutes. Whisk in the hot clam liquor and the vermouth; cook, stirring constantly, over low heat until the mixture is smooth. Gradually add the cream; stirring constantly, cook until this sauce is very smooth and thick—about two minutes.

Add the reserved clam mixture to the sauce; stir in a dash of Tabasco, a little nutmeg, and salt and pepper to taste. Spoon the filling into the baked pastry shell. Roll out the remaining dough to a 10-inch [25-cm.] circle; place this lid over the clam mixture. Press the overhanging dough under the rim of the pie plate to seal the edge; flute the edge. Cut a slit in the top to allow steam to escape. Bake the pie for 10 minutes at 400° F., then reduce the temperature to 350° F. [180° C.] and bake until golden brown—35 to 40 minutes.

BERT GREENE
BERT GREENE'S KITCHEN BOUQUETS

Clams Casino

To serve 4

2 dozen	littleneck or cherrystone clams, scrubbed, shucked and left on the half shell	2 dozen
	fresh lemon juice	
5 tbsp.	butter	75 ml.
3	garlic cloves, finely chopped	3
1 cup	finely chopped green pepper	¼ liter
6	slices bacon, cut into clam-sized pieces	6

Squeeze a little lemon juice over each clam on the half shell. Place the clams in a shallow baking pan.

Melt the butter in a saucepan, and add the garlic and the green pepper. Cook gently for three to five minutes. Spoon ½ to ¾ teaspoon [2 to 4 ml.] of the mixture over each clam and cover with a piece of bacon. Bake the clams in a preheated 425° F. [220° C.] oven until the bacon is crisp and brown—about 10 minutes.

JANE CHEKENIAN AND MONICA MEYER
SHELLFISH COOKERY

Clams Florentine

The clam shells called for in this recipe should be 4 to 5 inches [10 to 13 cm.] long. Such shells can be found—scoured by the surf—on most Atlantic beaches, or purchased at gift shops.

To serve 4

2 dozen	littleneck or small cherrystone clams, scrubbed, shucked and drained	2 dozen
3 tbsp.	butter	45 ml.
1 tbsp.	finely chopped onion	15 ml.
2 lb.	spinach, trimmed and stems removed, boiled in salted water for 2 minutes, drained, squeezed dry and finely chopped	1 kg.
	salt and pepper	
1 cup	Mornay sauce (recipe, page 164)	¼ liter

Melt the butter and in it cook the onion until transparent but not browned. Add the spinach and stir until it is heated through. Season the mixture rather highly with salt and pepper. Make a bed of the spinach mixture in four very large clam shells—and set them in a shallow baking pan. Arrange six clams on top of the spinach in each shell. Put a spoonful of Mornay sauce on top of each clam. Broil the clams under a preheated broiler until the sauce bubbles and they are hot.

MIRIAM UNGERER
GOOD CHEAP FOOD

Clam Pie

To serve 4

18	hard-shell clams, scrubbed	18
2 cups	white wine	½ liter
1	carrot, thinly sliced	1
1	onion, thinly sliced	1
1	bay leaf	1
1 tsp.	freshly ground black pepper	5 ml.
6 tbsp.	butter	90 ml.
2 tbsp.	flour	30 ml.
	salt	
1 lb.	small fresh mushrooms, trimmed	½ kg.
3 tbsp.	sherry or Madeira	45 ml.
½ lb.	short-crust dough (recipe, page 167)	¼ kg.
1	egg yolk, beaten with 2 tbsp. [30 ml.] water	1

In a nonreactive pot, steam the clams in the white wine with the carrot, onion, bay leaf and pepper until all of the clam shells open. Shuck the clams; strain the cooking liquid.

Melt half of the butter, stir in the flour, and add the strained clam liquid to make a velouté sauce. Stirring occasionally, simmer the sauce for at least 10 minutes, then season it to taste. Sauté the mushrooms in the remaining butter; season to taste. Combine the mushrooms, velouté sauce, clams and the sherry or Madeira. Cool the mixture well.

Pour the mixture into a deep 1-quart [1-liter] pie dish and top with the short-crust dough, rolled out to a thickness of about ¼ inch [6 mm.]. Cut a small hole in the center of the dough. Decorate the pie with leaves cut from the remaining dough, brush the top with the egg yolk mixed with water, and bake the pie in a preheated 450° F. [230° C.] oven for 15 minutes. Reduce the heat to 350° F. [180° C.] and bake the pie for about 20 minutes longer, or until nicely browned.

JAMES BEARD
JAMES BEARD'S NEW FISH COOKERY

Chicken Casalinga

To serve 4

1 dozen	littleneck clams, scrubbed	1 dozen
2½ lb.	frying chicken, cut into 8 pieces	1¼ kg.
	salt and pepper	
	paprika	
½ cup	flour	125 ml.
⅓ cup	oil	75 ml.
1	garlic clove	1
1	medium-sized onion, chopped	1
1 cup	chicken stock (recipe, page 166)	¼ liter
½ tsp.	dried marjoram leaves	2 ml.
1	bay leaf, crumbled	1
½	green pepper, seeded and cut into strips	½
½	sweet red pepper, seeded and cut into strips	½
4	tomatoes, quartered	4
½ lb.	large fresh mushrooms, sliced	¼ kg.

Sprinkle the chicken pieces with salt, pepper and paprika and dredge them with flour. In a skillet, heat the oil, add the garlic clove and brown the chicken pieces. When the chicken is brown, remove it and the garlic. Set the chicken aside in a warm place. In the same skillet, cook the onion until soft. Add the stock, marjoram, bay leaf, ½ teaspoon [2 ml.] of salt and ¼ teaspoon [1 ml.] of pepper. Scrape the skillet with a spatula until this sauce is well blended.

Layer the chicken, green and red pepper strips, tomato quarters and sliced mushrooms in a 2-quart [2-liter] casserole. Pour in the sauce, cover the casserole and bake it in a preheated 350° F. [180° C.] oven for 45 minutes. Add the clams and bake the casserole for an additional 10 minutes, or until the clams open. Serve over buttered rice or noodles.

JANE CHEKENIAN AND MONICA MEYER
SHELLFISH COOKERY

Steamed Soft-shell Clams, Eaton's Neck

To serve 4 to 6

100	soft-shell clams, rinsed	100
1 cup	water	¼ liter
1	small onion, sliced	1
8 tbsp.	butter, melted	120 ml.
1 tbsp.	fresh lemon juice or Worcestershire sauce	15 ml.

Put the clams in a large pot; add the water and onion; cover the pot tightly and set it over high heat. Bring the water to a simmer; do not let it come to a frothy boil. Cover the pot and steam the clams—stirring them once or twice with a wooden spoon—for three to four minutes, until they open. Discard any unopened clams. Transfer the rest to a deep dish. Strain the cooking liquid through cheesecloth and serve it in cups.

To make the sauce, melt the butter and flavor it with the lemon juice or Worcestershire. Serve the clams on plates; place a warmed container of butter sauce beside each plate.

J. GEORGE FREDERICK AND JEAN JOYCE
LONG ISLAND SEAFOOD COOK BOOK

Razor-Clam Cakes

To serve 4 or 5

2 cups	finely chopped razor-clam meat	½ liter
2	eggs	2
1 tsp.	dry mustard	5 ml.
½ tsp.	crumbled thyme	2 ml.
	Tabasco sauce	
½ tsp.	salt	2 ml.
	freshly ground black pepper	
¼ cup	finely chopped onion	50 ml.
¼ cup	finely chopped fresh parsley	50 ml.
4 cups	soft fresh bread crumbs	1 liter
6 tbsp.	butter	90 ml.
2 tbsp.	vegetable oil	30 ml.
1	lemon, cut into 4 or 8 wedges	1

In a deep bowl, beat the eggs, mustard, thyme, two or three drops of Tabasco, the salt and a few grindings of pepper together with a fork or wire whisk until the ingredients are well combined. Stir in the clam meat, onion and parsley, then 2½ cups [625 ml.] of the crumbs. Taste for seasoning. Divide the clam mixture into 10 equal portions and pat and shape each portion into a round cake about 3 inches [8 cm.] in diameter and ½ inch [1 cm.] thick. Spread the remaining 1½ cups [375 ml.] of bread crumbs on a plate and turn the

cakes in the crumbs to coat both sides evenly. Arrange the clam cakes on wax paper and refrigerate them for at least 15 minutes to firm the crumb coating.

Preheat the oven to its lowest setting. Line a shallow baking dish with paper towels and place it in the oven.

In a heavy 10- to 12-inch [25- to 30-cm.] skillet, melt 3 tablespoons [45 ml.] of the butter with 1 tablespoon [15 ml.] of the oil over medium heat. When the foam begins to subside, place three or four clam cakes in the hot fat and fry them for four or five minutes on each side, or until golden brown. Regulate the heat so that the cakes brown evenly, and add the remaining butter and oil by the spoonful when necessary. As the cakes brown, transfer them to the lined dish and keep them warm in the oven while you fry the rest.

Arrange the clam cakes attractively on a warmed platter and serve them at once, accompanied by the lemon wedges.

FOODS OF THE WORLD/AMERICAN COOKING: THE NORTHWEST

Portuguese Clam Fritters

Sea clams are deepwater bivalves 5 to 6 inches [13 to 15 cm.] long with tough but flavorful meat. They are fished commercially in New England, where they are also known as ocean quahogs. The large hard-shell clams called chowder clams may be substituted for them.

The linguiça called for in this recipe is a Portuguese, garlic-flavored, smoked pork sausage. Spanish chorizo or any other garlicky sausage may be used instead.

To serve 4

2 cups	sea clam meat, the stomach of each clam split open and rinsed, its siphons split and rinsed, and all the meat ground	½ liter
2	eggs, beaten	2
1	garlic clove, finely chopped	1
2 tbsp.	grated onion	30 ml.
3 tbsp.	milk	45 ml.
1 tbsp.	peeled and finely chopped *linguiça*	15 ml.
¼ tsp.	ground cumin	1 ml.
2 tbsp.	flour	30 ml.
½ tsp.	salt	2 ml.
	freshly ground black pepper	
	oil for deep frying	

Drain the ground clam meat and place it in a mixing bowl. Add the beaten eggs and stir well. Add the remaining ingredients and stir again. Heat oil in a heavy skillet to 375° F. [190° C.] and drop the mixture by the tablespoonful into the hot oil. Fry the fritters for about two minutes, or until brown on both sides. Drain the fritters on paper towels.

HOWARD MITCHAM
THE PROVINCETOWN SEAFOOD COOKBOOK

Mussels with a Special Mayonnaise
Moules Camarguaises

To serve 2 or 3

3 dozen	mussels, scrubbed and debearded	3 dozen
1 cup	dry white wine	¼ liter
1 cup	mayonnaise (recipe, page 165), made with fresh lemon juice	¼ liter
1 tbsp.	chopped fresh parsley	15 ml.

Set the mussels over high heat in a large, nonreactive pot and pour the wine over them. Cover and cook them for five minutes, shaking the pot frequently, then remove the mussels and discard the surplus half shells. (If the mussels are small, arrange them two to a half shell, but if they are of a good size leave them one in each shell.) Set the mussels aside to cool. Strain the cooking broth, boil to reduce it to about a quarter of its original volume, and cool.

Blend the mayonnaise with 2 tablespoons [30 ml.] of the reduced mussel broth. Spoon the mixture over the mussels, sprinkle with parsley and serve.

ALAN DAVIDSON
MEDITERRANEAN SEAFOOD

Mussels Bordeaux-Style
Moules à la Bordelaise

To serve 4 to 6

8 dozen	mussels, scrubbed and debearded	8 dozen
½ cup	white wine	125 ml.
2 tbsp.	butter	30 ml.
2	shallots, chopped	2
3	medium-sized tomatoes, peeled, seeded and chopped	3
	salt and pepper	
1	garlic clove, chopped	1
3 tbsp.	chopped fresh parsley	45 ml.
½ cup	fresh bread crumbs, soaked in milk and strained	125 ml.
1 tsp.	grated lemon peel	5 ml.

Place the mussels and the wine in a large, nonreactive pot, cover, and let the mussels open over high heat. Strain the mussels, reserving the cooking liquid, and remove the empty half shells.

In a small pan melt the butter, and in this sauté the shallots over low heat; add the tomatoes, seasonings, garlic, parsley and the bread crumbs. Increase the heat slightly and stir the sauce until the tomatoes are soft, then add a little of the strained cooking liquid from the mussels, and the grated

lemon peel. Put the mussels into a heavy enameled gratin dish, pour the sauce over them and simmer for three or four minutes, until the mussels are hot.

ELIZABETH DAVID
FRENCH COUNTRY COOKING

Mussels in the Style of Charente
Moules à la Charentaise

To serve 1

18	mussels, scrubbed and debearded	18
1	garlic clove	1
1	small onion, sliced	1
¼	bay leaf	¼
1	sprig thyme	1
6	sprigs fresh parsley, the leaves chopped and the stems reserved	6
1	carrot, sliced	1
1	strip orange peel	1
½ cup	white wine	125 ml.
⅓ cup	sour cream	75 ml.
1 tsp.	curry powder	5 ml.
	powdered saffron	
	cayenne pepper	
	orange-flower water (optional)	
2	egg yolks	2

Put the garlic, sliced onion, the bay leaf, thyme, parsley stems, carrot, orange peel and white wine in a nonreactive pan and cook over medium heat for about 10 minutes. Add the mussels, cover the pan and steam the mussels for about three minutes, until they open. As soon as they open, remove them from the heat. Break off and discard half of each shell and place the remaining meat-filled half in a baking dish. Keep the filled shells warm in a 200° F. [100° C.] oven.

Strain the mussel cooking liquid through a double layer of dampened cheesecloth. Put the strained liquid, a pinch of saffron and the sour cream in a skillet and cook the mixture over high heat until one third of the liquid has evaporated. Add the curry powder and a pinch of cayenne pepper. Take this preparation off the stove. Add the egg yolks and stir quickly to thicken the sauce.

Taste, correcting the seasoning by adding a drop of orange-flower water if the sauce seems too sharp.

Pour the sauce over the mussels. Dust them with the chopped parsley.

LE DUC
CRUSTACÉS, POISSONS ET COQUILLAGES

Mussels Steamed in Wine

Moules à la Marinière

To serve 6 to 8

6 dozen	mussels, scrubbed and debearded	6 dozen
1	onion, chopped	1
2	shallots, chopped	2
2½ cups	finely chopped fresh parsley	625 ml.
	freshly ground pepper	
10 tbsp.	butter, 3 tbsp. [45 ml.] cut into chunks	150 ml.
1½ cups	dry white wine	375 ml.
3 tbsp.	fresh lemon juice	45 ml.

Put the mussels into a nonreactive pot with the onions, shallots, parsley, pepper, 7 tablespoons [105 ml.] of the butter, and the wine. Cover and cook for a few minutes over high heat, shaking the pot several times. When all the mussels open, transfer them to a serving dish and keep them warm.

Strain the cooking liquid into a small, nonreactive saucepan. Over high heat, reduce the liquid to one third of its original volume. Off the heat, whisk in the butter chunks, and keep whisking until the sauce is thick and foamy. Whisk in the lemon juice and pour the sauce over the mussels.

ACADÉMIE CULINAIRE DE FRANCE
CUISINE FRANÇAISE

Creamed Mussels

Mouclade

To serve 3 or 4

4 dozen	mussels, scrubbed and debearded	4 dozen
⅔ cup	dry white wine	150 ml.
2	shallots, chopped	2
	salt and pepper	
	Curry sauce	
4 tbsp.	butter	60 ml.
¼ cup	flour	50 ml.
	salt and pepper	
1	garlic clove, finely chopped	1
1	egg yolk	1
1 tbsp.	fresh lemon juice	15 ml.
½ cup	heavy cream	125 ml.
1 tsp.	curry powder	5 ml.
	chopped fresh parsley	

Put the mussels in a large, nonreactive pot with the white wine, shallots, salt and pepper. Cover and cook over high heat, shaking the pot occasionally, until all the mussels have opened—about five minutes. Remove the mussels. Strain the cooking liquid through a sieve lined with cheesecloth and set over a bowl. Reserve the liquid. Discard one half shell from each mussel and arrange the mussels on a warmed platter; cover the mussels to keep them warm.

To make the sauce, first melt the butter in a saucepan and, using a wooden spoon, stir in the flour. Just as the mixture begins to turn golden, add the strained mussel cooking liquid and stir well. Season with salt and pepper and add the garlic. Simmer for 10 minutes over low heat, stirring all the time. In a bowl, whisk the egg yolk lightly; whisk in the lemon juice, cream and curry powder, then slowly pour in the sauce, stirring constantly.

Coat the mussels with the sauce and sprinkle them with chopped parsley. Serve at once.

ODETTE KAHN
LA PETITE ET LA GRANDE CUISINE

Mussels in Basil Sauce

Moules au Pistou

To serve 1

1 dozen	mussels, scrubbed and debearded	1 dozen
1 tbsp.	olive oil	15 ml.
3	garlic cloves, crushed to a paste	3
4	large tomatoes, peeled, seeded and coarsely chopped	4
¼ cup	heavy cream	50 ml.
	salt and pepper	
	cayenne pepper	
⅛ tsp.	sugar	½ ml.
1 tbsp.	kirsch	15 ml.
1½ cups	finely shredded fresh basil	375 ml.
1 tbsp.	finely chopped fresh parsley	15 ml.

Heat the oil in a sauté pan with the garlic, tomatoes, cream, salt and pepper, a pinch of cayenne and the sugar. Cook the mixture uncovered until about two thirds of the liquid has evaporated. Toss in the mussels, cover and cook them until the shells open—about three to four minutes. Remove each one from the pan as soon as it opens. Discard the shells, and keep the mussels warm in a covered dish. Continue to cook the sauce mixture to evaporate the juice from the mussels. Add the kirsch, adjust the seasoning if necessary and add half of the basil. Return the mussels to the pan and heat them for a few seconds. Pour the contents of the pan into a warmed dish, sprinkle the parsley and remaining basil on top, and serve at once.

JEAN AND PAUL MINCHELLI
CRUSTACÉS, POISSONS ET COQUILLAGES

Mussels in Fennel Sauce

Cassolette de Moules au Fenouil

To serve 4

6 dozen	mussels, scrubbed and debearded	6 dozen
8 tbsp.	butter, 5 tbsp. [75 ml.] cut into pieces	120 ml.
2 tbsp.	finely chopped shallots	30 ml.
1 cup	dry white wine	¼ liter
1 cup	finely chopped fennel	¼ liter
½ cup	court bouillon (recipe, page 162)	125 ml.
1¼ cups	heavy cream	300 ml.
	salt and freshly ground pepper	
	cayenne pepper	
	finely cut chives	
	finely chopped fennel leaves	

In a large pot, melt 3 tablespoons [45 ml.] of the butter. Add the shallot and sauté it until soft. Then add the mussels, wine, fennel and court bouillon. Cover the pot and bring the contents to a boil. Shaking the pot occasionally, steam the mussels for five to seven minutes, or until the shells open. Then remove the mussels, take the meat out of the shells and set the meat aside.

Strain the cooking liquid and boil it to reduce it to about 1 cup [¼ liter]. Add the cream and, stirring frequently, boil until this sauce lightly coats the back of a spoon. Gradually whisk in the butter pieces. Stir the mussels into the sauce and season the mixture with salt, pepper and cayenne. Add the chives and fennel leaves. Serve immediately.

ANTON MOSIMANN
CUISINE À LA CARTE

Mussels Baked with Potatoes

Cozze e Patate al Forno

To serve 6

5 dozen	mussels, scrubbed, debearded, steamed open and left on the half shell	5 dozen
2 lb.	potatoes, peeled and sliced	1 kg.
	salt and pepper	
¼ cup	chopped fresh parsley	50 ml.
6	plum tomatoes, 3 sliced, and 3 peeled, seeded and cut into chunks	6
3 tbsp.	olive oil	45 ml.
3 tbsp.	bread crumbs	45 ml.
2	garlic cloves, finely chopped	2

Coat a wide baking pan, about 2 inches [5 cm.] deep, with olive oil, then cover the bottom with the potatoes. Salt and pepper the potatoes. Strew 2 tablespoons [30 ml.] of the chopped parsley among the potatoes and pour 2 tablespoonfuls of olive oil over them. Lay the tomato slices on top of the potatoes. Place the mussels side by side on the tomatoes.

Next sprinkle bread crumbs over all. Moisten these with the remaining olive oil. Add salt and pepper, the remaining parsley and the garlic. Strew the tomato chunks over the top. Bake in a preheated 325° F. [160° C.] oven for one hour.

ALAN DAVIDSON
MEDITERRANEAN SEAFOOD

Mussels in Green Sauce

Moules au Vert

To serve 6

8 dozen	mussels, scrubbed and debearded	8 dozen
3 tbsp.	butter	45 ml.
1	onion, thinly sliced	1
10	sprigs parsley, finely chopped	10
½	celery rib, thinly sliced	½
	salt and pepper	
¾ cup	dry white wine	175 ml.
¾ cup	finely chopped fresh sorrel leaves	175 ml.
½ cup	finely chopped fresh chervil leaves	125 ml.
3	fresh sage leaves, finely chopped	3
½ tsp.	finely chopped fresh savory leaves	2 ml.
1 tbsp.	flour	15 ml.
2	egg yolks, lightly beaten	2
3 tbsp.	fresh lemon juice	45 ml.

Melt 1 tablespoon [15 ml.] of the butter in a large, nonreactive pot, and lightly sauté the onion, 1 tablespoon of the parsley, and the celery. Add the mussels and season with salt and pepper. Pour in the white wine, cover, and cook over high heat until all of the mussels have opened—about five minutes. Remove the mussels from the pot, shuck them and put the mussels in a warmed serving dish. Moisten them with some of the cooking liquid; cover and keep them warm.

Put another tablespoon of the butter in a saucepan with the sorrel, the remaining parsley, the chervil, sage and savory. Cook over low heat for about five minutes. Strain the mussel cooking liquid into the saucepan. Blend the remaining butter with the flour and whisk this *beurre manié* into the herb sauce. Cook gently for two minutes, or until the sauce is slightly thickened. Remove the sauce from the heat and blend in the egg yolks and lemon juice. Pour the sauce over the mussels and serve at once.

EMMANUELLE JANVIER
LES MEILLEURES RECETTES AUX FRUITS DE MER

Mussels Stuffed with Spinach

Moules aux Épinards

The technique of stuffing mussels is shown on page 51. A chopped hard-boiled egg may replace the bread crumbs.

To serve 4

32	large mussels, scrubbed and debearded	32
16	small mussels, scrubbed and debearded	16
2 lb.	spinach, parboiled for 1 minute, drained, squeezed dry and finely chopped	1 kg.
1½ cups	fresh bread crumbs, soaked in milk and squeezed dry	375 ml.
	salt and pepper	
¼ cup	olive oil	50 ml.
2	onions, finely chopped	2
4	large tomatoes, peeled, seeded and chopped	4

Put the small mussels into a pan containing a little simmering water. Cover and cook over high heat for about five minutes. When the shells open, drain and shuck the mussels. Mix them with about two thirds of the spinach, the bread crumbs, and salt and pepper. Open the large mussels with a knife, making sure that the flesh remains attached to both halves of each shell, and stuff the shells with the spinach mixture. Tie each mussel securely with string.

Heat the olive oil in a large pan and sauté the onions and tomatoes until the onions are soft. Mix in the remaining spinach, season, and add the stuffed mussels. Cover and cook gently for about 15 minutes. Transfer the mussels to a warmed serving dish, snip off the strings, pour the sauce over the mussels and serve at once.

C. CHANOT-BULLIER
VIEILLES RECETTES DE CUISINE PROVENÇALE

Skewered Mussels

Brochettes de Moules

To serve 4

4 dozen	large mussels, scrubbed, steamed open in white wine and shucked	4 dozen
5	thick slices bacon, cut into small strips	5
1	egg, lightly beaten in a shallow bowl with salt and pepper	1
½ cup	dry bread crumbs	125 ml.
3 tbsp.	oil	45 ml.

Thread four skewers with the mussels and bacon, arranging two mussels and one or two strips of bacon alternately. Put the bread crumbs in a shallow bowl. Roll the skewers first in the beaten egg, then in the bread crumbs, and sprinkle them lightly with oil. Preheat the broiler and broil the skewers for up to 15 minutes, or until browned, sprinkling them frequently with oil and turning them often.

LÉONE BÉRARD
POISSONS ET FRUITS DE MER

Baked Mussels

Gratinerad musslor

To serve 12

4 dozen	small mussels, scrubbed and debearded	4 dozen
1 cup	water	¼ liter
⅓ cup	Madeira or dry white wine	75 ml.
⅓ cup	finely chopped onion	75 ml.
1 tbsp.	finely chopped fresh parsley	15 ml.
1	bay leaf	1
3	whole allspice	3
	salt and pepper	
2 tbsp.	butter	30 ml.
1 tbsp.	flour	15 ml.
1 tsp.	Worcestershire sauce	5 ml.
1 tbsp.	fresh lemon juice	15 ml.
2	eggs, the yolks separated from the whites, the yolks lightly beaten and the whites stiffly beaten	2
¼ cup	dry bread crumbs	50 ml.

In a large kettle over high heat, bring to a boil the water, wine, onion, parsley, bay leaf and allspice, with a little salt and pepper added. Add the mussels, cover the kettle tightly, and steam the mussels for two to four minutes. Uncover the kettle and, as the mussel shells open, remove the mussels to a shallow, buttered baking dish. Discard the shells, but save the cooking liquid and strain it.

Melt the butter, stir in the flour smoothly, then add 1 cup [¼ liter] of the strained mussel liquid. Add the Worcestershire sauce, lemon juice, and a little salt and pepper. Let the sauce boil a moment longer, remove it from the heat and let it cool. Stir the egg yolks into the almost-cooled sauce. Then fold in the egg whites. Pour the sauce over the mussels in the baking dish and sprinkle the top with the bread crumbs. Bake the mussels in a preheated 375° F. [190° C.] oven for 10 to 15 minutes.

FLORENCE BROBECK AND MONIKA B. KJELLBERG
SMÖRGASBORD AND SCANDINAVIAN COOKERY

Spaghetti with Mussel Sauce
Spaghetti al Sugo di Mare

To serve 4 to 6

6 dozen	mussels, scrubbed and debearded	6 dozen
¾ cup	olive oil	175 ml.
2	garlic cloves, halved, green inner sprouts discarded, and chopped	2
⅛ tsp.	fresh oregano leaves	½ ml.
2 tbsp.	chopped fresh parsley	30 ml.
½ tsp.	dried rosemary	2 ml.
½	bay leaf	½
1 lb.	tomatoes, peeled, seeded and chopped	½ kg.
½	hot green chili, stemmed, seeded and chopped	½
	salt	
1 lb.	spaghetti	½ kg.

Put the mussels in a large saucepan with ¼ cup [50 ml.] of the oil. Heat them over high heat for about five minutes until they open. Take the mussels from the heat; remove and reserve their flesh. Strain the cooking liquid through a sieve lined with a double layer of dampened cheesecloth, and reserve. Over medium heat, brown the garlic in the remaining oil with the oregano, parsley, rosemary and bay leaf. Let these cook for a minute, then add the tomatoes, chili and salt. Simmer the sauce slowly for about 15 minutes; when it has reduced a little, add the mussels, leaving the pan on the heat for a few minutes. Cook the spaghetti in plenty of boiling salted water until it is half-cooked. Drain and turn into an earthenware bowl. Add the sauced mussels and the strained mussel stock. Bake in a preheated 375° F. [190° C.] oven for about 20 minutes, or until the spaghetti is fully cooked and the mussel stock absorbed.

FEAST OF ITALY

Willie's Curried Oysters

To serve 4

1½ pints	shucked oysters, with their liquor	¾ liter
2	medium-sized onions, chopped	2
4 tbsp.	butter	60 ml.
3 tbsp.	flour	45 ml.
1½ cups	half-and-half cream, or milk	375 ml.
1½ tbsp.	curry powder	22½ ml.
	salt and pepper	

Sauté the onions in the butter until they are pale yellow but not browned. Sprinkle them with the flour and stir the mix-

ture until blended. Add the half-and-half cream or milk slowly, stirring until the sauce is smooth and thick. Add the curry powder and seasonings to taste. Cook the oysters separately in their liquor over medium heat just until their edges curl—about two minutes. Add the oysters and their liquor to the onion sauce. Serve with rice.

MARIAN TRACY
THE SHELLFISH COOKBOOK

Doane's Famous Olympia Pepper Pan Roast

Olympia oysters, the only species native to the Pacific Coast, are tiny (1½ inches [4 cm.] long), delectable and rare; any variety of small Eastern oysters can be substituted.

To serve 2

½ pint	shucked Olympia oysters	¼ liter
2 tbsp.	butter	30 ml.
1 cup	chopped green pepper	¼ liter
1½ cups	ketchup	375 ml.
1 tsp.	Worcestershire sauce	5 ml.
	Tabasco sauce	
½ tsp.	salt	2 ml.

Melt the butter in a hot skillet and add the peppers. Stir together the ketchup, Worcestershire sauce, four or five drops of Tabasco sauce, and the salt, and pour the mixture into the skillet. Let the sauce simmer for about two minutes. Pour the Olympia oysters into the sauce. Let the oysters simmer until plump—about two minutes. Do not overcook them. Serve the oysters and sauce over hot buttered toast.

HELENE GLIDDEN
PACIFIC COAST SEAFOOD CHEF

Oysters Poulette

To serve 6

1 pint	shucked oysters, with their liquor	½ liter
1 tbsp.	flour	15 ml.
1 tbsp.	butter, melted	15 ml.
1½ cups	heavy cream, ½ cup [125 ml.] whipped	375 ml.
	salt and pepper	
	cayenne pepper	
2	egg yolks	2
1 tsp.	fresh lemon juice	5 ml.

Heat the oysters in their liquor until their edges begin to curl. Skim the liquor carefully, drain the oysters, and combine ¾ cup [175 ml.] of the liquor with ¾ cup [175 ml.] of the cream. In a saucepan, blend the flour and melted butter and gradually stir in the oyster liquor and cream mixture. Cook the cream sauce slowly, stirring constantly, until it thickens; season it to taste with salt, pepper and cayenne pepper, and take the saucepan off the heat.

In the top of a double boiler, beat the egg yolks with ¼ cup [50 ml.] of the cream. Add a little of the cream sauce, blend well, and add the rest of the sauce. Cook the mixture over simmering water, still stirring, until it just begins to thicken, then add the lemon juice and the oysters. Pour the mixture into a warmed serving dish and top it with the whipped cream. The perfect garnish for oysters poulette is a circle of puff-paste crescents, but small baking powder biscuits or triangles of toast will do nicely also.

NARCISSE CHAMBERLAIN AND NARCISSA G. CHAMBERLAIN
THE CHAMBERLAIN SAMPLER OF AMERICAN COOKING

Oyster Curry

Kastura Turcarri

To make the coconut milk called for in this recipe, pour about ½ cup [125 ml.] of hot water over ½ cup of freshly grated coconut. After five minutes, press the mixture through a cloth-lined sieve to extract the milk.

To serve 4

3 dozen	oysters, scrubbed, shucked and the liquor reserved	3 dozen
4 tbsp.	butter	60 ml.
2	onions, chopped	2
2 tbsp.	sesame seeds, slightly crushed	30 ml.
2 tsp.	ground turmeric	10 ml.
½ cup	desiccated coconut	125 ml.
1 cup	chicken stock (recipe, page 166)	¼ liter
3	bay leaves	3
½ cup	coconut milk	125 ml.
	salt	

Melt the butter, add the onions and fry them until lightly browned—about 10 minutes. Blend in the sesame seeds, turmeric and coconut, and fry for one minute. Add the stock and the bay leaves, cover and simmer over very low heat for 30 minutes.

Remove the bay leaves, add the coconut milk and cook over high heat, stirring constantly, for five minutes, or until this sauce is very thick. Add the oysters, oyster liquor and salt to taste. Simmer briefly until the oysters curl. Serve hot.

DHARAM JIT SINGH
CLASSIC COOKING FROM INDIA

Hot Oyster Stew

To serve 8

1 quart	shucked oysters, with their liquor	1 liter
8 tbsp.	butter, cut into pieces	120 ml.
8 cups	half-and-half cream, scalded	2 liters
2 tsp.	salt	10 ml.
1 tsp.	freshly ground white pepper	5 ml.
	paprika	
2 tbsp.	finely chopped fresh parsley	30 ml.

Heat the oysters in their liquor over high heat until their edges begin to curl—two to three minutes. Add the butter and the scalded half-and-half cream, still piping hot. Season with the salt and pepper, and pour the stew into a warmed tureen. Dust with paprika and sprinkle with the parsley. Do not boil or overcook this stew lest the oysters get rubbery.

JULIE DANNENBAUM
MENUS FOR ALL OCCASIONS

Oyster Puffs

To serve 4

1 pint	shucked oysters, with their liquor	½ liter
½ cup	half-and-half cream	125 ml.
2 tbsp.	butter	30 ml.
2 tsp.	salt	10 ml.
½ tsp.	sugar	2 ml.
1 cup	flour	¼ liter
4	eggs	4
	peanut oil for deep frying	

In a large, heavy saucepan, simmer the oysters in their liquor until the edges begin to curl. Remove the oysters from the liquor with a slotted spoon and pat them dry on paper towels. Chop the oysters fine. Pour ½ cup [125 ml.] of the oyster liquor into a saucepan and add the half-and-half cream, butter, salt and sugar; bring the mixture to a boil. Add the flour all at once. Stir this batter mixture constantly over low heat until it is smooth. Remove the batter from the heat. Let it cool for a few minutes before adding the eggs one at a time. Beat the mixture thoroughly after each egg is added. Blend in the chopped oysters and mix well.

Heat enough oil for deep frying to 375° F. [180° C.] in a large, heavy kettle or Dutch oven. A piece of bread dropped into the oil will almost instantly turn golden brown when the temperature is just right. Drop the batter into the oil by tablespoonfuls and fry the puffs until they are golden brown—about three to five minutes. Drain the puffs on paper towels. Serve them with cocktail sauce or tartar sauce.

THE GRAND CENTRAL OYSTER BAR & RESTAURANT SEAFOOD COOKBOOK

Oysters Fried on Skewers

Huîtres Frites en Brochettes

To deep fry the parsley called for in this recipe, drop a handful of rinsed and dried parsley into oil heated to 375° F. [190° C.]. Cook the parsley for a few seconds, then remove it from the pan and drain.

	To serve 4	
2 dozen	oysters, scrubbed, shucked and the liquor reserved	2 dozen
3 tbsp.	fresh lemon juice	45 ml.
1	egg, beaten	1
	fine fresh bread crumbs	
	deep-fried parsley	
1	lemon, quartered	1

Heat the oysters in a mixture of their liquor and the lemon juice for two minutes to stiffen them. Drain the oysters on a cloth and roll them in the beaten egg, then in the bread crumbs. Leaving a little space between them, thread six of the oysters onto each of four skewers. Plunge the oysters into preheated 375° F. [190° C.] oil for one or two minutes, or until the coating is golden brown. Drain the oysters on paper towels, and serve them with deep-fried parsley and a lemon quarter per skewer.

PAUL BOCUSE
PAUL BOCUSE'S FRENCH COOKING

Oysters with Black-Bean Sauce

The fermented black beans called for in this recipe are obtainable in Asian food stores.

	To serve 3 or 4	
1 pint	shucked oysters, drained, and cut into halves if large	½ liter
3 tbsp.	peanut oil	45 ml.
1½ tbsp.	fermented black beans, rinsed and mashed	22½ ml.
1	garlic clove, finely chopped	1
¼-inch	piece fresh ginger, peeled and finely chopped	6-mm.
1 tbsp.	light soy sauce	15 ml.
1 tsp.	rice wine or dry sherry	5 ml.
1 tsp.	cornstarch, mixed with 1 tbsp. [15 ml.] water	5 ml.
2 tbsp.	finely chopped scallion	30 ml.

Heat the oil in a wok or a skillet and add the black beans, garlic and ginger. Stir fry for 10 seconds and add the oysters,

soy sauce and wine. Do not stir. Let the oysters cook for 30 seconds, then carefully lift and stir them gently so they do not break. Cook for one or two minutes longer. Stir in the cornstarch mixture, add the chopped scallion and serve.

MARGARET GIN AND ALFRED E. CASTLE
REGIONAL COOKING OF CHINA

Flambéed Oysters

	To serve 2 to 3	
1 dozen	oysters, scrubbed, shucked and lightly rolled in fresh cracker crumbs	1 dozen
about 2 tbsp.	butter	about 30 ml.
1 tsp.	finely chopped fresh parsley	5 ml.
1 tsp.	finely chopped scallion	5 ml.
4	fresh mushrooms, sliced and sautéed in butter	4
1 cup	sour cream	¼ liter
½ tsp.	Worcestershire sauce	2 ml.
½ tsp.	dry mustard	2 ml.
3 tbsp.	Cognac, warmed over hot water	45 ml.

Sauté the oysters lightly in the butter in a chafing dish or saucepan. Add all of the other ingredients, except the Cognac, and blend the mixture well. Pour in the Cognac and light it. When the flames die, mix the sauce again, and serve the oysters at once on fresh toast triangles.

MIKE LINZ AND STAN FUCHS
THE LOBSTER'S FINE KETTLE OF FISH

Oyster-Asparagus Orlando

	To serve 6	
1 pint	small shucked oysters, with their liquor	½ liter
1 lb.	fresh mushrooms, sliced	½ kg.
1 tbsp.	finely chopped onion	15 ml.
3 tbsp.	butter	45 ml.
3 lb.	asparagus, tips broken off and trimmed, stalks reserved for another use	1½ kg.
½ tbsp.	flour	7 ml.
1 cup	heavy cream	¼ liter
½ tsp.	salt	2 ml.
½ tsp.	pepper	2 ml.
⅛ tsp.	grated nutmeg	½ ml.

Heat the oysters in their own liquor until they curl around the edges—about three minutes. Set them aside. Sauté the mushrooms and onion in 2 tablespoons [30 ml.] of the melted butter. Set the mushrooms aside. Put the asparagus tips into a pan, cover them with boiling salted water and cook them for three to five minutes, or until tender.

Meanwhile, melt the remaining butter in a skillet and blend in the flour. When this roux is lightly browned, add the cream. Stir constantly over low heat until the sauce is thickened. Add the salt, pepper and nutmeg. Stir in the mushroom mixture and the drained oysters.

Drain the asparagus tips and arrange them in a warmed serving dish. Top with the oyster-mushroom sauce.

SARAH D. ALBERSON
THE BLUE SEA COOKBOOK

Oysters Rockefeller

To serve 4 to 6

48	oysters, scrubbed and shucked, the deeper shells reserved	48
1 lb.	coarse salt	½ kg.
8 tbsp.	butter	120 ml.
8	slices bacon, cooked until crisp, drained and crumbled	8
10 oz.	spinach, stems removed and leaves finely chopped	300 g.
3 tbsp.	chopped fresh parsley	45 ml.
3 tbsp.	chopped celery leaves	45 ml.
3 tbsp.	chopped scallions	45 ml.
⅓ cup	dry bread crumbs	75 ml.
½ tsp.	salt	2 ml.
	Tabasco sauce	
1 tsp.	Pernod or *pastis*	5 ml.

For this dish oysters are usually arranged in their deeper shells, on a bed of coarse salt, in four or six shallow pans according to whether you are serving four or six people.

Melt the butter. Add the bacon crumbs and spinach, and the rest of the ingredients except the Pernod or *pastis*. Cook for five to 10 minutes over low heat, stirring the mixture until you have a lightly cooked stuffing. Taste, and adjust the seasonings. Divide the stuffing among the oysters. Place under a hot broiler or in a preheated 425° F. [220° C.] oven until the oysters are bubbling and lightly browned. Just before serving, put a few drops of Pernod or *pastis* on each oyster with an eye dropper. Serve in the pans of salt.

JANE GRIGSON
FISH COOKERY

Baked Oysters Italian

To serve 4 to 6

2 dozen	oysters, scrubbed, shucked and left on the half shell	2 dozen
1	small onion, finely chopped	1
1	celery rib, finely chopped	1
1 tbsp.	finely chopped fresh watercress	15 ml.
8 tbsp.	butter, melted	120 ml.
¾ cup	fresh bread crumbs	175 ml.
¼ cup	freshly grated Parmesan cheese	50 ml.
	ground anise	
	salt and pepper	

Combine the onion, celery, watercress, butter, bread crumbs and cheese. Season the mixture with a pinch of ground anise and salt and pepper to taste. Pour a thick layer of rock salt on the bottom of a large shallow baking dish. Pour the liquor out of the oysters. Spoon 1 tablespoon [15 ml.] of the blended mixture onto each oyster in the half shell. Arrange the shells on the bed of salt and bake them in a preheated 450° F. [230° C.] oven for five to eight minutes, until the tops of the oysters are lightly browned.

VICTOR BENNETT WITH ANTONIA ROSSI
PAPA ROSSI'S SECRETS OF ITALIAN COOKING

Oysters au Gratin

Gratinerade ostron

To serve 4

20 to 24	oysters, scrubbed, shucked and left on the half shell	20 to 24
3 tbsp.	butter	45 ml.
1	shallot, finely chopped	1
1	slice bacon, chopped	1
1 tsp.	grated horseradish	5 ml.
1 tsp.	chopped fresh basil leaves	5 ml.
	Worcestershire sauce	
	white pepper	

Place the oysters on a bed of coarse salt. Mix the butter with the other ingredients and top the oysters with this mixture. Bake in a preheated 450° F. [230° C.] oven until the fat melts and the topping browns—four to six minutes. Serve at once with toast or thinly sliced brown bread and butter.

J. AUDREY ELLISON (EDITOR)
THE GREAT SCANDINAVIAN COOK BOOK

Escaloped Oysters and Scallops

To serve 6 to 8

1 quart	shucked oysters	1 liter
1 lb.	shucked scallops	½ kg.
8 tbsp.	butter, melted	120 ml.
1 cup	fresh bread crumbs	¼ liter
1 tbsp.	celery seeds	15 ml.
	salt and pepper	
1 cup	cream	¼ liter

Mix the melted butter and bread crumbs together. Put a thin layer of this mixture in the bottom of a buttered 2-quart [2-liter] baking dish. Cover with half of the oysters and sprinkle them with celery seeds, salt and pepper. Add some of the cream. Cover with a layer of half of the scallops, sprinkle with seasonings, and add a layer of crumbs. Add the remaining oysters and the rest of the cream. Top with the remaining scallops and buttered crumbs. Bake in a preheated 400° F. [200° C.] oven for 30 minutes, or until the liquid is bubbly and the top is lightly browned.

PETER HUNT
PETER HUNT'S CAPE COD COOKBOOK

Baked Oysters with Champagne

Huîtres au Champagne

The oysters may also be prepared and served in individual salt-filled baking dishes.

To serve 2

1 dozen	oysters, scrubbed, shucked and the liquor reserved, the deeper half shells cleaned and reserved	1 dozen
½ cup	champagne or dry white wine	125 ml.
2	egg yolks	2
1 tsp.	cold water	5 ml.
1 tsp.	*crème fraîche*	5 ml.
	freshly ground pepper	

Preheat the oven to 475° to 500° F. [250° to 260° C.]. Through a cloth-lined sieve, filter the oyster liquor into a stainless-steel or enameled saucepan. Set the half shells in a shallow baking pan filled with coarse salt or fine white gravel. Warm the pan and shells over direct heat or, briefly, in the oven.

In a heavy saucepan, boil the champagne or white wine until it is reduced to about 2 tablespoons [30 ml.]. Allow this to cool to lukewarm. Meanwhile lightly whisk the egg yolks in a small bowl. Remove the saucepan from the heat, and whisk into the reduced champagne or white wine first the

cold water and *crème fraîche* and then the egg yolks. Put the saucepan back over low heat and, whisking constantly, warm the mixture—it must not become hotter than luke-warm (test with your finger)—until it thickens and becomes creamy. It is thick enough when the movement of the whisk exposes streaks of the bottom of the pan. Keep the sauce warm over lukewarm water.

Bring the oyster liquor to a simmer, add the oysters, and poach them for 30 seconds, or until their edges just begin to curl, turning them all over once. Drain the oysters, reserving the cooking liquor, and place each oyster in a half shell. Whisk the hot oyster liquor gradually into the egg-yolk sauce, season with pepper, and spoon a little of the sauce over each oyster. Bake the oysters in the preheated oven for 30 seconds, or until the sauce is glazed and golden. To serve, use tongs to transfer the half shells to two deep plates.

MICHEL GUÉRARD
MICHEL GUÉRARD'S CUISINE MINCEUR

Baked Oysters Alabama

To serve 4 to 6

2 dozen	oysters, scrubbed and shucked (about 1½ cups [375 ml.])	2 dozen
5 tbsp.	butter, 1 tbsp. [15 ml.] cut into small pieces	75 ml.
1	large onion, finely chopped	1
½ cup	finely chopped fresh parsley	125 ml.
1	celery rib, finely chopped	1
	Worcestershire sauce	
1	large egg, beaten	1
2 cups	finely crumbled saltine crackers	½ liter
	salt	

Melt 4 tablespoons [60 ml.] of the butter in a skillet. Add the onion, parsley and celery, and sauté until the vegetables are soft but not browned. Add the well-drained oysters—cut into halves if large—and a dash of Worcestershire sauce. Remove the skillet from the heat and add the beaten egg. Return the skillet to the heat, stirring lightly until the egg is cooked. Add 1 cup [¼ liter] of the cracker crumbs, salt to taste and mix well.

Place this mixture in a shallow buttered pan. Sprinkle the top with the remaining cracker crumbs and dot with the butter pieces. Bake in a preheated 450° F. [230° C.] oven for 10 minutes before serving.

JANE S. COLEMAN
GULF COAST GOURMET

Oysters Bienville

To serve 4 to 8

4 dozen	oysters, scrubbed, shucked and left on the half shell	4 dozen
½ lb.	medium-sized shrimp, rinsed, poached, shelled, deveined and finely chopped	¼ kg.
½ lb.	fresh mushrooms, finely chopped	¼ kg.
2 tbsp.	finely chopped shallots or scallions	30 ml.
5 tbsp.	butter	75 ml.
6 tbsp.	flour	90 ml.
¼ cup	dry white wine	50 ml.
1 ½ cups	fish stock (recipe, page 163)	375 ml.
¾ cup	milk	175 ml.
¾ cup	heavy cream	175 ml.
2	egg yolks	2
	salt and freshly ground black pepper	
2 tbsp.	anise-flavored liqueur (optional)	30 ml.
½ cup	freshly grated Parmesan cheese	125 ml.
	rock salt	

Sauté the mushrooms and the shallots in the butter over medium heat for about eight minutes, until the mushrooms give up their liquid. Sprinkle the mushrooms and shallots with the flour. Meanwhile, combine the wine and stock in a stainless-steel or enameled pot and bring them to a boil. Simmer the liquid for five minutes and add it to the mushroom mixture, stirring vigorously with a wire whisk. Stir in the milk. Combine the cream and egg yolks; add a little of the hot mixture to the cream and egg yolks, then stir this into the remaining hot mixture. Bring the sauce just to a boil and add salt, pepper and the shrimp. Add the anise-flavored liqueur, if desired.

Loosen the oysters on their half shells. Make a 1-inch-thick [2½-cm.] layer of rock salt in four piepans. Arrange one dozen oysters on the half shell in each pan. Place the pans in a preheated 450° F. [130° C.] oven and bake for about one minute, until the edges of the oysters start to curl. Carefully pour off the liquid from each shell and replace the shells on the rock salt. Spoon a generous amount of sauce over each oyster and sprinkle lightly with the Parmesan cheese. Return the oysters to the oven and bake for about three minutes, until lightly browned. Serve immediately.

JEAN HEWITT
THE NEW YORK TIMES SOUTHERN HERITAGE COOKBOOK

Deviled Oysters

To serve 8 to 12

8 dozen	small oysters, scrubbed and shucked (about 1 ½ quarts [1 ½ liters])	8 dozen
⅔ cup	flour	150 ml.
⅔ cup	oil	150 ml.
2 cups	finely chopped onions	½ liter
1 cup	finely chopped scallions	¼ liter
2	garlic cloves, finely chopped	2
1 ½ cups	finely chopped green peppers	375 ml.
1 cup	finely chopped celery	¼ liter
1	bay leaf	1
¼ tsp.	dried thyme leaves	1 ml.
8 tbsp.	butter	120 ml.
3 cups	sliced fresh mushrooms	¾ liter
¼ cup	fresh lemon juice	50 ml.
2 tsp.	salt	10 ml.
½ tsp.	black pepper	2 ml.
⅛ tsp.	cayenne pepper	½ ml.
2 tbsp.	Worcestershire sauce	30 ml.
1 ¼ cups	fresh crumbs, made from French bread	300 ml.

In a large, heavy skillet, make a dark brown roux by cooking the flour in the oil over low heat for 45 minutes to an hour, stirring the mixture frequently. Add the onions, scallions, garlic, green peppers, celery, bay leaf and thyme. Cook them until the vegetables are very tender—about 45 minutes. In a separate skillet, melt the butter, add 1 teaspoon [5 ml.] of the lemon juice and the mushrooms, and stir. Sauté the mushrooms until their liquid has evaporated—about five to seven minutes. Then add them to the sauce. Season the sauce with the salt, black pepper, cayenne pepper and Worcestershire sauce.

When ready to serve, heat the sauce. Drain the oysters, place them in a single layer in a shallow pan and bake them in a preheated 400° F. [200° C.] oven until just curled—about five to six minutes. Using a slotted spoon, transfer the oysters to the skillet containing the sauce. Add the remaining lemon juice and the bread crumbs. Blend well and pour the oyster mixture into a shallow baking dish or individual ramekins. Heat the deviled oysters in the 400° F. oven just until hot. Serve at once.

THE JUNIOR LEAGUE OF NEW ORLEANS
THE PLANTATION COOKBOOK

Stuffed Oysters, Williamsburg

If the walnut ketchup called for in this recipe is not available, substitute vinegar in which walnuts have been pickled. Alternatively, use wine vinegar.

This is an old colonial recipe, in use not only on Long Island but also along the Maryland and Virginia tidewater districts 200 years ago.

To serve 4

2 dozen	oysters, scrubbed, shucked, drained, chopped and their deeper shells cleaned and reserved	2 dozen
2	slices firm-textured white bread with the crusts removed, crumbled	2
1	small onion, finely chopped	1
1 tbsp.	chopped fresh parsley	15 ml.
2 tbsp.	finely chopped celery	30 ml.
1 tsp.	walnut ketchup	5 ml.
2 tbsp.	butter	30 ml.
2 or 3 tbsp.	fresh lemon juice	30 or 45 ml.
2 tsp.	grated lemon peel	10 ml.
	salt and pepper	
	cayenne pepper	
2	eggs, beaten	2
1 cup	bread crumbs, lightly fried in butter	250 ml.
1	lemon, cut into wedges	1

Put the oysters into a skillet and add the crumbled bread, onion, parsley, celery, walnut ketchup, butter, lemon juice and lemon peel, salt, pepper and a pinch of cayenne pepper. Cook for 15 minutes over low heat, stirring constantly. Then add the beaten eggs, mixing them in thoroughly. Fill the reserved oyster shells with this mixture, and place the shells in a shallow baking pan. Sprinkle the oyster filling with the fried bread crumbs, and brown the oysters in a preheated 425° F. [220° C.] oven for about 10 minutes. Serve garnished with the lemon wedges.

J. GEORGE FREDERICK AND JEAN JOYCE
LONG ISLAND SEAFOOD COOK BOOK

Oysters with Periwinkles in Butter Sauce

Huîtres Chaudes aux Bigorneaux

The technique of extracting periwinkles from their shells is demonstrated on pages 78-79. The technique of shucking oysters is demonstrated on pages 14-15.

To serve 4

2 dozen	oysters, scrubbed	2 dozen
1 lb.	periwinkles, rinsed	½ kg.
½ lb.	butter, cut into small pieces and chilled	¼ kg.
	freshly ground pepper, preferably white	
1½ tbsp.	fresh lemon juice	22½ ml.
Vinegar court bouillon		
1	onion, thinly sliced	1
2	carrots, thinly sliced	2
1	celery rib	1
1	sprig fresh thyme or ½ tsp. [2 ml.] crumbled dried thyme leaves	1
	coarse salt	
3 tbsp.	distilled white vinegar	45 ml.
4 cups	water	1 liter

Put the onion, carrot, celery and thyme in a large, heavy, nonreactive pot with a large pinch of coarse salt, the vinegar, and the water. Bring this court bouillon to a boil and let it simmer for 15 minutes. Drop the periwinkles into the pot. Bring the court bouillon to a boil again and skim the surface. Boil for three minutes, then remove the pot from the heat. Drain the periwinkles in a colander set over a bowl to catch the court bouillon. Then refresh the periwinkles by setting them under cold running water just long enough to cool them so that they can be handled. With the help of a pin or skewer, extract the periwinkles from their shells. Remove the black intestines and set the periwinkles aside in a bowl.

Put ½ cup [125 ml.] of the reserved court bouillon in a small saucepan and set it over low heat. Using a wire whisk, stir in the butter. The mixture should form a thick sauce. Taste for seasoning, adding pepper and lemon juice.

Shuck the oysters, reserving their liquor and the deeper shells. Warm the oysters and their liquor in a large, heavy saucepan over medium heat for about two minutes. Meanwhile, arrange the reserved oyster shells on two deep, heatproof platters and warm them in a preheated 300° F. [150° C.] oven. With a slotted spoon, place the oysters in the shells, cover them with the sauce and distribute the periwinkles over all. Broil the oysters under a preheated broiler for 20 seconds. Serve the oysters at once.

JEAN AND PIERRE TROISGROS
THE NOUVELLE CUISINE OF JEAN & PIERRE TROISGROS

Broiled Oysters in Bacon Blankets

Devils on Horseback

You can substitute clams for the oysters in this recipe.

	To serve 4	
2 dozen	oysters, shucked and drained	2 dozen
12	slices bacon, cut into halves	12
	lemon wedges	

Wrap each half slice of bacon around an oyster, fasten the bacon if necessary with wooden picks, and place the wrapped oyster on the rack of a broiler pan. Broil in a preheated broiler—about 3 inches [8 cm.] from the heat source—for three minutes on each side, or until the bacon is crisp and the edges of the oysters curl. Serve with the lemon wedges.

DAN AND INEZ MORRIS
THE COMPLETE FISH COOKBOOK

Oyster Pie Maryland

	To serve 6	
1 pint	shucked oysters, with their liquor	½ liter
½ cup	chopped green pepper	125 ml.
½ cup	chopped celery	125 ml.
4 tbsp.	butter, melted	60 ml.
5 tbsp.	flour	75 ml.
2 cups	milk	½ liter
2 tbsp.	chopped pimiento	30 ml.
1 tsp.	salt	5 ml.
⅛ tsp.	pepper	½ ml.
½ lb.	short-crust dough (recipe, page 167), rolled ⅛ inch [3 mm.] thick	¼ kg.

Cook the oysters in their liquor until their edges curl. Drain. Sauté the green pepper and celery in the butter until soft. Blend in the flour, add the milk and, stirring constantly, cook until the mixture becomes thick. Add the oysters, pimiento and seasonings, and heat again. Pour the mixture into a 1½-quart [1½-liter] casserole and top it with the rolled-out dough. Trim the edges of the dough and slash it in two or three places to let steam escape. Bake the pie in a preheated 425° F. [220° C.] oven for 15 minutes, or until the crust is brown.

SARAH D. ALBERSON
THE BLUE SEA COOKBOOK

Antoinette's Gratinéed Oysters

Huîtres Gratinées Antoinette

Pineau Charentais is an apertif that is made from white wine and Cognac.

	To serve 1	
6	oysters, scrubbed, steamed open, the meat removed, the cooking liquid strained and the deep half shells reserved	6
2 tbsp.	butter	30 ml.
2	shallots, finely chopped	2
½ cup	finely chopped fresh mushrooms	125 ml.
¾ cup	white wine	175 ml.
¾ cup	Pineau Charentais	175 ml.
	salt and pepper	
2 tbsp.	heavy cream	30 ml.
1	egg yolk	1
2 tbsp.	freshly grated Gruyère cheese	30 ml.
2 tbsp.	almonds, blanched, peeled and ground	30 ml.

In a nonreactive saucepan, melt the butter, and in it cook the shallots and mushrooms until they are soft but not brown. Moisten them with the two wines. Salt and pepper the mixture lightly and reduce it over medium heat until it is a wet paste. (It will look nasty, but taste good.)

In another saucepan over low heat, beat the cream and egg yolk, and when the mixture is thick enough to coat a spoon, add the contents of the other pan. Without letting this sauce boil, continue to stir it for a few more minutes. Taste and correct the seasoning.

Arrange the clean oyster shells in a gratin dish or heat-proof platter, then place an oyster on each shell and pour the reserved oyster liquor over them. Spoon the sauce over the oysters, and sprinkle it with the grated cheese and ground almonds. Run the dish under a preheated broiler for a minute or so to reheat the oysters and brown the sauce.

MADELEINE PETER
FAVORITE RECIPES OF THE GREAT WOMEN CHEFS OF FRANCE

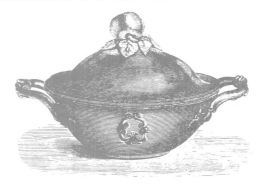

Baked Oysters, Fines Herbes

To serve 6

3 dozen	oysters, scrubbed, shucked and left on the half shell	3 dozen
¾ lb.	butter, softened	350 g.
9	shallots, grated	9
¼ cup	finely chopped fresh parsley	50 ml.
¼ cup	finely chopped fresh tarragon	50 ml.
¼ cup	finely cut chives	50 ml.
¼ cup	cracker crumbs	50 ml.
2 tsp.	fresh lemon juice	10 ml.

Fill six piepans with rock salt. Put the pans into a preheated 500° F. [260° C.] oven for 10 minutes. Make a paste of all the ingredients, except the oysters. Put a teaspoonful [5 ml.] of the paste on each oyster. Place six oysters in each pan. Run the oysters under a preheated broiler for just long enough to plump them—about three minutes—and serve them at once on the rock-salt beds.

CHARLOTTE ADAMS
THE FOUR SEASONS COOKBOOK

Hot Curried Oysters

Huîtres Chaudes de l'Île de Ré

To serve 1 or 2

8	oysters, scrubbed, shucked, and the liquor strained and reserved	8
2	shallots, chopped	2
1	garlic clove	1
1 tbsp.	butter	15 ml.
¼ cup	*crème fraîche*	50 ml.
½ tsp.	cayenne pepper	2 ml.
½ tsp.	powdered saffron	2 ml.
¾ tsp.	curry powder	4 ml.
	fresh lemon juice	

Put the oyster liquor into a pan with the shallots, garlic clove and the butter. Cook over medium heat until the butter melts, then simmer until the liquid is reduced to half its original volume. Add the *crème fraîche*, the cayenne, saffron and the curry. Stirring constantly, cook this sauce over low heat until it is thick and creamy. Add a few drops of lemon juice. Place the oysters in one or two individual gratin dishes. Pour the sauce over the oysters, and place the dishes under a preheated broiler for 10 seconds. Serve at once.

LE DUC
CRUSTACÉS, POISSONS ET COQUILLAGES

Oysters with Champagne Sauce

To serve 6

1 pint	shucked oysters	½ liter
1 tbsp.	cornstarch	15 ml.
¾ cup	heavy cream	175 ml.
1 cup	dry champagne, chilled	¼ liter
1 or 2	shallots	1 or 2
	Tabasco sauce	
	salt and pepper	
4	egg yolks	4

Measure the cornstarch into a small mixing bowl and stir in the cream. Pour this sauce base into a small, heavy, non-reactive pot and add the champagne. Spear each of the shallots on a wooden pick, add them to the sauce with a dash of Tabasco, and salt and pepper to taste. Bring the mixture to a simmer and cook it gently, uncovered, for 10 minutes.

Put the yolks into the same bowl used for the cream and beat them well. Remove the shallots from the champagne sauce and, while whisking, slowly pour the hot liquid into the beaten yolks. Return the sauce to the pot and taste it for salt and pepper. Cook over very low heat for a minute or less, whisking constantly and not allowing the sauce to boil. The sauce is finished when it will easily coat the back of a spoon and is quite thick.

While the sauce is simmering, place the oysters in six individual scallop shells. Spoon about 2 tablespoons [30 ml.] of hot champagne sauce over the oysters in each shell; the oysters must be completely covered by the sauce. Place the scallop shells under a preheated broiler for two or three minutes, or until the sauce bubbles. Place the shells on luncheon-size dishes and serve at once.

CAROL CUTLER
THE SIX-MINUTE SOUFFLÉ AND OTHER CULINARY DELIGHTS

Scallops in White Wine

Coquilles Saint-Jacques "Maître Paul"

This recipe will serve 10 to 12 people as an hors d'oeuvre.

To serve 6

1½ lb.	shucked sea scallops, cut into 2 or 3 slices	¾ kg.
7 tbsp.	butter	105 ml.
	salt and pepper	
3	shallots, very finely chopped	3
2 tbsp.	chopped fresh parsley	30 ml.
¼ cup	white wine	50 ml.

Put the scallops into a heavy enameled, stainless-steel or tin-lined saucepan. Add the remaining ingredients. Bring to a simmer over medium heat, cover, and cook for three to five minutes, or until the scallops are opaque. Remove the scallops with a slotted spoon, increase the heat, and boil the sauce for five to 10 minutes, or until it has been reduced to half of its original volume and is smooth, syrupy and the color of ivory. Return the scallops to the pan and heat them through. Serve immediately.

CURNONSKY
CUISINE ET VINS DE FRANCE

Bay Scallops Swimming in Their Bouillon

Coquilles Saint-Jacques à la Nage

To serve 4

1 to 1½ lb.	shucked bay scallops, rinsed and patted dry	½ to ¾ kg.
4 cups	fish stock (recipe, page 163), heated to boiling	1 liter
	coarse salt	
	freshly ground black pepper	
4	medium-sized carrots, scraped and cut into ¼-inch [6-mm.] dice	4
6 to 8	small white onions, thinly sliced	6 to 8
2 tsp.	sour cream	10 ml.
4 tbsp.	butter, cut into slivers	60 ml.
½	lemon	½
1 tbsp.	chopped fresh chervil, basil, tarragon or thyme leaves	15 ml.

Place the scallops in a 2-quart [2-liter] lidded saucepan, lightly salting and peppering them to taste, then covering the pot without turning on the heat. Put the diced carrots into a second 1½-quart [1½-liter] saucepan and pour over enough of the hot fish stock to cover them. Gently simmer, uncovered, until the carrots are just cooked but still quite crisp—usually in five to seven minutes.

When the carrots are done, add the onion slices. The instant the liquid returns to a boil, turn off the heat. Working fast, pour the carrots and onions with their hot bouillon over the waiting scallops, adding enough additional hot bouillon to cover the scallop mixture by about half an inch [1 cm.]. Turn the heat fairly high and, timing from the precise moment when the liquid returns to a boil, cook the scallops for exactly two minutes—not a second more, or they will become leathery. Meanwhile, warm four soup plates.

With a slotted spoon, lift out the scallops and the vegetables, dividing them equally among the four warm soup plates. Keep them all warm. Now add more hot bouillon to the scallop bouillon until the volume in the saucepan is

about 3 cups [¾ liter]. Bring it to a rolling boil and keep it bubbling hard to reduce it. When it is just beginning to develop a mildly glutinous body, turn off the heat and carefully stir in the sour cream. Now enrich the sauce by performing the small operation known in the French cuisine as *monter au beurre*—mounting with butter. Turn the heat back up to merry bubbling and arm yourself with a wooden spoon, then drop in the butter—sliver by sliver—stirring continuously until each sliver is melted across the surface, but not incorporated into the bouillon. Add a couple of squeezes of lemon juice, just enough to give the slightest sense of tartness. Taste, and adjust salt and pepper as required. Turn off the heat and stir in the fresh herb leaves. Pour the bouillon sauce, in equal portions, into the four soup plates with the scallops and the vegetables, and serve instantly.

ROY ANDRIES DE GROOT
REVOLUTIONIZING FRENCH COOKING

Scallops with Saffron

Coquilles Saint-Jacques au Saffron

This is a recipe from Maxim's restaurant in Paris. To make the rice pilaf accompaniment for this dish, sauté ½ cup [125 ml.] of white rice in a little oil or butter in a saucepan; add 1 cup [¼ liter] of boiling water. Cover and cook gently until all the liquid is absorbed—about 20 minutes.

To serve 4

1 lb.	shucked sea scallops, rinsed and patted dry	½ kg.
5 tbsp.	butter	75 ml.
1	shallot, chopped	1
¼ tsp.	powdered saffron	1 ml.
	salt and pepper	
1 tsp.	Cognac	5 ml.
1 tsp.	dry vermouth	5 ml.
2	large tomatoes, peeled, seeded and coarsely chopped	2
¼ lb.	mushrooms, thinly sliced (about 1 cup [¼ liter])	125 g.
2 cups	heavy cream	½ liter

Heat the butter in a nonreactive sauté pan and add the shallot. As soon as the shallot turns transparent, add the scallops and saffron, and season with salt. Cover and stew for two minutes. Add the Cognac and vermouth, then the tomatoes, mushrooms and cream. Cover and stew for eight minutes.

Remove the scallops and arrange them in a warmed serving dish. Cook the sauce, uncovered, over medium-high heat until it thickens slightly. Taste for salt and pepper. Coat the scallops with the sauce. Serve with a rice pilaf.

LES PRINCES DE LA GASTRONOMIE

Bay Scallops with Caviar Butter

Coquilles Saint-Jacques au Caviar

If Calvados is unavailable, do not substitute applejack but use a good Cognac or a well-aged Armagnac. Sea scallops may also be used; cut them into ¼-inch [6-mm.] slices before frying. Use only fine imported caviar. If you cannot afford it, omit it; the sauce will still be good.

To serve 6

1½ lb.	shucked bay scallops, rinsed and patted dry	¾ kg.
⅔ cup	fish stock (recipe, page 163)	150 ml.
⅓ cup	dry Champagne, or an excellent dry white wine	75 ml.
3 tbsp.	chopped shallots	45 ml.
	salt and pepper	
½ tsp.	potato starch	1 ml.
¼ cup	heavy cream	50 ml.
16 tbsp.	unsalted butter	240 ml.
2 tbsp.	Calvados, Cognac or Armagnac	30 ml.
1 to 2 oz.	beluga *malossol* caviar	30 to 60 g.
	lemon juice	

Place the fish stock, Champagne, shallots and a pinch of salt and pepper in a 9-inch [23-cm.] skillet. Set the skillet over medium heat and slowly cook until all but ¼ cup [50 ml.] of the liquid has evaporated. Mix the potato starch and cream and stir these into the reduced wine to thicken it. Bring the liquid to a boil and whisk in all but 2 tablespoons [30 ml.] of the butter. Strain the sauce into a clean saucepan and keep it warm over very low heat.

Do not clean the skillet, but leave it on medium heat and add the remaining 2 tablespoons of butter. By the time the butter has melted, the sauce left in the skillet will have turned to a light-brown glaze. Add the scallops and toss them over high heat until they appear milky white; this should not require more than two minutes. Remove the pan from the heat. Salt and pepper lightly. Heat the Calvados or other chosen spirit in a small pan, ignite it and pour it flaming into the pan of scallops. Shake the pan over high heat until the flames die. Remove the scallops to a warmed shallow dish and keep them warm.

Reduce the juices in the skillet over high heat to about 2 tablespoons of glaze. Strain them into the reserved warm sauce. Add the caviar to the sauce. Correct the seasoning by adding salt, if necessary, and pepper. Add a few drops of lemon juice. Should the caviar make the sauce a bit too salty, rebalance the taste by adding lemon juice. Pour the sauce over the scallops. Serve the assembly on warm plates.

This dish does not wait, but is waited for by guests already sitting at the dinner table.

MADELEINE M. KAMMAN
WHEN FRENCH WOMEN COOK

Baked Scallops

To serve 8

2 lb.	shucked bay or sea scallops, rinsed and patted dry, the sea scallops cut into quarters	1 kg.
	salt and freshly ground black pepper	
2 tbsp.	fresh lemon juice	30 ml.
¼ cup	dry white wine	50 ml.
2 tbsp.	butter, melted	30 ml.
½ cup	heavy cream	125 ml.
½ cup	fresh bread crumbs	125 ml.

Put the scallops into a large mixing bowl, add salt and pepper to taste, then the lemon juice and white wine. Using your hands or a fork and spoon, toss all the ingredients together.

Generously butter a shallow 12-by-16-inch [30-by-40-cm.] baking dish. Using a rubber spatula, scrape the scallop mixture and all of its liquid into the baking dish, then add the cream. Sprinkle the top evenly with the bread crumbs, then dribble the melted butter over the crumbs. Set the baking dish on the middle shelf of a preheated 400° F. [200° C.] oven and bake for 12 to 14 minutes, or until the bread crumbs are pale gold.

JOHN CLANCY AND FRANCES FIELD
CLANCY'S OVEN COOKERY

Scallops with Garlic

To serve 2 or 3

1¼ lb.	shucked scallops, rinsed and patted dry	⅔ kg.
6 tbsp.	butter	90 ml.
3	large garlic cloves, finely chopped	3
1 tbsp.	flour	15 ml.
1	ripe tomato, peeled, seeded and chopped	1
6	scallions with the green tops, chopped	6
	fresh thyme leaves	
⅓ cup	vermouth	75 ml.
2 tbsp.	fresh lemon juice	30 ml.
½ tsp.	salt	2 ml.
⅛ tsp.	freshly ground pepper	½ ml.
2 tbsp.	finely chopped fresh parsley	30 ml.

If using sea scallops, cut them into quarters. In a large skillet, melt 2 tablespoons [30 ml.] of the butter. Add one third of the garlic; cook over medium heat for one minute. Add one third of the scallops; cook over high heat, stirring constantly, until golden, five to six minutes. Transfer the scallops to a warmed serving platter. Repeat the process with the remaining butter, garlic and scallops. Keep the cooked scallops warm in a preheated 225° F. [110° C.] oven.

Sprinkle the flour into the butter remaining in the skillet and stir until all of the liquid is absorbed. Add the tomato, scallions and a pinch of thyme; cook over medium heat until the tomato is soft, about five minutes. Gradually stir in the vermouth and lemon juice; cook until the sauce is syrupy, about five minutes. Stir in the salt and pepper.

Pour the sauce over the scallops and sprinkle with the chopped parsley. Serve hot.

BERT GREENE
BERT GREENE'S KITCHEN BOUQUETS

Broiled Scallops with Mushrooms and Ham

To serve 6

2 lb.	shucked scallops, rinsed	1 kg.
2	shallots, finely chopped, or 2 tsp. [10 ml.] chopped scallions	2
	salt and pepper	
2 tbsp.	brandy	30 ml.
½ cup	dry white wine	125 ml.
2	sprigs fresh parsley	2
1	bay leaf, broken in half	1
18	mushroom caps	18
2	slices boiled ham	2
6 tbsp.	butter	90 ml.
3	lemons, halved	3

If you use large sea scallops, quarter them. Place the scallops in a flat dish. Chop the shallots or scallions and sprinkle them over the scallops along with the salt and pepper. Pour on the brandy and white wine. The liquid should not completely cover the scallops; they are meant to marinate, not swim in the wines. Turn the scallops a few times with your hands. Tuck in the parsley and bay-leaf pieces. Cover the dish and let it stand at room temperature for at least one hour; two or three hours are even better. (The scallops can marinate overnight in the refrigerator, but add 2 tablespoons [30 ml.] of oil to the marinade.) Turn occasionally.

Rinse the mushroom caps and let them dry. If they are large, cut them in halves or quarters; the mushrooms should not be larger than the scallops. Dice the ham into ¼-inch [6-mm.] or slightly smaller squares. Melt the butter.

Discard the parsley and bay-leaf pieces and lift the scallops out of the marinade, shaking off the excess liquid. Place the scallops in a gratin dish. Add the ham and mushroom caps and mix all together with your hands. Sprinkle lightly with salt and pepper. Pour over the scallops three fourths of the melted butter and place the dish under a preheated broiler. Broil for three minutes.

Toss the scallops and mushrooms with a spatula and sprinkle with the remaining melted butter. Broil for two or three minutes longer. Take the gratin dish to the table and serve from it onto individual plates. Place a lemon half on each plate.

CAROL CUTLER
THE SIX-MINUTE SOUFFLÉ AND OTHER CULINARY DELIGHTS

French-Style Scallops and Mushrooms

To serve 6

1 lb.	shucked sea scallops, rinsed and patted dry	½ kg.
1 lb.	small fresh mushrooms, trimmed and thinly sliced	½ kg.
5 tbsp.	butter	75 ml.
¾ cup	dry white vermouth	175 ml.
¼ cup	water	50 ml.
1	bay leaf	1
½ tsp.	salt	2 ml.
⅛ tsp.	white pepper	½ ml.
3 tbsp.	flour	45 ml.
1 cup	light cream	¼ liter
½ cup	fresh bread crumbs, mixed with 1 tbsp. [15 ml.] melted butter	125 ml.

In a 10-inch [25-cm.] skillet, heat 2 tablespoons [30 ml.] of the butter; add the mushrooms and sauté them rapidly and briefly so as not to gather juices; reserve the mushrooms.

Place the scallops in a nonreactive saucepan with the vermouth, water, bay leaf, salt and pepper. Bring the liquid to the boiling point and simmer until the scallops are just opaque through—about five minutes; do not overcook them, or the scallops will toughen. Drain the scallops; strain and reserve 1 cup [¼ liter] of the cooking liquid. Cut each of the scallops into four chunks and reserve them.

In a saucepan over low heat, melt the remaining 3 tablespoons [45 ml.] of butter; stir in the flour. Add the reserved scallop cooking liquid and the cream; cook and stir constantly over low heat until this sauce is thickened. Add the sautéed mushrooms and the quartered scallops. Spoon the mixture into six scallop or other baking shells; sprinkle with the buttered bread crumbs. Bake in a preheated 400° F. [200° C.] oven until bubbling hot and golden—about 10 minutes.

CECILY BROWNSTONE
CECILY BROWNSTONE'S ASSOCIATED PRESS COOK BOOK

Galician Scallops
Vieiras Gallegas

To serve 4

1¼ lb.	shucked scallops, finely chopped	600 g.
1	medium-sized onion, finely chopped	1
1	garlic clove, crushed to a paste	1
1 tbsp.	finely chopped fresh parsley	15 ml.
	salt and pepper	
2 tbsp.	fresh bread crumbs	30 ml.
1 tbsp.	olive oil	15 ml.

Combine the scallops, onion, garlic, parsley, salt and pepper. Mix well with the bread crumbs and olive oil. Fill four baking shells or ramekins with the mixture. Bake in a preheated 400° F. [200° C.] oven for 10 minutes, or until golden.

JEANNETTE AGUILAR
THE CLASSIC COOKING OF SPAIN

Scallops with Mushrooms
Coquilles Saint-Jacques à la Ménagère

The technique of opening scallops is demonstrated on pages 16-17. Scrub the insides of the concave shells and reserve them for serving scallops or other fish dishes. The technique for preparing court bouillon is shown on pages 22-23.

To serve 6

1 dozen	sea scallops, shucked and the concave half shells scrubbed and reserved	1 dozen
20 tbsp.	butter	300 ml.
½ lb.	fresh button mushrooms, thinly sliced	¼ kg.
2 tbsp.	flour	30 ml.
2	egg yolks, lightly beaten	2
¼ cup	fine fresh bread crumbs	50 ml.
Court bouillon		
1 cup	water	¼ liter
½ cup	dry white wine	125 ml.
1	sprig thyme	1
½	bay leaf	½
1	medium-sized onion, finely chopped	1
	salt and pepper	

Prepare the court bouillon. Poach the scallop muscles and corals in this court bouillon for four minutes. Strain the scallops and reserve the cooking liquid. Set the corals aside and cut the scallop muscles into slices ¼ inch [6 mm.] thick.

Heat 4 tablespoons [60 ml.] of the butter in a skillet, toss in the mushrooms and sauté them rapidly, then add the scallop slices, mix well and remove the pan from the heat. Cover the mixture to keep it hot.

In a sauté pan, melt 7 tablespoons [105 ml.] of the butter. Add the flour and cook gently, stirring frequently, for 10 minutes to make a roux. Remove the pan from the heat and cool the roux. Stir 2 tablespoons [30 ml.] of the court bouillon into the egg yolks; heat the remaining court bouillon and add it to the roux, stirring until you have obtained a smooth sauce. Bring the sauce to a boil, stirring with a whisk, and cook for one minute. Off the heat, thicken the sauce with the egg yolks. Continue to whisk the sauce while heating it. Remove the pan from the heat when the mixture approaches the boiling point: Do not let the sauce boil, or the egg yolks will cook and form small lumps. Whisk in 7 tablespoons of the butter and check the seasoning.

Plunge six of the concave scallop shells into boiling water, drain them and wipe them dry. Place 1 tablespoon [15 ml.] of the sauce into each shell. Then add to each shell the meat of about two sliced scallops, some mushrooms and, finally, two pieces of coral. Cover with the sauce and sprinkle the bread crumbs over the top. Melt the remaining butter and sprinkle it over the bread crumbs. Brown the scallops in a preheated 475° F. [250° C.] oven for five or six minutes.

Serve the scallops on top of a folded napkin on a platter.

PAUL BOCUSE
THE NEW CUISINE

Scallops with Gin

To serve 4 or 5

1 lb.	shucked scallops, rinsed	½ kg.
4 tbsp.	butter	60 ml.
1 tbsp.	oil	15 ml.
about ¾ cup	flour	about 175 ml.
¾ cup	gin	175 ml.
1 cup	heavy cream	¼ liter
1½ tbsp.	fresh lemon juice	22½ ml.
	salt and pepper	
1 tsp.	chopped fresh tarragon	5 ml.
1 tbsp.	chopped fresh parsley	15 ml.

Heat the butter and oil together in a large skillet; use two skillets if necessary to keep the scallops in a single layer. While the butter is heating, spread the flour on a dish or a large piece of waxed paper. Add the scallops to the flour. Toss to coat the scallops thoroughly with flour, shake off the excess flour, and add the scallops to the skillet when the butter is hot and foamy.

Cook the scallops over high heat just long enough to give them a nice light-brown coating; this should take no more than one or two minutes. Keep turning them with a wide spatula. Pour in the gin, cream and lemon juice, and sprinkle with salt and pepper. Reduce the heat to medium, cover the pan, and simmer for two minutes for tiny bay scallops, or three to four minutes for larger scallops. Spoon the hot scallops with the cream sauce into warm scallop shells or individual serving dishes. Sprinkle lightly with the chopped parsley and tarragon. In addition to a fork, each diner should have a teaspoon for the delicious sauce.

CAROL CUTLER
THE SIX-MINUTE SOUFFLÉ AND OTHER CULINARY DELIGHTS

Crab

Soft-shell Crabs in Black-Bean and Chili Sauce

The volatile oils in chilies may irritate your skin. Wear rubber gloves when handling them. The fermented black beans called for in this recipe are obtainable in Asian food stores.

	To serve 2 to 4	
4	soft-shell crabs, rinsed, cleaned and patted dry	4
1 cup plus 2 tbsp.	oil	280 ml.
2 tbsp.	fermented black beans, rinsed in hot water, drained and mashed to a paste	30 ml.
4	garlic cloves, finely chopped	4
½ tsp.	finely chopped fresh ginger	2 ml.
2	dried hot red chilies, torn into small pieces, the seeds reserved	2
½ cup	chopped green pepper	125 ml.
1	scallion, including the green part, cut into pea-sized pieces	1
1 tsp.	cornstarch, mixed with 2 tbsp. [30 ml.] water	5 ml.
	Wine sauce	
1½ tbsp.	Chinese shaoh sing wine or pale dry sherry	22½ ml.
½ tsp.	sugar	2 ml.
2 tbsp.	thin soy sauce	30 ml.
¼ cup	chicken stock (recipe, page 166)	50 ml.

In a wok, heat 1 cup [¼ liter] of the oil to 375° F. [190° C.]. Add the crabs and deep fry them until they turn golden.

Drain the crabs and discard the oil. Clean and dry the wok.

Combine the black beans, garlic, ginger and chilies, and set aside. Combine the sauce ingredients and set aside. Heat the wok over high heat. Swirl in the remaining oil. When the oil is hot, add the black-bean mixture. Stir fry the mixture for about 30 seconds. Add the green pepper and scallion and stir fry for about 10 seconds. Stir in the sauce. Put the cooked crabs back into the wok. Cover, turn the heat to low and cook until the sauce comes to a boil. Stir in the cornstarch and cook until the sauce is thickened. Serve at once.

MAI LEUNG
THE CLASSIC CHINESE COOK BOOK

Chesapeake Bay Soft-shell Crabs

If desired, crabs may be deep fried in oil at 375° F. [190° C.] for two to three minutes, or until browned.

	To serve 6	
12	soft-shell crabs, rinsed and cleaned	12
	salt and pepper	
	flour (optional)	
	butter or oil for frying	

Dry crabs with paper towels, and sprinkle them with salt and pepper. Lightly coat with flour, if desired. Fry the crabs in a skillet, in just enough fat to prevent sticking, until browned—about five minutes on each side.

MARYLAND SEAFOOD MARKETING AUTHORITY
MARYLAND SEAFOOD COOKBOOK 1

Baked Soft-shell Crabs

	To serve 4 to 6	
1 dozen	small soft-shell crabs, rinsed and cleaned	1 dozen
4 tbsp.	butter, melted	60 ml.
	salt and pepper	
1 cup	fine dry bread crumbs	¼ liter

Dip each crab in the melted butter and sprinkle it with salt and pepper; then roll each crab in the bread crumbs. Place the crabs in a shallow, buttered baking pan and bake them in a preheated 400° F. [200° C.] oven for 15 minutes, or until browned. Serve with tartar sauce.

PHILLIP MASON
SHELLFISH COOKBOOK

Sautéed Soft-shell Crabs

To serve 4 to 6

1 dozen	small soft-shell crabs, rinsed and cleaned	1 dozen
½ cup	whole-wheat flour	125 ml.
¼ tsp.	cayenne pepper	1 ml.
⅛ tsp.	black pepper	½ ml.
8 to 12 tbsp.	butter	120 to 180 ml.
1	small garlic clove, crushed to a paste	1
2 tbsp.	fresh lemon juice	30 ml.
1 tbsp.	finely chopped fresh parsley	15 ml.

Season the flour with the cayenne and black pepper. Dredge the crabs all over with the seasoned flour. Melt 8 tablespoons [120 ml.] of the butter in a large, heavy skillet and when hot, add as many of the crabs as will fit in one layer without crowding. Sauté the crabs until golden brown—about one or two minutes on each side. With tongs, transfer the crabs to a warmed platter. Add the remaining crabs to the skillet—along with more butter, if necessary—and sauté them similarly. Add the garlic to the butter remaining in the skillet and stir quickly. Then add the lemon juice. Pour this sauce over the crabs and sprinkle with parsley.

SHERYL AND MEL LONDON
THE FISH-LOVERS' COOKBOOK

Soft-shell Crabs with Almonds

The technique of preparing soft-shell crabs for frying is demonstrated on pages 20-21.

To serve 6

12 to 18	soft-shell crabs, rinsed and cleaned	12 to 18
1 cup	clarified butter	¼ liter
1 cup	almonds, blanched, peeled and slivered	¼ liter
½ cup	flour, seasoned with ½ tsp. [2 ml.] salt and pepper to taste	125 ml.
2 tbsp.	fresh lemon juice	30 ml.
2 tbsp.	chopped fresh parsley	30 ml.
6	lemon wedges	6

Sauté the almonds in 2 tablespoons [30 ml.] of the clarified butter in a heavy pan until golden, then place them in a 250° F. [120° C.] oven to keep them hot.

Wash the crabs and pat them dry. Roll them in the seasoned flour, and sauté them in the remaining butter until golden on both sides—about six minutes. Transfer the crabs to a heatproof platter and keep them warm in the oven.

Add the lemon juice and parsley to the butter remaining in the pan, and heat briefly. Pour the butter and the almonds over the crabs. Garnish with lemon wedges. Serve at once.

LILLIAN LANGSETH-CHRISTENSEN AND CAROL STURM SMITH
THE SHELLFISH COOKBOOK

Deep-fried Stuffed Crabs

Rellenong Alimango

To make 8 to 10

12	medium-sized blue crabs, poached, meat extracted and the body shells rinsed and drained, or substitute 1 lb. [½ kg.] crab meat, picked over	12
	vegetable oil	
½ cup	thinly sliced scallions	125 ml.
1 tsp.	finely chopped garlic	5 ml.
1	small tomato, peeled, seeded and coarsely chopped	1
1¼ tsp.	salt	6 ml.
	freshly ground black pepper	
2	eggs, the yolks separated from the whites	2
1	head romaine lettuce, washed, separated into leaves and chilled	1
1	firm tomato, cut into 6 wedges	1
2	lemons, each cut into 6 wedges	2

In a heavy 8- to 10-inch [20- to 23-cm.] skillet, heat 3 tablespoons [45 ml.] of oil over medium heat until a light haze forms above it. Drop in the scallions and garlic and stir for two to three minutes. When the scallions are soft and transparent, add the chopped tomato and stir for five minutes, or until most of the liquid in the pan evaporates. Mix in the crab meat, 1 teaspoon [5 ml.] of the salt and a few grindings of pepper. Stirring constantly, cook over low heat until the mixture is quite dry. Do not let the crab brown. Remove from the heat, taste for seasoning and set the mixture aside.

With a wire whisk or a rotary or electric beater, beat the egg whites and the remaining salt in a deep bowl until the whites are stiff. In a separate bowl, with the same beater, beat the egg yolks until they thicken slightly. Fold the yolks gently but thoroughly into the beaten whites.

To assemble each *alimango*, spoon about ¼ cup [50 ml.] of the crab meat mixture into the reserved crab shells or into natural scallop shells (not china or plastic), mounding the meat slightly in the center. With a rubber spatula, spread a 1-inch [2½-cm.] layer of the egg mixture over the crab meat.

Depending on the size and meatiness of the crabs, there may be only enough filling for eight to 10 of the shells.

Pour enough oil into a large heavy skillet to form a ½-inch [1-cm.] layer. Heat until the oil is very hot but not smoking. Fry the *alimango* three or four at a time. Slide each one gently into the skillet, shell side down, and—constantly dribbling hot oil over the top with a large spoon—cook for two minutes, or until the top is puffed and golden.

Arrange the lettuce on a platter, place the *alimango* on it, and garnish with the tomato and lemon wedges.

FOODS OF THE WORLD/PACIFIC AND SOUTHEAST ASIAN COOKING

Crab with Peking Sauce

Jiang-bao Qing-xie

The technique of cutting up a crab is shown on pages 20-21.

To serve 1

½ to ¾ lb.	blue crab, scrubbed, poached, cleaned, cut up and the claws cracked	¼ kg. to 350 g.
1 cup	oil	¼ liter
1 tsp.	finely chopped scallions	5 ml.
2 tsp.	finely chopped fresh ginger	10 ml.
½ cup	fish or chicken stock (recipes, pages 163 and 166)	125 ml.
2 tsp.	rice wine or dry sherry	10 ml.
1 tsp.	salt	5 ml.
1 tbsp.	red-bean paste, mixed with 1 tbsp. [15 ml.] water	15 ml.
½ tsp.	sugar	2 ml.
2 tsp.	soy sauce	10 ml.
2 tsp.	cornstarch, mixed with 2 tsp. [10 ml.] water	10 ml.

Heat the oil in a wok over medium-high heat. Add the crab pieces and deep fry them, stirring for 15 to 20 seconds. Remove the crab pieces and drain them. Leave only 4 to 6 tablespoons [60 to 90 ml.] of the oil in the wok. Heat the oil over medium heat, then add the scallions and ginger. Stir fry briefly, then return the deep-fried crab to the wok. Stir fry for a few moments.

Add the stock, wine and salt. Stir well for a few seconds, then pull the crab pieces up from the center of the wok onto the sides. Add the red-bean sauce, sugar and soy sauce to the liquid in the bottom of the wok. Stir well, then let the pieces of crab return to the bottom of the wok. Stir. Give the mixture of cornstarch and water a stir and then add this to the contents of the wok. Stir over medium heat until the sauce thickens and adheres to the crab pieces. Transfer the crab to a warmed serving dish and serve hot.

ROBERT A. DELFS
THE GOOD FOOD OF SZECHWAN

Broiled Crab Legs in Herb Butter

To serve 2

2 lb.	king crab legs, defrosted	1 kg.
8 tbsp.	butter	120 ml.
1 or 2	garlic cloves, crushed to a paste (optional)	1 or 2
2 tbsp.	chopped fresh parsley	30 ml.
1 tsp.	basil	5 ml.
1 tsp.	tarragon	5 ml.
	salt and pepper	

Melt the butter and add the garlic (if using), the herbs, and salt and pepper to taste. Place the crab legs in a shallow baking dish, pour half of the butter over them and broil them in a preheated broiler for 10 to 15 minutes—depending on the size of the legs—turning them once. Alternatively, bake the legs in a preheated 450° F. [230° C.] oven for about 15 minutes, or until brown.

Split the legs down each side with scissors, loosen the shells, baste the crab meat with the remaining butter and serve at once.

ANNE WILLAN (EDITOR)
GRAND DIPLÔME COOKING COURSE, VOLUME 3

Joe's Marinated Cracked Crab

The techniques of cleaning and cutting up poached crab are demonstrated on pages 32-33.

To serve 4

two 3 lb.	Dungeness crabs, scrubbed, poached, cleaned, cut up and the claws cracked	two 1½ kg.
1 cup	olive oil	¼ liter
⅓ cup	red wine vinegar	75 ml.
3	large garlic cloves, finely chopped or crushed to a paste	3
¾ tsp.	salt	4 ml.
¼ tsp.	freshly ground black pepper	1 ml.
½ cup	chopped fresh parsley	125 ml.

Place the crab in a deep bowl. Shake or beat together the oil, vinegar, garlic, salt, pepper and parsley. Pour this mixture over the crab and let it stand in a cool place for about one and one half hours; turn the crab occasionally. To serve, heap the crab onto a platter; pour any excess marinating sauce into individual bowls and serve it as a dipping sauce.

SHIRLEY SARVIS
CRAB & ABALONE: WEST COAST WAYS WITH FISH & SHELLFISH

Hogan's All-Crab Cioppino

The technique of cutting up a crab is shown on pages 20-21.

To serve 4 to 6

three 2 to 3 lb.	Dungeness crabs, scrubbed, cleaned, cut up, claws cracked, crab fat reserved	three 1 to 1½ kg.
2	large onions, finely chopped	2
½ cup	olive oil	125 ml.
3	large garlic cloves, finely chopped	3
2 cups	tomato sauce (recipe, page 165)	½ liter
1 tsp.	salt	5 ml.
½ tsp.	black pepper	2 ml.
1 lb.	spaghetti, boiled, drained, sprinkled with Parmesan cheese and black pepper	½ kg.
	chopped fresh parsley	

In a large kettle, sauté the onions in the oil until golden. Stir in the garlic, then the tomato sauce, crab fat, salt and pepper. Simmer for five minutes, stirring occasionally. Add the crab and simmer for 10 minutes. Serve the crab on heated shallow platters with spaghetti alongside. Spoon the sauce over the crab and spaghetti. Sprinkle with the parsley.

SHIRLEY SARVIS
CRAB & ABALONE: WEST COAST WAYS WITH FISH & SHELLFISH

Crab Meat Casserole

To serve 4 to 6

1 lb.	crab meat, picked over	½ kg.
4 tbsp.	butter	60 ml.
4	large mushrooms, thinly sliced	4
2 tsp.	grated mild-flavored onion	10 ml.
2	tomatoes, peeled and thickly sliced	2
	salt and cayenne pepper	
1 cup	heavy cream	¼ liter
2 tsp.	finely chopped fresh parsley	10 ml.
1 tsp.	finely cut chives	5 ml.
3 tbsp.	brandy	45 ml.
1½ cups	cooked white rice	375 ml.

Melt the butter in a fireproof casserole; add the mushrooms and cook for five minutes over low heat. Add the onion and tomatoes and cook for another five minutes. Then add the crab meat, leaving it in as large lumps as possible. Season with salt and cayenne pepper and heat through; then add the

cream, stirring gently. Boil for no longer than one minute, then add the parsley, chives and brandy. Serve at once from the casserole into shallow soup plates, each containing a few spoonfuls of cooked rice.

THE JUNIOR LEAGUE OF CHARLESTON
CHARLESTON RECEIPTS

Crab Creams

To serve 6

1 lb.	crab meat, picked over	½ lite
3 tbsp.	clarified butter	45 ml
½ cup	sliced fresh mushrooms	125 ml
2 tbsp.	flour	30 ml
1½ cups	milk or half-and-half cream	375 ml
½ tsp.	salt	2 ml
⅛ tsp.	white pepper	½ ml
	cayenne pepper	
¼ cup	dry white wine	50 ml
	chopped fresh parsley, plus parsley sprigs	

Pastry shells

2	eggs, beaten	2
1 tsp.	salt	5 ml
about 1 cup	flour	about ¼ lite
	oil for deep frying	

To the beaten eggs, add the salt and sift in just enough flour to make a stiff dough. Knead the dough very lightly until it is smooth. Roll the dough very thin and cut it into six rounds, about 3 inches [8 cm.] in diameter. In a saucepan, heat the oil to 375° F. [190° C.] and deep fry the rounds, one at a time, for only 15 to 20 seconds. As the dough browns, it will mound in the middle and ripple at the edges, forming a scallop-like shell. When nicely brown, turn the shell with tongs and quickly brown the other side. Lift the pastry shell, let it drain a moment and lay it on thick paper toweling. Keep the shells warm in a 250° F. [120° C.] oven. Fry the other shells.

Melt the clarified butter over medium-low heat, and sauté the mushrooms until tender. Remove the mushrooms with a slotted spoon, and drain them on paper towels.

With a wooden spoon, stir the flour into the butter, and stir and cook until all is smooth and bubbly. Heat the milk and gradually stir it into this roux; stir until thickened. Stir in salt, pepper and cayenne. Add the crab meat, the mushrooms and the wine, and gently blend while the mixture heats through. Remove it from the heat.

Place each pastry shell on a dessert-sized plate and fill the shell with the crab mixture, dividing it evenly. Sprinkle a bit of fresh parsley leaf on top of each shell and tuck a few sprigs of parsley under its edges.

FRANCES MAC ILQUHAM
FISH COOKERY OF NORTH AMERICA

Crab Meat Risotto

Risotto con Polpa di Granchio

To serve 6

1 lb.	crab meat, picked over	½ kg.
4 tbsp.	butter	60 ml.
2 cups	white rice	½ liter
4 cups	fish stock (recipe, page 163), heated	1 liter
	olive oil	
1	garlic clove, coarsely chopped	1
1	medium-sized tomato, peeled, seeded and coarsely chopped	1
	salt and pepper	
	chopped fresh parsley	

Melt the butter in a saucepan and sauté the rice until it absorbs all of the butter. Add the hot fish stock. Cook over moderately high heat, without stirring, for about 10 minutes. Meanwhile, heat ½ cup [125 ml.] of olive oil in a saucepan and sauté the garlic. Add the tomato and, stirring frequently, cook over high heat until this sauce is thick—about 10 minutes. Off the heat, add the crab meat—reserving a few pieces. Stir the crab meat mixture into the rice. Season with salt and pepper. When the rice is *al dente,* turn the risotto out onto a serving dish. Garnish with the reserved crab meat and sprinkle with a little olive oil and parsley.

FEAST OF ITALY

Spicy Crab Cakes

To make 8 or 9 crab cakes

1 lb.	crab meat, picked over	½ kg.
2 tbsp.	mayonnaise (recipe, page 165)	30 ml.
1 tbsp.	prepared mustard	15 ml.
1 tsp.	Worcestershire sauce	5 ml.
1 tsp.	finely chopped fresh parsley	5 ml.
¼ tsp.	salt	1 ml.
1	large egg	1
8 tbsp.	butter	120 ml.
½ cup	oil	125 ml.

Mix the mayonnaise, mustard, Worcestershire sauce, parsley, salt and egg together in a small bowl. Add this mixture to the crab meat and barely mix, using a spoon—not your hands. Make into flat cakes, each about 2½ inches [6 cm.] in diameter, handling the mixture as little as possible. Melt the butter in the oil in a large, heavy skillet set over medium-high heat—the mixture should form a layer about ½ inch [1 cm.] deep. Fry the cakes in the butter mixture for about two minutes on each side, or until golden brown. Drain the cakes on paper towels and serve at once.

MARIAN TRACY
THE SHELLFISH COOKBOOK

Crab with Prosciutto

To serve 6

¾ lb.	lump crab meat, picked over (about 1½ cups [375 ml.])	350 g.
24	thin slices prosciutto	24
12 tbsp.	butter	180 ml.
1 tsp.	Worcestershire sauce	5 ml.
½ tsp.	Tabasco sauce	2 ml.
3 tbsp.	fresh lemon juice	45 ml.
2 tbsp.	finely chopped fresh parsley	30 ml.
	freshly ground black pepper	

Arrange four slices of prosciutto on a flat surface, each slice slightly overlapping the next one. In the center, place about 4 tablespoons [60 ml.] of the crab meat. From a narrow end, roll up the prosciutto to form a tube with crab meat filling. Repeat with the remaining prosciutto and crab meat to make six rolls.

In a large skillet, melt the butter; place the prosciutto rolls in the butter and cook over medium heat. When heated, the prosciutto will cling to the crab meat. Turn the rolls only once and cook them until the prosciutto begins to brown and crisp—about 10 minutes in all. Transfer the rolls to a warmed platter and keep them hot.

To the juices remaining in the skillet, add the Worcestershire sauce, the Tabasco and the lemon juice. Heat the mixture, stirring with a wooden spoon; pour this sauce over the prosciutto rolls. Sprinkle the tops with the parsley and pepper, and serve at once.

THE GREAT COOKS COOKBOOK

Crab Cakes

To serve 3 or 4

2 cups	crab meat, picked over	½ liter
¼ cup	milk	50 ml.
2 tbsp.	finely chopped fresh parsley	30 ml.
	salt	
½ cup	fresh bread crumbs	125 ml.
2	eggs, well beaten	2
1 tsp.	Worcestershire sauce	5 ml.
4 tbsp.	butter	60 ml.
	lemon wedges	
	tartar sauce *(recipe, page 165)*	

Blend the crab meat with the milk, parsley, salt to taste, bread crumbs, eggs and Worcestershire sauce. Shape into four to six cakes, fry in butter on both sides until golden brown—about six to eight minutes in all. Serve the cakes with lemon wedges and tartar sauce.

RUTH A. SPEAR
COOKING FISH AND SHELLFISH

Donegal Crab Pie

To serve 3 or 4

½ lb.	cooked crab meat, picked over	¼ kg.
1½ lb.	puff-pastry dough *(recipe, page 167)*	¾ kg.
1 tbsp.	finely chopped celery	15 ml.
2 tbsp.	finely chopped fresh parsley	30 ml.
¾ cup	hard cider	175 ml.
	salt and pepper	
6	eggs, plus 1 egg white	6
1¼ cups	milk	300 ml.
¼ tsp.	grated nutmeg	1 ml.

Roll 1 pound [½ kg.] of the dough ¼ inch [6 mm.] thick and use it to line a piepan or quiche dish, 12 inches [30 cm.] across and 1 inch [2½ cm.] deep. Refrigerate the pie shell for an hour. Roll the remaining dough into a round to serve as a cover for the pie and chill it also.

Flake the crab meat and put it in the pie shell, followed by the celery, parsley, cider, salt and pepper. Beat the eggs and milk together and add them. Sprinkle the mixture with the nutmeg. Put the cover on the pie, trim the edges and brush the top with the egg white. Bake the pie in a preheated 425° F. [225° C.] oven for 25 minutes, or until the pastry is puffed and golden brown. Serve the pie at once.

ALAN DAVIDSON
NORTH ATLANTIC SEAFOOD

Trout Stuffed with Crab

The technique of stuffing trout is shown on pages 74-75.

To serve 2

½ lb.	crab meat, shredded and picked over	¼ kg.
1 tbsp.	butter	15 ml.
2 tbsp.	heavy cream	30 ml.
2 tsp.	chopped fresh parsley	10 ml.
2	whole trout (about ½ lb. [¼ kg.] each), cleaned, with or without heads	2
	salt and freshly ground pepper	
2 tbsp.	fresh lemon juice	30 ml.

In a skillet, melt the butter and add the crab meat, stirring until the crab meat is thoroughly coated with butter. Add the cream and the parsley. Season the trout inside and out with salt and pepper. Stuff each trout, beginning at the tail end, and sew it up with heavy thread and a large darning needle, or use skewers to close the openings. Lay the stuffed trout in a buttered baking dish and sprinkle them with the lemon juice. Bake the fish in a preheated 350° F. [180° C.] oven for 15 minutes. The trout are done when they flake easily when tested with a fork.

ALICE WATSON HOUSTON
THE AMERICAN HERITAGE BOOK OF FISH COOKERY

Deviled Crabs

To serve 6

¾ lb.	crab meat, picked over	350 g.
½	small onion, finely chopped	½
2	large fresh mushrooms, finely chopped	2
1	garlic clove, finely chopped	1
4 tbsp.	butter, 2 tbsp. [30 ml.] melted	60 ml.
2 tbsp.	flour	30 ml.
1½ tsp.	dry mustard	7 ml.
	Tabasco sauce	
⅛ tsp.	freshly grated nutmeg	½ ml.
1 tsp.	Worcestershire sauce	5 ml.
1 cup	clam broth or milk	¼ liter
2	egg yolks, beaten	2
2 tbsp.	cracker crumbs	30 ml.

In a large skillet over medium heat, sauté the onion, mushrooms and garlic in 2 tablespoons [30 ml.] of the butter until soft—about five minutes. Stir in the flour and the seasonings, and then slowly add the clam broth or milk, stirring constantly. When the sauce is smooth, remove the skillet from the heat and stir in the egg yolks carefully. Fold in the crab meat. Pile the mixture into large scallop shells or buttered ½-cup [125-ml.] ramekins. Sprinkle with the cracker crumbs, and then dribble melted butter over the tops. Bake in a preheated 400° F. [200° C.] oven for eight to 10 minutes, or until browned.

MIKE LINZ AND STAN FUCHS
THE LOBSTER'S FINE KETTLE OF FISH

Polly Hamblet's Deviled Crab

To prepare crab shells for use as baking vessels, poach four crabs, remove the claws and legs, extract the meat from the body shells and scrub the shells thoroughly. The meat can be used for this recipe or reserved for another use.

To serve 4

1 lb.	crab meat, picked over	½ kg.
1¾ cups	cracker crumbs, crushed	425 ml.
2	celery ribs, finely diced	2
1	medium-sized onion, finely chopped	1
8 tbsp.	butter, melted	120 ml.
¼ cup	milk	50 ml.
1 tsp.	dry mustard	5 ml.
½ tsp.	salt	2 ml.
	cayenne pepper	
2 tbsp.	finely chopped fresh parsley	30 ml.
1 tbsp.	finely chopped green pepper	15 ml.

Combine the crab meat with the crumbs, celery and onion, and moisten with the melted butter and milk. Season with the mustard, salt, cayenne, parsley and green pepper. Mix thoroughly. Pile the mixture into four prepared crab shells or a buttered shallow 1-quart [1-liter] casserole, and bake in a preheated 350° F. [180° C.] oven for about 30 minutes, or until the top surface is well browned.

JAMES BEARD
JAMES BEARD'S FISH COOKERY

Crab Mousse with Caviar

To serve 12

1 lb.	crab meat, picked over	½ kg.
2 cups	heavy cream, whipped	½ liter
⅓ cup	meat stock (recipe, page 166), at room temperature	75 ml.
1 to 2 tbsp.	brandy	15 to 30 ml.
¼ cup	caviar	50 ml.

Place the crab meat in the work bowl of a food processor and process it until smooth. Then push the mixture through a

drum sieve so that it is silky smooth. Stir in about ½ cup [125 ml.] of the whipped cream, then fold in another ½ cup.

Slowly stir the remaining whipped cream in its bowl and, at the same time, pour in the stock. Fold the mixture into the crab meat with the brandy. When the mixture is smooth, divide it among twelve ¾-cup [175-ml.] ramekins. Do not smooth the tops; let them peak. Chill the mousse for about two hours, or until it sets.

Just before serving, top each portion with 1 teaspoon [5 ml.] of the caviar.

TOM MARGITTAI AND PAUL KOVI
THE FOUR SEASONS

Crab Mousse with Cucumber Sauce

To serve 4

¾ lb.	crab meat, picked over	350 g.
1 tbsp.	unflavored powdered gelatin	15 ml.
½ cup	fresh clam juice	125 ml.
1 tbsp.	fresh lemon juice	15 ml.
1 tbsp.	finely cut chives	15 ml.
2 tbsp.	thinly sliced pimiento	30 ml.
½ cup	heavy cream, whipped	125 ml.
½ cup	sour cream	125 ml.
	salt and cayenne pepper	
	Boston or Bibb lettuce leaves, washed	

Cucumber sauce

1	large cucumber (or 2 small ones), peeled, halved, seeded, chopped and drained	1
1 cup	mayonnaise (recipe, page 165)	¼ liter
½ tsp.	salt	2 ml.
2 tbsp.	fresh lemon juice	30 ml.
1 tsp.	Dijon mustard	5 ml.
2 tbsp.	finely chopped scallion tops	30 ml.
1 tbsp.	sour cream	15 ml.

Soak the gelatin in the clam juice and then heat the mixture gently until the gelatin has completely dissolved. In a bowl, mix the lemon juice, chives, pimiento and crab meat together, then stir in the clam-juice mixture. Gently fold in the whipped cream and the sour cream. Season to taste. Rinse a 1-quart [1-liter] mold with cold water and pour in the crab-mousse mixture. Chill until firm—about three to four hours. Meanwhile, stir the cucumber-sauce ingredients together until blended, and chill for at least 30 minutes.

Unmold the mousse on the lettuce leaves. Serve with the cucumber sauce.

JANE CHEKENIAN AND MONICA MEYER
SHELLFISH COOKERY

Crayfish, Malaysian Prawns and Shrimp

Poached Crayfish

Écrevisses

To serve 4

2 lb.	crayfish, rinsed and deveined	1 kg.
1	onion, thickly sliced	1
8	sprigs fresh parsley	8
	salt and pepper	
½ cup	red wine	125 ml.

Put the crayfish into a 3-quart [3-liter] nonreactive saucepan. Add all of the other ingredients. Cover the pan and cook over high heat for about 10 minutes, stirring the crayfish three times. The crayfish are cooked when they are red all over. To serve, remove the onion and parsley, arrange the crayfish in a mound on a deep, warmed platter and pour the cooking liquid over them.

JULES GOUFFÉ
LE LIVRE DE CUISINE

Boiled Crayfish

Kokning av Kräftor

To serve 4

4 lb.	crayfish, rinsed and deveined	2 kg.
	salt	
	dill sprigs	

Allow sufficient water to cover the crayfish completely and add 4½ to 6 teaspoons [22 to 30 ml.] salt for every 1¼ quarts [1¼ liters] of water in the pot. (Use the lesser amount if the crayfish are to be kept for more than 10 to 12 hours, because they will steep in the cooking liquid until served.) Add some dill and boil until the water is strongly flavored with the dill.

Take out the dill and add the crayfish, eight to 10 at a time, to the boiling water. Each time the water returns to a boil, add another batch of crayfish and a little dill. When the water returns to a boil after the last addition of crayfish, count five to eight minutes of cooking time, depending on the size and number of the crayfish. Transfer the cooked crayfish to a bowl containing several sprigs of dill. Pour the cooking liquid over them and allow them to cool.

At serving time, lift out and drain the cold crayfish. Arrange them in a dish and garnish with fresh sprigs of dill. Serve with toast and butter.

J. AUDREY ELLISON (EDITOR)
THE GREAT SCANDINAVIAN COOK BOOK

Crayfish for a Crowd

To serve 6 to 8

5 lb.	medium-sized crayfish, rinsed and deveined	2½ kg.
1	celery rib, diced	1
1	onion, diced	1
4 cups	water	1 liter
1½ tsp.	salt	7 ml.
¼ tsp.	black pepper	1 ml.
1	bouquet garni, made with 4 sprigs parsley, 1 sprig thyme and a bay leaf, tied inside a little cheesecloth bag	1
8	slices stale bread	8
¼ cup	white wine	50 ml.
4 tbsp.	butter	60 ml.

Add the celery and onion to the water with the salt, pepper and bouquet garni. Bring the mixture to a rolling boil and add the crayfish. Reduce the heat and simmer for 15 minutes, stirring once or twice. Strain off the liquid and set it aside. You may also now dispose of the bouquet garni.

When the crayfish are cool enough to handle, clean them and extract the meat from their tails. Add enough water to the reserved cooking liquid to make 2 quarts [2 liters]. Place this stock back on the stove over gentle heat and add the stale bread. Stir until the bread and stock are well blended. Add the wine and bring the mixture to a boil, stirring constantly. Just before serving, add the crayfish meat and the butter. Serve immediately.

PHILLIP MASON
SHELLFISH COOKBOOK

Gratin of Braised Crayfish Tails

To serve 4

2 lb.	crayfish, rinsed	1 kg.
6 tbsp.	butter	90 ml.
1	large onion, finely chopped	1
2	carrots, chopped	2
1	celery rib, chopped (optional)	1
1	bay leaf, crumbled	1
1 tsp.	crumbled dried thyme or mixed dried herbs (thyme, oregano, savory, marjoram)	5 ml.
	salt	
¼ cup	Cognac	50 ml.
2 cups	dry white wine	½ liter
	cayenne pepper	
⅓ cup	flour	75 ml.
5 cups	fish stock (recipe, page 163)	1¼ liters
⅔ cup	heavy cream	150 ml.

Melt 2 tablespoons [30 ml.] of the butter in a large sauté pan, add the chopped vegetables and the crumbled herbs, and season with salt. Cook over low heat, stirring from time to time, for 10 minutes, or until the vegetables are softened but not colored. Increase the heat, add the crayfish, pour on the Cognac and set it alight. Extinguish the flames by pouring on the wine. Season with cayenne, cover the pan and simmer for five minutes. Set the mixture aside to cool. When the crayfish are cool enough to handle, pull each of them in half, shell and devein the tails and set them aside; reserve the debris—heads, claws and shells—separately.

Melt the remaining butter in a heavy saucepan, stir in the flour, and add the stock to make a fish velouté. Simmer and skim the sauce for at least an hour, until about two thirds of the liquid has evaporated. In a mortar or food processor, reduce all of the crayfish debris to a paste, a small portion at a time. Add this paste, with the vegetables and juices from the sauté pan, to the velouté. Bring the liquid to a boil and simmer for five to 10 minutes. Pass the sauce first through a food mill, discarding the shells that remain behind, and then through a fine sieve, discarding the fine debris that remains behind. You should have a thick purée. Stir the cream into the sauce.

Arrange the crayfish tails tightly in a single layer in a gratin dish, and pour the sauce over them. Bake the crayfish in a preheated 425° F. [220° C.] oven for 10 minutes, or until the sauce is bubbling gaily. If the surface has not yet formed an irregular burnished gratin, pass the dish beneath the broiler for a few moments before serving.

PETITS PROPOS CULINAIRES

Fernand Point's Crayfish Gratin
Gratin de Queues d'Écrevisses Fernand Point

To serve 4 to 6

4 lb.	crayfish, rinsed	2 kg.
6 tbsp.	unsalted butter, 3 tbsp. [45 ml.] softened	90 ml.
3½ tbsp.	chopped onion	52 ml.
3½ tbsp.	chopped carrot	52 ml.
¼ cup	Cognac	50 ml.
2 cups	dry white wine	½ liter
½ cup	water	125 ml.
1 tsp.	tomato purée	5 ml.
1	small bouquet garni, made with several sprigs of tarragon	1
	salt and pepper	
	cayenne pepper	
2 tbsp.	flour	30 ml.
1 cup	heavy cream	¼ liter
3½ tbsp.	truffles, cut into julienne	52 ml.
½ cup	hollandaise sauce (recipe, page 166)	125 ml.

Plunge the crayfish into boiling water for five minutes. Drain them immediately, remove the tails and claws, and shell the tails. Set the tails and claws aside. Pound the crayfish heads and shells in a mortar.

In a saucepan, sauté the pounded shells in 1 tablespoon [15 ml.] of the butter; add the chopped onion and carrot. Ignite half of the Cognac and, when the flames die, pour it over the mixture. Pour in the white wine and water to moisten the mixture. Add the tomato purée and the bouquet garni. Season the mixture to taste with salt and pepper and a dash of cayenne. Cook over very low heat for about 20 minutes. Then rub the mixture through a very fine sieve and thicken this sauce with a *beurre manié* made by mixing the flour with 3 tablespoons [45 ml.] of the butter.

Sauté the reserved crayfish tails and claws in the remaining butter. Deglaze the pan with the remaining Cognac. Add the cream and the crayfish sauce. After adding the truffles, bring the mixture to the boiling point for a few minutes; then, off the heat, mix in the hollandaise sauce. Correct the seasoning, and spoon the crayfish and the sauce into individual ovenproof porcelain gratin dishes. Place the dishes under a preheated broiler to brown the sauce lightly. Serve immediately.

PAUL BOCUSE
PAUL BOCUSE'S FRENCH COOKING

Crayfish Tails Gratinéed with Hollandaise Sauce
Écrevisses au Gratin

	To serve 4	
4 lb.	medium-sized crayfish, rinsed, poached for 2 minutes, shelled and deveined	2 kg.
3 tbsp.	shellfish butter (recipe, page 164), made with crayfish shells	45 ml.
3 tbsp.	Cognac, warmed	45 ml.
2 cups	heavy cream	½ liter
¼ cup	hollandaise sauce (recipe, page 166)	50 ml.
	salt and freshly ground pepper	

Warm the shellfish butter, quickly sauté the crayfish, add the Cognac and ignite it. When the flame dies, remove the crayfish from the pan and arrange them in a gratin dish. Add 1½ cups [375 ml.] of the cream to the contents of the pan and bring it to a boil. Stirring frequently, boil this sauce until it is thick enough to coat the back of a spoon. Add the hollandaise sauce and the rest of the cream, and adjust the seasoning. Pour the sauce over the crayfish and broil under a preheated broiler until the surface of the sauce is browned—about five minutes.

ANTON MOSIMANN
CUISINE À LA CARTE

Braised Crayfish Bordelaise-Style
Écrevisses à la Bordelaise

	To serve 4	
3 lb.	crayfish, rinsed and deveined	1½ kg.
14 tbsp.	butter	210 ml.
1	medium-sized carrot, finely diced	1
2	shallots, finely chopped	2
3 tbsp.	finely chopped fresh parsley	45 ml.
¼ tsp.	thyme	1 ml.
1	bay leaf	1
	salt and pepper	
2½ cups	white wine	625 ml.
⅔ cup	Cognac	150 ml.
	cayenne pepper	

In a large, nonreactive sauté pan, melt 2 tablespoons [30 ml.] of the butter over low heat and in it cook the vegetables, herbs, salt and pepper, without letting them color. Pour in the wine. As soon as the mixture comes to a boil, add the crayfish and the Cognac. Set the Cognac alight and, after the flames die, simmer the crayfish until well cooked—about 10 minutes. Remove the crayfish with a slotted spoon, drain them, put them in a warmed serving dish and cover them to keep them hot.

Boil the sauce until one third of the liquid has evaporated. Remove the pan from the heat, whisk the remaining butter into the sauce and add a pinch of cayenne pepper. Pour the sauce over the crayfish and serve at once.

ARISTIDE QUILLET
LA CUISINE MODERNE

South Indian Prawn Curry
Jhinga Kari

To make the coconut milk called for in this recipe, pour about 2 cups [½ liter] of hot water over 2 cups of freshly grated coconut. After five minutes, press the mixture through a cloth-lined sieve to extract the milk. Ghee is clarified butter. Curry (or kari) leaves are sweet and pungent; they are obtainable dried in Indian food stores—which also sell desiccated coconut, rice flour and ghee.

The paprika is used to give the curry the desired red color, which in India would come from adding a large amount of cayenne pepper.

	To serve 4 to 6	
2 lb.	Malaysian prawns, shelled	1 kg.
1 tbsp.	desiccated coconut	15 ml.
1 tbsp.	rice flour	15 ml.
2 cups	coconut milk	½ liter
2 tbsp.	ghee or oil	30 ml.
12	curry leaves	12
2	medium-sized onions, finely chopped	2
5	garlic cloves, finely chopped	5
1 tbsp.	finely grated fresh ginger	15 ml.
2 tbsp.	Madras curry powder	30 ml.
1 tsp.	cayenne pepper (optional)	5 ml.
2 tsp.	paprika	10 ml.
1½ tsp.	salt	7 ml.
2 tbsp.	fresh lemon juice	30 ml.
	cooked white rice	

Put the desiccated coconut into a dry pan and toast it over medium heat, shaking the pan or stirring constantly until the coconut is golden brown. Remove the coconut from the pan and do the same with the rice flour. Put both into a blender container with about ½ cup [125 ml.] of the coconut milk and blend until the mixture is smooth and the coconut is very finely ground.

Heat the *ghee* or oil in a saucepan and fry the curry leaves for one minute. Add the onions, garlic and ginger, and fry until they turn golden brown, stirring with a wooden spoon. Add the curry powder, cayenne pepper and paprika, and fry over low heat, stirring. Do not let the spices burn. Add the blended mixture, the remaining coconut milk and the salt; stir while bringing the sauce to the simmering point. Do not cover the pan. Simmer the sauce gently for 15 minutes, stirring occasionally. Add the prawns, stir to mix, then simmer for 10 minutes, or until the prawns are cooked and the gravy is thick. Stir in the lemon juice. Serve with rice.

CHARMAINE SOLOMON
THE COMPLETE ASIAN COOKBOOK

Malaysian Prawns in Coconut

Udang Masak Lemak

To make the santan, or coconut cream, called for in this recipe, shell and grate a fresh coconut. Pour ¾ cup [175 ml.] of boiling water over the grated coconut, and let it stand for 20 minutes. Strain through a sieve, pressing hard to extract all of the liquid.

To serve 2

1 lb.	medium-sized Malaysian prawns, shelled	½ kg.
2 tsp.	coconut or peanut oil	10 ml.
1	large red onion, finely sliced	1
¼ tsp.	ground turmeric	1 ml.
¾ cup	santan	175 ml.

Heat the oil in a saucepan, add the onion and the turmeric, and fry over medium heat for one minute. Add the prawns and the *santan,* and simmer for eight to 10 minutes, without allowing the mixture to boil, until the prawns are cooked and the sauce has thickened. Serve in heated bowls with a separate dish of boiled rice.

LILIAN LANE
MALAYAN COOKERY RECIPES

Shrimp in Dill Sauce

To serve 8

1½ lb.	small shrimp, poached, drained, shelled and deveined	¾ kg.
4 tbsp.	butter	60 ml.
2 tbsp.	oil	30 ml.
¼ cup	flour	50 ml.
1 cup	milk	¼ liter
	salt and pepper	
1 cup	finely cut fresh dill	¼ liter
½ cup	chicken stock *(recipe, page 166)*	125 ml.
1 cup	sour cream	¼ liter
2 to 3 tbsp.	vinegar or fresh lemon juice	30 to 45 ml.

In a saucepan, melt the butter in the oil over medium heat. Combine the flour with the milk, season with salt and pepper, and—stirring constantly—pour the milk into the pan. Stir in 1 tablespoon [15 ml.] of the dill. Keep stirring until this sauce starts to thicken. Remove the sauce from the heat and dilute it with the chicken stock. Taste for seasoning. Bring the sauce to a boil, add the shrimp and the sour cream, then add most of the dill and the vinegar or lemon juice. Serve sprinkled with the remaining dill.

LOUIS SZATHMÁRY
THE CHEF'S SECRET COOK BOOK

Shrimp Steamed in Vermouth

Scampi Stufati nel Vermut

To serve 4 to 6

2 lb.	shrimp, rinsed	1 kg.
1 cup	dry white vermouth	¼ liter
1 cup	water	¼ liter
⅓ cup	thinly sliced yellow onion	75 ml.
⅓ cup	thinly sliced celery	75 ml.
⅓ cup	thinly sliced carrots	75 ml.
3	parsley sprigs	3
1	bay leaf	1
¼ tsp.	thyme	1 ml.
3	peppercorns	3

Simmer the vermouth, water, onion, celery, carrots, parsley, bay leaf, thyme and peppercorns in a tightly covered enameled casserole for 15 minutes. Add the shrimp and simmer, covered, for five minutes, shaking the casserole frequently. Let the shrimp cool in the liquid. Shell and devein them.

FRANCESCO GHEDINI
NORTHERN ITALIAN COOKING

Shrimp Boiled in Beer

To serve 4

1 lb.	shrimp, rinsed	½ kg.
1½ cups	beer	375 ml.
1 tsp.	celery seeds	5 ml.
2	garlic cloves	2

Put the beer in a 2-quart [2-liter] saucepan, add the celery seeds and garlic and bring to a boil. Put in the shrimp, cover the pot and bring the beer back to a boil. Remove the pot from the heat and let the shrimp cool, covered. Shake the pot from time to time so that all of the shrimp have a chance to steep in the seasoned beer. Drain the cooled shrimp in a colander and serve them warm or cold.

MOLLY FINN
SUMMER FEASTS

Shrimp Poached in Coconut Milk with Fresh Herbs

Yerra Moolee

To make the coconut milk, pour about 3 cups [¾ liter] of hot water over 3 cups of freshly grated coconut. Wait for five minutes, then press the mixture through a cloth-lined sieve to extract the milk. The volatile oils in hot chilies may irritate your skin. Wear rubber gloves when handling them.

To serve 6

2 lb.	medium- to large-sized shrimp, shelled and deveined	1 kg.
7 tbsp.	vegetable oil	105 ml.
2 cups	finely chopped onions	½ liter
2 tsp.	finely chopped garlic	10 ml.
1½ tbsp.	crushed fresh ginger	22½ ml.
2	hot green chilies, stemmed, seeded and finely chopped	2
¼ tsp.	ground turmeric	1 ml.
2 tbsp.	ground coriander seeds	30 ml.
3 cups	coconut milk	¾ liter
1½ tsp.	coarse salt	7 ml.
2 tbsp.	finely chopped fresh coriander leaves, or substitute 1 tbsp. [15 ml.] dried coriander leaves	30 ml.

Heat the oil in a large heavy-bottomed pan, and add the onions. Over high heat, fry the onions until they turn golden brown—about 10 minutes—stirring constantly to prevent burning. Reduce the heat to medium, add the garlic, ginger and chilies, and fry for an additional two minutes. Add the turmeric and ground coriander seeds, stir rapidly for 15 seconds, then add the coconut milk and salt. Cook the sauce, uncovered, until it thickens—about 10 minutes. Stir frequently to ensure that the sauce does not stick and burn.

Add the shrimp, mix, reduce the heat to medium low, cover, and simmer for five to seven minutes, or until the shrimp are cooked through. Do not overcook the shrimp or they will become tough and chewy. Check for salt, stir in the coriander leaves and serve.

JULIE SAHNI
CLASSIC INDIAN COOKING

Shrimp with Spices in Beer

To serve 6 to 8

6 lb.	large shrimp, rinsed	3 kg.
4 cups	beer	1 liter
1 tbsp.	salt	15 ml.
¼ cup	chopped fresh parsley	50 ml.
1	onion, chopped	1
1	celery rib, chopped	1
1 tsp.	mustard seeds	5 ml.
1 tsp.	celery seeds	5 ml.
1 tsp.	caraway seeds	5 ml.
1 tsp.	sesame seeds, toasted	5 ml.
1 tsp.	anise seeds	5 ml.
1 tsp.	cardamom seeds	5 ml.
1 tsp.	dried thyme leaves	5 ml.
1 tsp.	dried marjoram leaves	5 ml.
½ tsp.	cayenne pepper	2 ml.
¼ tsp.	curry powder	1 ml.

Open the beer an hour or so before you plan to start cooking to allow it to become flat at room temperature.

Place the shrimp in a large, nonreactive kettle with all of the remaining ingredients, including the beer. Bring to a boil. Cover the kettle and boil over high heat for eight minutes, stirring occasionally. Remove the kettle from the heat. Drain the shrimp and reserve the cooking liquid. Shell and devein the shrimp. Serve them in a deep tureen with the cooking liquid, accompanied by individual serving bowls of any sauce you choose.

INGEBORG DAHL JENSEN
WONDERFUL WONDERFUL DANISH COOKING

Shrimp in Pumpkin Seed Sauce

Camarones en Pipián

Raw pumpkin seeds—hulled but neither roasted nor salt-ed—are obtainable in health-food stores. The volatile oils in hot chilies may irritate your skin. Wear rubber gloves when you are handling them.

To serve 6 to 8

1½ lb.	medium-sized shrimp, rinsed	¾ kg.
1½ cups	water	375 ml.
1 tsp.	salt	5 ml.
	freshly ground pepper	
1 cup	hulled raw pumpkin seeds	¼ liter
1½ tbsp.	fresh coriander leaves	22½ ml.
3	fresh hot green chilies	3
¼ cup	chopped onion	50 ml.
1 tbsp.	unsalted butter	15 ml.
⅔ cup	sour cream	150 ml.

Put the shrimp into a saucepan with the water, salt and pepper and bring to a boil. Reduce the heat and simmer, turning the shrimp constantly so that they cook evenly, for about three minutes, or until the shrimp are opaque. Drain the shrimp and reserve the cooking liquid in the pan. As soon as the shrimp are cool enough to handle, shell and devein them. Add the shrimp shells to the reserved cooking liquid, cover the pan and simmer for 10 minutes. Strain and reserve the broth, discarding the shells.

In a heavy ungreased skillet, toast the pumpkin seeds lightly, stirring them constantly, until they begin to swell up and start to pop about—do not let them brown. In a blend-er, combine the shrimp broth, coriander, chilies and onion, add the toasted seeds and blend until the mixture is smooth. Melt the butter in the skillet. Add the pumpkin-seed sauce and cook over very low heat for about 10 minutes, stirring constantly and scraping the bottom of the pan: Add the sour cream, stir the shrimp into the sauce and heat them. You may need to dilute the sauce a bit; if so, add a little hot water.

DIANA KENNEDY
RECIPES FROM THE REGIONAL COOKS OF MEXICO

Shrimp Laced with Mild Spices

Masala Jheengari

The white poppy seeds in this recipe thicken and enrich the sauce, and give it a special nutty aroma. They are obtainable at Asian food stores. The volatile oils in hot chilies may irri-tate your skin. Wear rubber gloves when handling them.

To serve 6

2 lb.	large- to medium-sized shrimp, shelled and deveined	1 kg.
4 cups	water	1 liter
½ tsp.	ground turmeric	2 ml.
½ cup	light vegetable oil	125 ml.
1½ cups	finely chopped onions	375 ml.
2 tsp.	finely chopped garlic	10 ml.
1½ tsp.	ground roasted white poppy seeds	7 ml.
1 tsp.	ground cumin	5 ml.
2 tsp.	ground coriander	10 ml.
1½ tsp.	paprika	7 ml.
¼ cup	unflavored yogurt	50 ml.
1½ tsp.	coarse salt	7 ml.
2	fresh hot green chilies, stemmed, seeded and finely chopped, or substitute ½ teaspoon [2 ml.] cayenne pepper	2
¼ cup	heavy cream	50 ml.
2 tbsp.	finely chopped fresh coriander leaves	30 ml.

Bring the water to a boil over high heat. Add the shrimp and the turmeric and cook for four minutes. Immediately drain the shrimp, reserving the cooking liquid, and set them aside.

Heat the oil in a large, heavy-bottomed pan, preferably one with a nonstick surface, and add the onions. Over high heat, fry the onions until they turn golden brown—about eight minutes—stirring constantly to prevent burning. Add the garlic, and cook for an additional half minute. Reduce the heat, and add the ground poppy seeds, cumin, coriander and paprika. Stir rapidly for five seconds, and add half of the reserved liquid in which the shrimp were cooked. Increase the heat to high and boil rapidly, uncovered, for 10 minutes. Add the remaining liquid, and continue boiling, uncovered, until the sauce reduces to a thick, pulpy gravy—about 20 minutes. Stir occasionally to ensure that the sauce does not stick to the pan.

Add the yogurt, salt, and chilies or cayenne pepper, and continue cooking for an additional two or three minutes, stirring constantly. Add the cooked shrimp, and stir to mix. Reduce the heat, cover, and gently simmer for a couple of minutes, or until the shrimp are heated through and absorb some of the luscious gravy. Turn off the heat, and stir in the cream. Let the dish rest for at least one hour.

When ready to serve, gently simmer the shrimp until heated through. Check for salt, stir in the chopped coriander leaves and serve sprinkled with a few more chopped leaves.

JULIE SAHNI
CLASSIC INDIAN COOKING

Shrimp with Green Mayonnaise

Crevettes au Vert

To serve 4

½ lb.	shrimp, poached, shelled and deveined	¼ kg.
5 oz.	fresh button mushrooms, chopped (about 2 cups [½ liter])	150 g.
2	eggs, hard-boiled, peeled and mashed with a fork	2
⅔ cup	green mayonnaise (recipe, page 165)	150 ml.

Mix the shrimp, mushrooms and eggs together, arrange on a platter, mask with the green mayonnaise, and serve.

LA CUISINE LYONNAISE

Pear and Shrimp Curry

To make the curry paste called for in this recipe, combine 1 tablespoon [15 ml.] each of ground coriander and caraway, 1 teaspoon [5 ml.] each of ground turmeric and black pepper, ¼ teaspoon [1 ml.] of cayenne pepper, ½ teaspoon [2 ml.] of grated nutmeg, 2 tablespoons [30 ml.] of anchovy paste and 2 teaspoons [10 ml.] of vinegar.

The rice flour called for in this recipe is obtainable at Asian food stores.

To serve 4

½ to 1 lb.	shrimp, shelled and deveined	¼ to ½ kg.
2 tbsp.	butter	30 ml.
1	small onion, chopped	1
½ cup	peeled, chopped apple	125 ml.
½ cup	halved, seeded, deribbed and diced green pepper	125 ml.
¾ cup	halved, seeded, deribbed and diced red pepper	175 ml.
2 tbsp.	rice flour	30 ml.
1 tsp.	curry powder	5 ml.
2½ cups	fish stock (recipe, page 163)	625 ml.
1 tsp.	chutney	5 ml.
1½ tbsp.	fresh lemon juice	22½ ml.
2	pears, quartered, peeled, cored and sliced	2
1 tsp.	curry paste	5 ml.
¼ cup	seedless raisins	50 ml.
	salt	
	boiled white rice	

Melt the butter and in it sauté the onion until it is transparent, but not brown. Add the apple and peppers and cook gently for three or four minutes. Stir in the rice flour and curry powder, and cook for five minutes. Add the stock gradually; stir in the rest of the ingredients and add salt to taste. Simmer for 25 minutes. Serve over boiled rice.

BARBARA HARGREAVES (EDITOR)
THE SPORTING WIFE

Velvet Creamed Shrimp

Jheenga Malai Khasa

The volatile oils in hot chilies may irritate your skin. Wear rubber gloves when handling them.

To serve 6

2 lb.	medium- to large-sized shrimp, shelled and deveined	1 kg.
1 cup	dessicated coconut	¼ liter
¾ cup	unflavored yogurt	175 ml.
2 tsp.	finely chopped garlic	10 ml.
1 tbsp.	peeled and finely chopped fresh ginger	15 ml.
2	hot green chilies, stemmed and seeded	2
½ cup	vegetable oil	125 ml.
3-inch	cinnamon stick	8-cm.
8	whole cloves	8
8	green cardamom pods	8
⅔ cup	finely chopped onions	150 ml.
3 tbsp.	ground blanched almonds	45 ml.
1½ cups	boiling water	375 ml.
1½ tsp.	coarse salt	7 ml.
2 tbsp.	finely chopped fresh coriander leaves	30 ml.

Place a skillet over medium heat. When it is hot, add the dessicated coconut and toast it, stirring and tossing, until the coconut turns a dark caramel brown—about five to eight minutes. Transfer the toasted coconut to the container of an electric blender or food processor. Add the yogurt, garlic, ginger and green chilies, and run the machine until the mixture is finely puréed. Set aside.

Heat the oil over medium heat in a shallow pan with a nonstick surface. When the oil is hot, add the cinnamon, cloves and cardamom. When the spices get slightly puffed and begin to brown—about half a minute—add the onions. Increase the heat to high and, stirring constantly to prevent burning, fry the onions until they turn caramel brown—about 10 minutes. Add the ground almonds, stir rapidly for half a minute, and add the coconut purée. Cook the mixture uncovered until the oil begins to separate from the sauce—about three minutes.

Add the boiling water and salt. Reduce the heat, cover, and simmer for five minutes. Add the shrimp, and stir well to distribute them evenly into the sauce. Continue cooking, covered, for five to seven minutes, or until the shrimp are cooked through but still tender. Check for salt, and serve the shrimp sprinkled with the chopped coriander leaves.

JULIE SAHNI
CLASSIC INDIAN COOKING

Shrimp Creole

To serve 4 to 6

2 lb.	shrimp, shelled and deveined	1 kg.
⅔ cup	vegetable oil	150 ml.
½ cup	flour	125 ml.
1¾ cups	thinly sliced scallions	425 ml.
1 cup	chopped onions	¼ liter
½ cup	chopped green pepper	125 ml.
⅓ cup	chopped celery	75 ml.
4 tsp.	finely chopped garlic	20 ml.
3 tbsp.	finely chopped fresh parsley	45 ml.
2 cups	drained canned Italian-style whole peeled tomatoes	½ liter
1 cup	tomato sauce (recipe, page 165)	¼ liter
1 tbsp.	finely chopped chives	15 ml.
¼ cup	red wine	50 ml.
4	bay leaves, crushed	4
6	whole allspice	6
2	whole cloves	2
2 tsp.	salt	10 ml.
¾ tsp.	freshly ground black pepper	4 ml.
¼ tsp.	cayenne pepper	1 ml.
¼ tsp.	chili powder	1 ml.
¼ tsp.	ground mace	1 ml.
¼ tsp.	dried basil	1 ml.
½ tsp.	dried thyme	2 ml.
4 tsp.	fresh lemon juice	20 ml.
2 cups	water	½ liter
3 cups	boiled white rice	¾ liter

In a heavy 6- to 8-quart [6- to 8-liter] pot, heat the oil and gradually add the flour, stirring constantly. Cook over low heat, stirring constantly, until a medium brown roux (the color of rich peanut butter) is formed—about 30 minutes. Remove the pot from the heat and add the scallions, onions, green pepper, celery and parsley. Mix them well with the roux, then return the pot to low heat and cook, stirring constantly, until the vegetables begin to brown—about 15 minutes. Mix in the tomatoes and tomato sauce, then add the chives, wine, seasonings and lemon juice and mix again.

Increase the heat under the pot and bring the mixture to a boil. Add the water and mix thoroughly. When the mixture boils up again, reduce the heat and simmer for 45 minutes. Add the shrimp and allow the mixture to come to a boil again, then cover, reduce the heat slightly and simmer for 20 minutes. Remove the pot from the heat and allow the mixture to stand, covered, at room temperature for about 10 minutes before serving. Serve over boiled rice.

RIMA AND RICHARD COLLIN
THE PLEASURES OF SEAFOOD

Shrimp in Tomato Sauce with Almonds and Pine Nuts

Gambas a la Menorquína

To serve 3 or 4

2 cups	shelled cooked small shrimp	½ liter
⅓ cup	olive oil	75 ml.
1 cup	chopped onion	¼ liter
3 cups	fresh or canned tomatoes, peeled, seeded and chopped	¾ liter
½ cup	ground blanched almonds	125 ml.
⅓ cup	pine nuts	75 ml.
4	garlic cloves, chopped	4
2 tbsp.	chopped fresh parsley	30 ml.
3 tbsp.	water	45 ml.
¼ tsp.	cayenne pepper	1 ml.
	salt	

Heat the oil in a skillet, and in it cook the onion until soft and golden. Add the tomatoes. Cook uncovered for 15 to 20 minutes, stirring often. In a blender, grind the almonds, pine nuts, garlic, parsley and water to a paste. Stir this paste into the tomato sauce. Stirring constantly, cook for five minutes. If the sauce is very thick, thin it with up to 1 cup [¼ liter] of boiling water. Season with cayenne pepper and salt. Fold in the shrimp. Allow the mixture to heat through. Serve it on a bed of boiled rice.

PAULA WOLFERT
MEDITERRANEAN COOKING

Shrimp with Cashew Nuts

Black or dark soy sauce is extracted from fermented soybeans, caramel, flour, salt and water; it has a salty, slightly sweet taste. Light or thin soy sauce is extracted from soybeans, flour, salt and water after slow fermentation in the sun. It has a salty and savory flavor and is the variety of soy sauce commonly sold in America.

To serve 6

1 lb.	shrimp, shelled and deveined	½ kg.
⅛ tsp.	salt	½ ml.
½ tsp.	pale dry sherry	2 ml.
1 tbsp.	egg white	15 ml.
5 tbsp.	peanut oil	75 ml.
⅓ cup	raw cashews	75 ml.
¼ cup	Chinese dried mushrooms, soaked in water for 30 minutes, drained, stemmed and the caps cut into squares	50 ml.
⅓ cup	quartered water chestnuts	75 ml.
1	scallion, including the green top, cut into ¼-inch [6-mm.] pieces	1
1 tsp.	sesame-seed oil	5 ml.

Soy and sherry sauce

1 tbsp.	light soy sauce	15 ml.
½ tsp.	black soy sauce	2 ml.
1 tsp.	pale dry sherry	5 ml.
¼ tsp.	sugar	1 ml.

Combine the shrimp, salt, sherry and egg white in a bowl, cover, refrigerate the shrimp and let marinate for at least 30 minutes. Combine the sauce ingredients and set aside.

In a wok, heat the oil until very hot but not smoking. Add the cashews, reduce the heat to low and fry the cashews slowly until they are golden brown. Remove the nuts and drain them on paper towels. Reheat the oil over medium heat. Brown the mushrooms slightly. Add the water chestnuts and the shrimp mixture. Stir fry until the shrimp turn whitish pink—about one minute. Stir in the sauce mixture and add the scallion. Stir fry for about 15 seconds. Add the sesame-seed oil and the cashews. Mix well; serve at once.

MAI LEUNG
THE CLASSIC CHINESE COOK BOOK

Shrimp Tarragon

To serve 4

1½ lb.	medium-sized shrimp, shelled and deveined	¾ kg.
4 tbsp.	butter, plus 1 tbsp. [15 ml.] blended with 1 tbsp. flour	60 ml.
2 tbsp.	finely chopped shallots	30 ml.
½ tsp.	dried tarragon	2 ml.
	black pepper	
1 tsp.	fresh lemon juice	5 ml.
3 tbsp.	Cognac, warmed	45 ml.
¾ cup	heavy cream	175 ml.

Melt the 4 tablespoons [60 ml.] of butter in a chafing dish and, when it is hot, add the shrimp. Sprinkle with salt. Cook the shrimp until they are pink on both sides—approximately four minutes.

Sprinkle the shrimp with the shallots, tarragon, pepper and lemon juice and continue cooking, stirring. Sprinkle the shrimp with the warm Cognac; ignite. Spoon the sauce over the shrimp as the flame burns. When the flame dies, pour the cream over the shrimp and bring the sauce to a boil. Whisk the butter-flour mixture into the sauce and stir until the sauce thickens. Serve immediately.

JEAN HEWITT
THE NEW YORK TIMES LARGE TYPE COOKBOOK

Shrimp Panned with Corn

To serve 4

1¼ lb.	shrimp, shelled with the tails left intact, and deveined	600 g.
4 tbsp.	butter	60 ml.
1 tbsp.	olive oil	15 ml.
1½ cups	corn kernels, cut from about 3 large ears	375 ml.
4	small garlic cloves, finely chopped	4
¼ cup	dry white wine	50 ml.
2 tbsp.	fresh lemon juice	30 ml.
2 tbsp.	finely chopped fresh parsley or a combination of parsley and chervil	30 ml.
	salt and freshly ground pepper	
	lemon wedges	

Put the butter and olive oil in a heavy skillet and set over medium heat. When the butter has melted, stir in the corn kernels and cook for four or five minutes. Increase the heat and add the shrimp; stir and cook for one or two minutes, or until the shrimp just begin to turn opaque. Add the chopped garlic; cook and stir for 30 seconds. Pour in the wine, add the lemon juice, and stir and cook for a few moments longer until the liquid bubbles up around the shrimp and glazes them. Stir in the chopped herbs and season with salt and pepper. Turn the panned mixture out onto a serving plate and garnish it with lemon wedges.

LISA YOCKELSON
THE EFFICIENT EPICURE

Deep-fried Shrimp and Vegetables
Tempura

Rice flour is obtainable at Asian food stores.

The secret of a good tempura batter is to avoid overmixing. An overmixed batter will result in heavy and excessively crusty tempura.

To serve 6

1½ lb.	large shrimp, shelled with the tails left intact, and deveined	¾ kg.
½ cup	green beans, trimmed and cut into shrimp-sized pieces	125 ml.
½ cup	peeled eggplant, cut into shrimp-sized pieces	125 ml.
½ cup	peeled zucchini, cut into shrimp-sized pieces	125 ml.
	oil for deep frying	
1	white radish, peeled and grated	1
2 tbsp.	grated horseradish	30 ml.
1 tbsp.	peeled and grated fresh ginger	15 ml.
Tempura batter		
1	egg	1
1 cup	water	¼ liter
1¼ cups	rice flour or all-purpose flour	300 ml.
Flavored soy sauce		
¼ cup	soy sauce	50 ml.
½ cup	fish stock *(recipe, page 163)*	125 ml.
2 tsp.	sugar	10 ml.

Slit the undersection of each shrimp to prevent excessive curling. Prepare the batter by beating the egg and water together, then adding the flour and mixing lightly. Two or three stirs should be enough, but some lumps may remain.

Fill a deep pan at least three quarters full with oil and heat until very hot. To test the oil temperature, make a small ball of flour and water and drop it in; the temperature is just right if the ball floats to the surface immediately. Fry the shrimp and vegetables in small batches: Dip them one at

a time into the batter and drop them into the hot oil. Large bubbles will form. When these bubbles become small, the tempura is done. Drain and serve hot.

Meanwhile, mix the sauce ingredients in a small pan and warm the sauce over low heat. Serve the sauce in individual bowls together with separate dishes of white radish, horseradish and ginger. Each diner stirs as much of each condiment as he chooses into his bowl of sauce, then dips a hot tempura piece into the sauce mixture and eats it.

TATSUJI TADA
JAPANESE RECIPES

Pan-fried Shrimp
Crevettes à la Pôele

Use the whole shrimp—head, tails and all—sold in New England fish markets. Small San Francisco Bay shrimp will also be delicious prepared this way. Sort the shrimp, one by one, to be certain you discard the baby sole or flounder, the baby starfish and the crabs that are always caught with them. Do not wash the shrimp.

To serve 6

2 lb.	Maine shrimp	1 kg.
2 tbsp.	butter	30 ml.
	pepper	
⅔ cup	heavy cream	150 ml.
⅓ cup	sour cream	75 ml.
	salt (optional)	

Heat a large skillet very well so that the butter will sizzle when it is added. Add the butter and swish it around the pan quickly so that it turns *noisette*—nut brown—but does not burn. The taste of the *noisette* butter is the key to the final taste of the dish. Add the shrimp, put the skillet over high heat and sauté the shrimp until all of the shells turn red. Remove the skillet from the heat; cover it and let the shrimp steam for about three minutes. Remove the shrimp to a platter; keep them warm.

Add a generous grinding of pepper to the juices in the pan. Add the cream and reduce the liquid by half. Add the sour cream. Mix well. Return the shrimp to the skillet and reheat them thoroughly. Add salt only if necessary, and more pepper to taste.

To eat, put the skillet on the table; serve the shrimp with a loaf of crisp French bread and a bar of unsalted butter. Eat each shrimp as you peel it: First remove the head; then remove the first link of the tail shell. Pinch the last link of the tail shell between the index finger and thumb of your left hand at the same time that you pull out the already shelled first link with your right hand. Eat the shrimp tail meat. (Keep all of the heads and shells to make a shrimp butter.)

MADELEINE M. KAMMAN
WHEN FRENCH WOMEN COOK

Grilled Shrimp

Gambas a la Plancha

To serve 4

1 lb.	large shrimp, rinsed	½ kg.
	olive oil	
	salt	

Coat a cast-iron griddle or skillet with olive oil and set it over high heat. When the oil is hot, put on the shrimp and sprinkle them with salt. Turn them over when they start turning opaque. Remove them from the griddle or skillet after four minutes. Grilled shrimp should be left juicy, never thoroughly cooked. Serve them hot, still in their shells.

D. E. POHREN
ADVENTURES IN TASTE: THE WINES AND FOLK FOOD OF SPAIN

Jim Lee's Puff Shrimp

Fau Jah Ha

Do not use unbleached flour; it will turn gray instead of golden brown. Puff shrimp need not be served at once, because the coating will not turn limp and soggy. Keep them in a preheated 180° F. [85° C.] oven and the shrimp will be hot and crisp for half an hour or longer.

To serve 2 or 3

1½ lb.	large shrimp, shelled with the tails left intact, and deveined	¾ kg.
½ tsp.	garlic juice, extracted with a garlic press	2 ml.
¼ tsp.	salt	1 ml.
1½ cups	flour	375 ml.
1 tbsp.	baking powder	15 ml.
½ tsp.	salt	2 ml.
½ cup	vegetable oil	125 ml.
1 cup	cold water	¼ liter
8 to 12 cups	oil for deep frying	2 to 3 liters
	fresh coriander or watercress sprigs	
	lettuce leaves (optional)	

With a sharp knife, cut each shrimp from the underside almost through to the back. Be careful not to sever the halves completely. Remove any black veins and rinse the shrimp well. Place the shrimp on paper towels and pat them dry. Arrange the shrimp on a plate or platter, their split sides up. Rub a little garlic juice on each shrimp. Sprinkle a touch of salt on each shrimp. Put them aside.

Place the flour, baking powder and salt in a mixing bowl. Mix thoroughly. Add the vegetable oil a little at a time, while stirring with a wooden fork or spoon until all of the ingredients form a ball and the sides of the bowl are clean. Add the water a little at a time, while stirring until the dough becomes the consistency of pancake batter. (The thicker the batter, the thicker the crust will be on the cooked shrimp.) Place the shrimp and the batter conveniently near your cooking vessel.

Heat the oil in a wok or a deep-frying vessel to 360° F. [182° C.]. You can also test the temperature of the oil by putting a drop of batter in it. If the batter sizzles, puffs up and floats, the oil is ready.

Take each shrimp by the tail and dip it into the batter. Put the shrimp directly into the hot oil, one at a time. As each shrimp turns golden brown, remove it from the oil with tongs and place it on paper towels to drain. Arrange the shrimp on a serving plate and garnish the plate with coriander or watercress. A few leaves of lettuce under the shrimp will help to make the dish look fuller and prettier, and will allow any excess oil to drain.

CECILY BROWNSTONE
CECILY BROWNSTONE'S ASSOCIATED PRESS COOK BOOK

Shrimp Tempura

Sake is also called rice wine, although it is more closely related to beer. It is available at liquor stores, either in stock or on special order.

Green beans and other vegetables are often coated with batter and fried with the shrimp, as are pieces of fish.

To serve 4

1 lb.	jumbo shrimp, shelled with the tails left intact, and deveined	½ kg.
1 cup	flour	¼ liter
2 tbsp.	soy sauce	30 ml.
2	eggs	2
⅔ cup	milk	150 ml.
	fat or oil for deep frying	
	Dipping sauce	
½ cup	dry sherry or sake	125 ml.
¼ cup	soy sauce	50 ml.
1 tbsp.	peeled and grated fresh ginger	15 ml.
1 tsp.	sugar	5 ml.

Dip the shrimp in a batter made with the flour, soy sauce, eggs and milk. Fry the shrimp in deep fat or oil heated to 370° F. [188° C.] until they are golden brown. Serve the fried shrimp with a sauce made from the sherry, soy sauce, ginger and sugar.

HELEN BROWN
HELEN BROWN'S WEST COAST COOK BOOK

Scampi in Wine

To serve 2 to 4

1 lb.	large shrimp, shelled with the tails left intact, and deveined	½ kg.
8 tbsp.	butter	120 ml.
1	large garlic clove, finely chopped	1
2 tsp.	finely chopped fresh parsley	10 ml.
3 tbsp.	fresh lemon juice	45 ml.
⅓ cup	dry white wine	75 ml.
	salt	
	pepper	

Melt the butter, add the garlic and parsley and brown lightly. Blend in the lemon juice, wine, and salt and pepper to taste. Add the shrimp and sauté them quickly, stirring until they are tender—approximately five minutes. Serve the sauce over the shrimp.

VICTOR BENNETT WITH ANTONIA ROSSI
PAPA ROSSI'S SECRETS OF ITALIAN COOKING

Indonesian Shrimp Cakes

Garnalengehakt

To serve 4

1½ lb.	shrimp, shelled, deveined and finely chopped	¾ kg.
5	potatoes, boiled, peeled and mashed	5
1	small leek, trimmed to 1 inch [2½ cm.] above the white part, washed and finely chopped	1
	salt and pepper	
	freshly grated nutmeg	
2 tbsp.	milk	30 ml.
1	egg, lightly beaten	1
½ cup	dry bread crumbs	125 ml.
4 tbsp.	butter	60 ml.
½ cup	fish stock *(recipe, page 163)*	125 ml.

Mix the shrimp with the mashed potatoes, leek, salt, pepper, nutmeg, milk and egg. Form flat rounds of the mixture and

turn them lightly in the bread crumbs. In a large skillet, fry these cakes in 3 tablespoons [45 ml.] of the butter until they are golden brown. Remove them from the skillet. Add the remaining butter and the fish stock to the skillet and boil the liquid to reduce it a little. Return the cakes to the pan and simmer them for a few minutes until heated through.

EMMA W. K. STEINMETZ
ONZE RIJSTTAFEL

Indian Shrimp with Yogurt and Coriander

To serve 6

2 lb.	medium-sized shrimp, shelled and deveined	1 kg.
½ tsp.	crushed, dried mint leaves	2 ml.
¼ tsp.	dried red pepper flakes	1 ml.
2¼ tsp.	ground turmeric	11 ml.
½ tsp.	ground coriander	2 ml.
1 tsp.	grated fresh ginger or ½ tsp. [2 ml.] ground ginger	5 ml.
2	garlic cloves, finely chopped	2
½ tsp.	ground cumin	2 ml.
4 tbsp.	butter	60 ml.
1	medium-sized onion, grated	1
1 cup	unflavored yogurt, lightly whisked	¼ liter
1 tsp.	mild, light honey	5 ml.
2 tbsp.	finely chopped fresh coriander leaves	30 ml.
1½ tbsp.	fresh lemon juice	22½ ml.
	cooked brown rice	

Place the shrimp in a bowl and add the mint, red pepper flakes, turmeric, ground coriander, ginger and cumin. Mix until the shrimp are well coated and let them stand at room temperature for one hour. Then melt 3 tablespoons [45 ml.] of the butter in a deep, heavy skillet and add the onion; stir and cook until the onion is fairly dry, but not brown. Add the remaining butter and the shrimp mixture. Cook, stirring and turning the shrimp gently until they start to turn color all over, then reduce the heat. Stir the yogurt and honey together, add them to the skillet, cover and simmer for three minutes. Uncover the skillet and cook for three minutes more. Add the fresh coriander and lemon juice, and serve the shrimp at once—spooned over hot, cooked brown rice that will absorb the sauce.

SHERYL AND MEL LONDON
THE FISH-LOVERS' COOKBOOK

Sauté of Jumbo Shrimp

The volatile oils in hot chilies may irritate your skin. Wear rubber gloves when handling them.

	To serve 3 or 4	
1 lb.	jumbo shrimp, shelled and deveined	½ kg.
	peanut oil	
2	green peppers, halved, seeded, deribbed and coarsely diced	2
4	fresh tiny hot chilies, stemmed, seeded and halved, or ¼ tsp. [1 ml.] hot pepper sauce	4
2 or 3	leeks, white parts only, thinly sliced	2 or 3
	peeled and finely shaved fresh ginger	
1	garlic clove, finely chopped	1
2 tbsp.	soy sauce	30 ml.
1 tbsp.	salt	15 ml.
2 tbsp.	cider vinegar	30 ml.
	Egg-white batter	
2	egg whites	2
2 tbsp.	white wine	30 ml.
2 tbsp.	cornstarch	30 ml.
	salt	

Crosscut the jumbo shrimp in two, making a small slash in each piece to prevent shrinking.

Pour enough oil into a wok or deep-frying pan to make a layer about 2 inches [5 cm.] deep, and heat it to 360° F. [182° C.]. Beat the egg whites with a whisk until barely frothy. Dissolve the cornstarch and salt in the wine and whisk the mixture into the egg whites. Whisk to a frothy, fluid stickiness. Dip a few shrimp at a time into the batter and deep fry them to a light gold—about two minutes. Place the fried shrimp on absorbent paper and keep them warm in a preheated 250° F. [120° C.] oven.

Heat ¼ cup [50 ml.] of oil in a sauté pan or wok and, over high heat, sauté the peppers, chilies, leeks, a few shavings of ginger and the garlic for one minute. Stir in the soy sauce, salt and vinegar, bring the mixture to a boil, add the fried shrimp and serve at once.

FRANCES MAC ILQUHAM
FISH COOKERY OF NORTH AMERICA

Shrimp with Hot Garlic Sauce

Gambas al Ajillo

	To serve 2 or 3	
1 lb.	shrimp, shelled and deveined	½ kg.
	salt	
¼ cup	olive oil	50 ml.
4	garlic cloves, sliced	4
1	dried hot red chili, stemmed, seeded and cut into 4 pieces	1

Salt the shrimp. Heat the oil in a skillet. Add the garlic and chili and sauté until the garlic is light brown. Add the shrimp and cook over high heat, stirring the shrimp with a wooden spoon for about three minutes. Serve immediately.

D. E. POHREN
ADVENTURES IN TASTE: THE WINES AND FOLK FOOD OF SPAIN

Shrimp Croquettes

Garnalenkroketten

	To serve 4	
1 lb.	very small shrimp, shelled and deveined, or medium-sized shrimp, shelled, deveined and coarsely chopped	½ kg.
2 tbsp.	butter	30 ml.
1	onion, finely chopped	1
1	medium-sized potato, boiled, peeled and mashed	1
	salt and freshly ground pepper	
	grated nutmeg	
1 tbsp.	chopped fresh parsley	15 ml.
2 or 3 tbsp.	milk	30 or 45 ml.
1 cup	fresh bread crumbs	¼ liter
1	large egg, beaten with 2 tbsp. [30 ml.] water	1
	oil for deep frying	

Melt the butter in a pan and cook the onion until transparent. Transfer the onion to a bowl and mix with the shrimp, potato, parsley, a pinch of nutmeg, and salt and pepper to taste. Add enough milk to moisten the mixture, and let it cool. Shape the mixture into eight to 12 cork-shaped croquettes and roll these first in the bread crumbs, then in the beaten egg, and again in the bread crumbs. Deep fry the croquettes in oil preheated to 375° F. [190° C.] until they are evenly browned—three to four minutes.

TON VAN ES
HET VOLKOMEN VISBOEK

Special Broiled Shrimp

To serve 3 or 4

2 lb.	shrimp, shelled and deveined	1 kg.
1 cup	oil	¼ liter
1 tbsp.	ground turmeric	15 ml.
¼ tsp.	ground black pepper	1 ml.
3	garlic cloves, crushed to a paste	3
1 tbsp.	chopped fresh basil leaves	15 ml.
1 tbsp.	chopped fresh mint leaves	15 ml.
	salt	
1½ tsp.	cayenne pepper, mixed with 1 tbsp. [15 ml.] vinegar	7 ml.

Make a marinade of the oil, spices, garlic, herbs and salt. Add the shrimp, mix well, cover, and marinate in the refrigerator overnight.

Remove the shrimp from the marinade, and place them on the rack of a broiling pan. Broil the shrimp 6 inches [15 cm.] from the heat in a preheated broiler for six to 10 minutes—depending on their size. Turn the shrimp once while broiling them, and baste them with the marinade.

DHARAM JIT SINGH
CLASSIC COOKING FROM INDIA

Shrimp Stuffed with Shrimp and Mushrooms

The technique of butterflying and stuffing shrimp is demonstrated on pages 74-75.

To serve 6

27	large shrimp, peeled and deveined	27
6 tbsp.	butter, 4 tbsp. [60 ml.] cut into small pieces	90 ml.
¾ cup	finely chopped celery	175 ml.
1	large garlic clove, finely chopped	1
4	large mushrooms, finely chopped	4
¼ tsp.	black pepper	1 ml.
1 tbsp.	fresh lemon juice	15 ml.
1 cup plus 2 tbsp.	fresh whole-wheat bread crumbs	¼ liter plus 30 ml.
¼ cup	finely chopped fresh parsley	50 ml.
1	egg, lightly beaten	1
2 tbsp.	grated Gruyère cheese	30 ml.

Butterfly 18 of the shrimp. Coarsely chop the others: There should be about ¾ cup [175 ml.]. Set the shrimp aside.

Heat 2 tablespoons [30 ml.] of the butter in a skillet and add the onion, celery and garlic. Stirring constantly, cook until the vegetables are wilted. Add the mushrooms, pepper and lemon juice. Stir and cook for three minutes. Remove the skillet from the heat and stir in the chopped shrimp, 1 cup [¼ liter] of the bread crumbs, all of the parsley and the egg. Spoon an equal portion of this stuffing mixture on top of each butterflied shrimp.

Butter a baking dish large enough to hold the shrimp in one layer and arrange the shrimp in the dish. Sprinkle the shrimp with a mixture of the remaining 2 tablespoons [30 ml.] of bread crumbs and the grated cheese, and dot them with the pieces of butter. Place the shrimp about 5 inches [13 cm.] from the heat of a preheated broiler and broil them until the shrimp are cooked through and the stuffing has browned—five to seven minutes. Baste the shrimp once with the juices that will collect in the dish.

SHERYL AND MEL LONDON
THE FISH-LOVERS' COOKBOOK

Shrimp in Tomato Sauce with Feta Cheese

Garidhes a la Turkolimano

To serve 4

1½ to 2 lb.	medium-sized shrimp, shelled and deveined	¾ to 1 kg.
½ cup	chopped onion	125 ml.
3 tbsp.	olive oil	45 ml.
1	garlic clove, chopped	1
2 cups	tomato sauce *(recipe, page 165)*	½ liter
¼ cup	dry white wine	50 ml.
¼ cup	chopped fresh parsley	50 ml.
	salt and freshly ground black pepper	
	cayenne pepper	
1 cup	crumbled feta cheese	¼ liter

In a skillet, cook the onion in the olive oil until soft and golden. Add the garlic, tomato sauce, wine, half of the parsley, salt, pepper and a pinch of cayenne pepper. Simmer uncovered for 15 minutes, stirring often. The sauce should be rather thick.

Add the shrimp to the sauce and cook for five minutes. Sprinkle the feta cheese into an oiled baking dish, cover the cheese with the shrimp and the tomato sauce, and bake in a preheated 450° F. [230° C.] oven for 10 minutes. Sprinkle the baked shrimp with the remaining parsley and serve at once.

PAULA WOLFERT
MEDITERRANEAN COOKING

Thorny Shrimp Balls Filled with Sweet Chestnuts

Igaguri

Kombu is dried kelp—a species of seaweed; it is sold in sheets, and must be washed in cold water and then soaked before it is used. Mirin is a sweet rice wine. Somen are thin vermicelli made from white wheat flour. All three products are available where Japanese foods are sold. To make the sweet chestnuts called for in this recipe, slash raw chestnuts on their flat sides, parboil them for two or three minutes, then drain and peel them. Simmer the peeled chestnuts in 2 cups [½ liter] of water for 20 minutes, then drain and set them aside. Boil the chestnuts a third time in a mixture of 1 cup [¼ liter] of water and 3 tablespoons [45 ml.] of sugar for 20 minutes. Stir in 2 more tablespoons [30 ml.] of sugar and cook the chestnuts for another five minutes. Let them cool to room temperature in the cooking liquid. Drain them before using.

To make 6 shrimp balls

2 lb.	large shrimp, shelled and deveined	1 kg.
1	3-inch [8-cm.] square of *kombu*, washed	1
⅓ cup	flour	75 ml.
¼ tsp.	salt	1 ml.
1 tbsp.	*mirin*, or substitute 2 tsp. [10 ml.] pale dry sherry	15 ml.
1	egg white	1
6	small white turnips, peeled	6
3 oz.	*somen*, or substitute any thin noodle, cut into 1-inch [2½-cm.] lengths (about 1½ cups [375 ml.])	90 g.
	vegetable oil	
6	sweet chestnuts	6

Soak the *kombu* in ½ cup [125 ml.] of water for 30 minutes. Stir in the flour, mix the ingredients to a paste, and set aside.

Purée the shrimp, a few at a time, in an electric blender or put them twice through the finest blade of a meat grinder. Then, with an electric beater or large spoon, beat into the purée the salt, *mirin*, egg white and 6 tablespoons [90 ml.] of the flour-and-*kombu* paste. Continue to beat until smooth.

With a small, sharp knife, trim the turnips into ½-inch [1-cm.] balls. Divide the shrimp mixture into six parts and, moistening your hands with cold water, shape them into six balls. Make an indentation in the top of each ball and force a turnip into it. Pat the shrimp mixture into shape again, enclosing the turnip. Spread the cut noodles out on a sheet of wax paper. Then roll the shrimp balls about in them until they adhere and protrude like thorns.

Pour into a deep fryer or skillet enough oil to come 3 inches [8 cm.] up the sides. Set the pan over high heat until the oil registers 375° F. [190° C.] on a deep-frying thermometer. Deep fry the shrimp balls three or four at a time for two

to three minutes, or until they are golden brown. Remove and drain them on paper towels.

With a chopstick or the point of a knife, make a hole in the top of each ball and spread it open gently. Remove each turnip and insert a sweet chestnut in its place. Serve the shrimp balls at room temperature.

FOODS OF THE WORLD: THE COOKING OF JAPAN

Scallop-stuffed Shrimp

The technique of butterflying shrimp is demonstrated on pages 74-75.

To serve 2

1 lb.	jumbo shrimp	½ kg.
6 oz.	shucked scallops, finely chopped	175 g.
¼ cup	fresh bread crumbs	50 ml.
¼ cup	freshly grated Parmesan cheese	50 ml.
	paprika	
1	garlic clove	1
3 tbsp.	butter, melted	45 ml.
¼ cup	dry white wine or dry sherry (optional)	50 ml.

Shell the shrimp, leaving the tails intact. Devein and butterfly them. Stuff each shrimp with ½ tsp. [2 ml.] of chopped scallops, and arrange the shrimp in a buttered baking dish. Combine the bread crumbs and cheese and sprinkle this mixture over the scallop stuffing. Top each shrimp with a dash of paprika. Put the garlic clove through a press, add it to the melted butter and drizzle this over the shrimp. Basting two or three times with white wine or sherry, if using, bake the shrimp in a preheated 350° F. [180° C.] oven for 15 minutes, or until the stuffing is golden brown and the shrimp feel firm to the touch. Serve immediately.

RUTH A. SPEAR
COOKING FISH AND SHELLFISH

Shrimp Gratin

Gratin de Queues de Crevettes

To serve 2

½ lb.	shrimp, shelled and deveined	¼ kg.
5 tbsp.	butter	75 ml.
	pepper	
3 tbsp.	Cognac	45 ml.
1 cup	heavy cream	¼ liter
3 or 4	green outer leaves of Bibb or Boston lettuce, finely shredded	3 or 4

In a covered, nonreactive pan over low heat, cook the shrimp in 3 tablespoons [45 ml.] of the butter, adding a little pepper, but no salt. After two or three minutes, add the Cognac and cook the shrimp uncovered until most of the liquid has evaporated. Add the heavy cream; let it simmer for a few seconds, then remove the pan from the heat, but cover it to keep the shrimp warm.

In another covered pan, cook the shredded lettuce in the remaining butter for a few minutes over low heat. Add the lettuce to the shrimp, stirring to ensure they are well mixed. Adjust the seasoning. Transfer the mixture to a gratin dish and bake it in a preheated 425° F. [220° C.] oven for five minutes, or until the surface is bubbling and lightly browned. Serve very hot.

FERNAND POINT
MA GASTRONOMIE

Skewered Shrimp

Spiedini di Scampi

The original version of this recipe calls for scampi—miniature Mediterranean lobsters that are rarely obtainable in North America.

	To serve 6	
2 lb.	jumbo shrimp, rinsed	1 kg.
18	bay leaves	18
	salt and freshly ground pepper	
¼ cup	olive oil	50 ml.
6 tbsp.	butter	90 ml.
2	garlic cloves, lightly crushed	2
⅓ cup	brandy	75 ml.
	Worcestershire sauce	
3	salt anchovies, filleted, soaked in water for 30 minutes, drained and patted dry	3
1 tbsp.	Dijon mustard	15 ml.
1 tsp.	fresh lemon juice	5 ml.

Thread four shrimp onto each of six skewers, alternating the shrimp with the bay leaves. Season with salt and pepper. Oil a baking pan and suspend the skewers over it—resting the ends of the skewers on the rims of the sides of the pan. Brush the skewered shrimp with oil and bake them in a preheated 350° F. [180° C.] oven for about 15 minutes, turning the skewers two or three times and basting the shrimp with the remaining oil.

Meanwhile, in a small pan, melt 2 tablespoons [30 ml.] of the butter and in it sauté the garlic until golden. Discard the garlic, add the brandy and a few drops of Worcestershire sauce, and cook over high heat until the liquid is reduced to about half of its original volume. In a mortar, pound the remaining butter with the anchovies and stir them into the brandy mixture, together with the mustard and lemon juice.

Pour the brandy sauce onto six warmed serving plates, arrange the skewers on top of each plate, and serve the shrimp very hot.

LUIGI CARNACINA AND LUIGI VERONELLI
LA BUONA VERA CUCINA ITALIANA

Bugey Shrimp Turnovers

Chaussons à la Nantua

Bugey has the reputation of having the best cuisine in France. Brillat-Savarin was born in Belley, which was once the county seat of Bugey.

	To make twelve 2½-by-4-inch [6-by-10-cm.] square turnovers	
1½ lb.	medium-sized shrimp, rinsed	¾ kg.
4 cups	court bouillon (recipe, page 162), made with white wine	1 liter
2 lb.	puff-pastry dough (recipe, page 167)	1 kg.
1	egg, beaten	1
	Nantua sauce with cream	
2 cups	white sauce (recipe, page 164)	½ liter
½ cup	heavy cream	125 ml.
3 tbsp.	shellfish butter (recipe, page 164), made with shrimp	45 ml.
½ tsp.	brandy	2 ml.
	cayenne pepper	

Simmer the shrimp in the court bouillon over medium heat for one minute. Drain the shrimp, reserving and straining 1 cup [¼ liter] of the cooking liquid. Shell and devein the shrimp—reserving their shells, if desired, for the shellfish butter—and set them aside.

Combine the white sauce with the reserved cup of shrimp cooking liquid and, stirring frequently, cook over medium heat until the mixture is reduced to half its original volume. Stir in the cream, shellfish butter, brandy and a pinch of cayenne pepper. Set this sauce aside off the heat.

Roll out the puff-pastry dough to a thickness of ¼ inch [6 mm.]. Cut it into rectangular pieces 2¼ inches [6 cm.] wide and 4 inches [10 cm.] long. Put several shrimp, three or four depending on size, and 1 tablespoon [15 ml.] of sauce on one end of each piece of dough. Fold the rectangle in half to enclose the shrimp filling; press the edges together to seal the turnovers. Brush the tops with the beaten egg, put the turnovers on lightly buttered baking sheets, and bake them in a preheated 400° F. [200° C.] oven for 15 minutes, or until the pastry is puffed and golden brown.

Heat the remaining sauce gently over low heat and serve it with the turnovers.

NINA FROUD AND TAMARA LO
INTERNATIONAL FISH DISHES

Shrimp de Jonghe

This recipe is named for a Dutch family who owned the De Jonghe Hotel in Chicago around the turn of the century and served this dish in their restaurant.

To serve 6

2 lb.	medium-sized shrimp, shelled and deveined	1 kg.
¾ cup	dry white wine	175 ml.
½ tsp.	black pepper	2 ml.
4 tbsp.	butter, softened	60 ml.
1 cup	fresh bread crumbs	¼ liter
2	garlic cloves, crushed to a paste	2
2 tsp.	dried basil	10 ml.
½ tsp.	salt	2 ml.
1 tbsp.	chopped fresh parsley	15 ml.

Coat the bottom and sides of a large gratin dish with butter. Place the shrimp in the dish; they should cover the bottom while slightly overlapping each other. Add the wine and sprinkle the shrimp with pepper. Blend all of the remaining ingredients together in a small bowl. Dot the surface of the shrimp with the butter mixture. Be sure that the dots are of the same size and that all the shrimp are covered. Bake in a preheated 350° F. [180° C.] oven for 20 to 25 minutes, or until the surface is browned. Serve immediately.

LOUIS SZATHMÁRY
THE CHEF'S SECRET COOK BOOK

Broiled Spanish Shrimp with Saffron

To serve 6

2 lb.	large shrimp, shelled with the tails left intact, and deveined	1 kg.
1 tsp.	crushed saffron threads or ⅛ tsp. [½ ml.] powdered saffron	5 ml.
1	large shallot, chopped, or 2 scallions, white parts only, chopped	1
2	small garlic cloves, finely chopped	2
½ tsp.	finely chopped fresh thyme or ¼ tsp. [1 ml.] crumbled dried thyme	2 ml.
3 tbsp.	olive oil	45 ml.
⅓ cup	fresh lemon juice	75 ml.
8 tbsp.	butter, melted	120 ml.
1 tbsp.	finely chopped fresh parsley	15 ml.

Prepare a marinade with the saffron, shallot, garlic, thyme, olive oil and lemon juice. Add the shrimp and toss them to coat them evenly. Refrigerate and marinate for one and one half hours, turning the shrimp once or twice.

Lift out the shrimp from the marinade. Do not dry them. Place them on the rack of a broiling pan. Pour the marinade into the melted butter, heat the mixture just to the boiling point and reserve it as a sauce.

Broil the shrimp, turning them once. Allow two to three minutes for each side, until the shrimp turn pink and opaque. Arrange them on a warmed platter and sprinkle them with the parsley. Serve the hot butter-marinade sauce in a sauceboat to spoon over the shrimp at the table.

SHERYL AND MEL LONDON
THE FISH-LOVERS' COOKBOOK

Crown of Shrimp in Aspic

The technique of making an aspic mold is demonstrated on pages 82-83. As an alternative, you may substitute scallops for half of the shrimp.

To serve 12

¾ lb.	small shrimp, poached and shelled	350 g.
4 cups	clarified fish aspic (recipe, page 163), cooled	1 liter
4	tomatoes, peeled, seeded and cut into quarters, the juice from the seeds reserved	4
1	small celery heart	1
¾ cup	mayonnaise (recipe, page 165)	175 ml.

Set a 1½-quart [1½-liter] ring mold over a pan of ice water. When it is very cold, add a little of the cool but still-liquid aspic and tilt the mold until the sides and base are coated. Chill the mold until the aspic is firmly set; repeat the coating process if necessary.

Arrange the tomato quarters on the aspic, rounded sides down, their points toward the outside rim of the mold. Spoon enough of the liquid aspic over the tomatoes to hold them in place; chill the mold in a pan of ice water until the aspic sets. Fill the mold alternately with layers of shrimp and cool aspic, letting each layer of aspic set before adding another layer of shrimp and aspic. Cover the filled mold with plastic wrap; chill for two hours, or until the aspic is firmly set.

Cut the celery into julienne and let them stand in ice water for about 30 minutes until they curl at the ends; drain the strips thoroughly.

To serve, dip the mold into warm water and turn it out onto a platter. Fill the center of the aspic with the celery curls. Press the reserved juice from the tomato seeds through a strainer, mix it with the mayonnaise and serve this sauce in a separate container.

ANNE WILLAN (EDITOR)
GRAND DIPLÔME COOKING COURSE, VOLUME 14

Shrimp-stuffed Baked Pike

To serve 4

11 tbsp.	butter, 4 tbsp. [60 ml.] cut into small pieces	165 ml.
¼ cup	vegetable oil	50 ml.
2½ to 3 lb.	pike, cleaned but with head and tail left on	1¼ to 1½ kg.
	Shrimp and bread-crumb stuffing	
½ lb.	shrimp, shelled, deveined and finely chopped	¼ kg.
1 cup	soft fresh bread crumbs	¼ liter
1 tbsp.	very finely chopped fresh parsley	15 ml.
⅛ tsp.	ground mace	½ ml.
½ tsp.	salt	2 ml.
	freshly ground black pepper	
1	egg yolk	1

In a small pan, melt 4 tablespoons [60 ml.] of the butter with the oil over medium heat. Remove the pan from the heat and, with a pastry brush, spread about 1 tablespoon [15 ml.] of the mixture evenly over the bottom of a baking-serving dish large enough to hold the fish comfortably. Set the remaining butter-and-oil mixture aside.

Melt 3 tablespoons [45 ml.] of the remaining butter in a 6- to 8-inch [15- to 20-cm.] skillet and brown the bread crumbs, stirring them often until they are golden. Place the shrimp in a mixing bowl, and with a rubber spatula scrape the contents of the skillet over the shrimp. Add the parsley, mace, salt and a few grindings of pepper, and beat vigorously with a wooden spoon until the mixture is a thick, smooth paste. Beat in the egg yolk and the pieces of butter.

Wash the fish inside and out under cold running water and dry it thoroughly with paper towels. Loosely fill the cavity of the fish with the shrimp stuffing, then close the opening with small skewers, crisscrossing them with kitchen cord as if lacing a turkey. Place the fish in the baking dish and brush the top with 1 or 2 tablespoons [15 or 30 ml.] of the butter-and-oil mixture. Bake uncovered in the middle of a preheated 375° F. [190° C.] oven for 30 minutes, basting the fish every 10 minutes with the remaining butter-and-oil mixture. Serve at once, directly from the baking dish.

FOODS OF THE WORLD/AMERICAN COOKING: THE NORTHWEST

Shrimp Mousse

To serve 4 to 6

¾ lb.	shrimp, poached, shelled and deveined, ⅓ cup [75 ml.] left whole and the rest puréed (about 1 cup [¼ liter] purée)	350 g.
½ cup	cold water	125 ml.
1 tbsp.	unflavored powdered gelatin	15 ml.
⅔ cup	mayonnaise *(recipe, page 165)*	150 ml.
⅓ cup	heavy cream	75 ml.
½ tsp.	salt	2 ml.
¼ tsp.	freshly ground white pepper	1 ml.
¼ tsp.	ground coriander	1 ml.
⅛ tsp.	ground cumin	½ ml.
1/16 tsp.	cayenne pepper	¼ ml.
⅛ tsp.	ground mace	½ ml.
1 tsp.	fresh lemon juice	5 ml.
2 tsp.	sugar	10 ml.
2 tbsp.	thinly sliced scallion tops	30 ml.

Put the cold water in a small saucepan and sprinkle the gelatin over it. Cook over very low heat, stirring constantly with a wooden spoon or spatula, until the gelatin is dissolved—about three minutes.

Pour the dissolved gelatin into a large mixing bowl to cool. Add all of the remaining ingredients except the whole shrimp and the scallions. Using an electric mixer, whip at low speed until the ingredients are thoroughly blended, then at high speed until the mousse appears creamy. Pour about ⅓ cup [75 ml.] of the mousse into a 4-cup [1-liter] mold, then press the whole boiled shrimp in a decorative pattern into the mousse. Set the mold in the freezer for 12 to 14 minutes until the mousse appears firmly set. Add the scallion tops to the mousse mixture remaining in the bowl and whip briefly, just long enough to distribute the scallions evenly. Remove the mold from the freezer, fill it with the remainder of the mousse, then cover the mold with foil, and chill the mousse on the top shelf of the refrigerator for three to four hours.

When ready to serve, carefully slide a thin, sharp knife around the edge between the mousse and the mold, then dip the bottom of the mold in warm water for about eight seconds. Wipe the bottom with a towel, cover the top with a serving plate, then invert both. Rap the mold firmly. If the mousse does not slip out onto the plate, repeat the knife and warm water operations. Slice the mousse at the table.

RIMA AND RICHARD COLLIN
THE PLEASURES OF SEAFOOD

Pickled Shrimp

To serve 4

1 lb.	shrimp, poached, shelled and deveined	½ kg.
¾ cup	olive oil	175 ml.
3	garlic cloves, crushed to a paste	3
2	onions, sliced and separated into rings	2
½ cup	wine vinegar	125 ml.
½ tsp.	dry mustard	2 ml.
2 tbsp.	chopped fresh parsley	30 ml.
2 tbsp.	finely cut fresh dill	30 ml.
	salt and freshly ground black pepper	
1 tsp.	sugar	5 ml.

In a large bowl, combine all of the ingredients. Cover and refrigerate overnight. Serve the shrimp on greens with two spoonfuls of marinating liquid poured over each portion.

THE GREAT COOKS COOKBOOK

Shrimp in Puff Pastry

Feuilleté de Crevettes Cardinal

To make the vol-au-vent, cut 18 ovals from puff-pastry dough (recipe, page 167) rolled ⅛ inch [3 mm.] thick; prick each one. Score a lid in six ovals. Stack the ovals in threes on a baking sheet with the scored ovals on top. Brush with beaten egg yolk, chill for 20 minutes and bake for 30 minutes at 400° F. [200° C.]. Cool for 10 minutes, cut out the lids and scrape out the raw dough. Dry for 10 minutes in a 300° F. [150° C.] oven.

To serve 6

1¼ lb.	shrimp, shelled and deveined	600 g.
3 tbsp.	shellfish butter *(recipe, page 164)*	45 ml.
¼ cup	Cognac	50 ml.
¾ cup	dry white wine	175 ml.
½ cup	fish stock *(recipe, page 163)*	125 ml.
2 tbsp.	*beurre manié*, made by mixing 1 tbsp. [15 ml.] butter with 1 tbsp. flour	30 ml.
¾ cup	heavy cream, 1 tbsp. [15 ml.] whipped	175 ml.
3 tbsp.	hollandaise sauce *(recipe, page 166)*	45 ml.
	salt and pepper	
6	small, oval vol-au-vent	6

Brown the shrimp in the shellfish butter; add the Cognac and ignite it; when the flames die, add the white wine. Allow to cook gently for five minutes; remove the shrimp and keep them hot. Add to the cooking liquid the fish stock and the cream, reduce the liquid by a quarter, and thicken it with the *beurre manié*. Add the shrimp to the sauce; stir in the

whipped cream and hollandaise. Adjust the seasoning. Fill the vol-au-vent with the mixture. Serve very hot.

A. E. SIMMS (EDITOR)
FISH AND SHELL-FISH

Shrimp Quenelles

Quenelles de Crevettes

The technique of making quenelles is shown on pages 84-85.

To serve 6

½ lb.	shrimp, shelled and deveined	¼ kg.
¼ lb.	sole or flounder fillet, skinned and cut into 1-inch [2½-cm.] pieces	125 g.
2	egg whites	2
1 cup	heavy cream	¼ liter
¾ tsp.	salt	4 ml.
¼ tsp.	white pepper	1 ml.
⅛ tsp.	cayenne pepper	½ ml.
	fish stock *(recipe, page 163)* (optional)	

Thick shrimp sauce

2 oz.	shrimp, shelled, deveined, poached and diced (about ⅓ cup [75 ml.])	60 g.
1½ cups	fish velouté sauce *(recipe, page 163)*	375 ml.
⅓ cup	fish stock *(recipe, page 163)*	75 ml.
⅓ cup	heavy cream	75 ml.
1 tbsp.	tomato sauce *(recipe, page 165)*, reduced to 1 tsp. [5 ml.]	15 ml.

To make the sauce, combine the fish velouté sauce, fish stock and heavy cream in a pan. Over high heat, reduce the mixture by one quarter. Strain it through a fine-meshed sieve. Adjust the seasoning. Keep the sauce warm over hot water. At serving time, stir in the tomato sauce and diced shrimp.

To make the quenelles, finely grind both the shrimp and fish in a food grinder or, preferably, a food processor. Transfer this forcemeat to a bowl. Slowly add the egg whites and heavy cream, mixing continuously. Season the mixture with the salt, white pepper and cayenne. Dip a large soupspoon in hot water and scoop up a heaping amount of the mixture. Using another spoon, round the mixture to make a neat, egg-shaped quenelle and push it into a large buttered sauté pan or fireproof cooking dish. Cover the quenelles with simmering salted water or fish stock. Cover the pan or dish and simmer the quenelles for three minutes. Turn the quenelles over, cover, and let them cook for three more minutes—or until they rise to the surface of the cooking liquid. Drain the quenelles on paper towels, arrange them on a serving dish, and cover each quenelle with shrimp sauce.

JEAN F. NICOLAS
THE COMPLETE COOKBOOK OF AMERICAN FISH AND SHELLFISH

Lobster

Poached Lobsters with Savory White Butter Sauce
Homards à la Nage et Beurre Blanc
This recipe is from the Lucas Carton restaurant in Paris.

To serve 4

four 1 lb.	lobsters	four ½ kg.
	White-wine court bouillon	
2 cups	dry white wine	½ liter
2	carrots, sliced	2
2	onions, sliced	2
4	shallots, sliced	4
1	small garlic clove	1
1	sprig thyme	1
1	small bay leaf	1
12	sprigs parsley	12
	salt and pepper	
½ cup	thinly sliced fennel stalks	125 ml.
about 1 cup	water	about ¼ liter
	Savory white butter sauce	
2 tbsp.	finely chopped shallots	30 ml.
⅔ cup	vinegar	150 ml.
1 cup	dry white wine	¼ liter
	salt and pepper	
7 tbsp.	butter, chilled and cut into small pieces	105 ml.

Mix the court-bouillon ingredients in a large nonreactive pot and boil for five minutes, adding more water, if necessary, to keep the solid ingredients completely covered: Plunge the lobsters into the pot, cover and simmer for 15 minutes.

Meanwhile, make the sauce. Put the shallots into a small nonreactive pan with the vinegar and half of the wine. Season with salt and pepper, and boil until the liquid is reduced to half its original volume. Add the remaining wine, and return the mixture to a boil. Vigorously whisk in the butter until the sauce is thick and creamy. Remove the pan from the heat before the last piece of butter is absorbed.

Drain the lobsters and arrange them on a platter. Serve the sauce separately in a warmed sauceboat.

LES PRINCES DE LA GASTRONOMIE

My Great-grandmother's Lobster Newburg

The lobster called for in this recipe will yield about 4 cups [1 liter] of meat. Shrimp, scallops or crab meat—or a combination of all three—may be substituted for the lobster or used with it.

To serve 6 to 8

one 4 lb.	lobster, poached, shelled and cut into small pieces	one 2 kg.
4 tbsp.	butter	60 ml.
2 tsp.	salt	10 ml.
¼ tsp.	cayenne pepper	1 ml.
¼ tsp.	freshly grated nutmeg	1 ml.
1 cup	heavy cream	¼ liter
4	egg yolks	4
2 tbsp.	brandy	30 ml.
2 tbsp.	dry sherry	30 ml.

Heat the butter in a skillet and add the lobster. Cook slowly for a few minutes. Add the salt, cayenne pepper and nutmeg. Lightly beat the cream with the egg yolks and add the mixture to the pan, stirring constantly. Finally, add the brandy and sherry as the mass begins to thicken. Serve in vol-au-vent cases or on toast.

THE JUNIOR LEAGUE OF CHARLESTON
CHARLESTON RECEIPTS

Lobster in Madeira Sauce
Homard à la Duchesse

To serve 2 or 3

one 2 lb.	lobster, poached and shelled	one 1 kg.
2 tbsp.	butter	30 ml.
¾ cup	Madeira	175 ml.
	salt	
	cayenne pepper	
1 cup	heavy cream	¼ liter
3	egg yolks	3

Slice the lobster meat and sauté the pieces briefly in the butter. Add the Madeira, salt and a pinch of cayenne pepper. Reduce the heat to low and simmer the lobster for about five minutes, or until the pan juices are well reduced. Beat the cream with the egg yolks and pour this mixture over the lobster. Stir well, and tilt the pan back and forth so that all of the lobster pieces are coated with sauce. Serve as soon as the sauce is hot and just beginning to thicken; do not let it boil.

NARCISSA G. CHAMBERLAIN AND NARCISSE CHAMBERLAIN
THE FLAVOR OF FRANCE IN RECIPES AND PICTURES, VOLUME 2

Lobster Stew

Navarin de Homards

The technique of splitting a lobster is shown on pages 18-19.

To serve 4

two 1¼ lb.	female American lobsters	two 600 g.
6	small potatoes, peeled	6
½ lb.	very tender green beans, trimmed	¼ kg.
2	medium-sized carrots, cut into small ovals	2
1	medium-sized turnip, cut into small ovals	1
⅓ cup	freshly shelled green peas	75 ml.
8 to 9 tbsp.	unsalted butter	120 to 135 ml.
3	shallots, finely chopped	3
6	small boiling onions	6
	salt and pepper	
1 cup	dry white wine	¼ liter
1 cup	chicken stock (recipe, page 166)	¼ liter
	fresh tarragon leaves	
	fresh chervil leaves	

Put the potatoes and string beans into separate pans of boiling salted water and blanch them; allow about eight minutes for the potatoes and two minutes for the beans to make sure that the vegetables remain firm. Blanch the carrots and turnips, starting with cold salted water, allowing eight minutes for the carrots and four minutes for the turnips. Drain each vegetable, rinse it in cold water and drain it again.

Put the green peas into boiling salted water and cook at a simmer for four to six minutes. Drain, rinse in cold water and drain the peas again. Set the vegetables aside.

Plunge a knife into the lobster at the center of the point where the tail and body join. This will kill the lobster instantly. Slice off the tail and cut it crosswise into four sections. Split the body lengthwise; remove the small pouch of membrane, which contains the stomach, at the top, and the intestine, which runs down the center. Reserve the coral. Break the lobster claws.

In a saucepan, heat 7 tablespoons [105 ml.] of the butter and sauté the pieces of lobster in it for three or four minutes. Add the shallots and onions and stir them briefly. Add the blanched vegetables, salt and freshly ground pepper. Cook for about five minutes, stirring to blend the ingredients thoroughly. Add the wine and stock. Cover and cook for approximately 10 minutes.

Remove the pan from the heat; pour the cooking juices into another saucepan and set them over high heat to reduce them. Keep the lobster warm. Blend the reserved coral with an equal amount of the remaining butter. After the juices have reduced to half their original volume—in about 15

minutes—add the butter-coral mixture and bring to the boiling point. Then add the tarragon and the chervil.

Pour the sauce over the lobster, bring to the boiling point again, continuing to stir, and cook for another five minutes. Serve immediately.

PAUL BOCUSE
PAUL BOCUSE'S FRENCH COOKING

Baked Lobster with Bread Stuffing

To serve 2

two 1 lb.	lobsters, halved, the tomalley and coral—if any—extracted and reserved	two ½ kg.
2 cups	fresh bread crumbs	½ liter
¼ tsp.	finely chopped garlic	1 ml.
	salt and pepper	
2 tbsp.	finely chopped shallots or onion	30 ml.
8 tbsp.	butter, melted	120 ml.
	lemon wedges	

Combine the lobster tomalley and coral—if any—with the bread crumbs, garlic, salt and pepper, shallots or onion, and 2 tablespoons [30 ml.] of the butter. Mix well and stuff lightly into the body cavities of the lobster. Bake in a preheated 400° F. [200° C.] oven for 15 to 25 minutes, or until the meat is opaque and lightly browned. Serve at once with the lemon wedges and the remaining melted butter.

DAN AND INEZ MORRIS
THE COMPLETE FISH COOKBOOK

Lobster Fra Diavolo

To serve 4

two 1½ to 2 lb.	lobsters	two ¾ to 1 kg.
½ cup	olive oil	125 ml.
½ cup	chopped green pepper	125 ml.
2 tbsp.	chopped fresh flat-leafed parsley	30 ml.
2	garlic cloves, chopped	2
2 tbsp.	chopped fresh basil, or 1 tbsp. [15 ml.] dried basil	30 ml.
2 cups	canned Italian-style plum tomatoes, chopped	½ liter
2 tbsp.	tomato paste	30 ml.
⅛ tsp.	crushed red pepper	½ ml.
1 lb.	linguini or spaghettini	½ kg.

Put all of the ingredients except the lobsters and the linguini or spaghettini into a large, nonreactive pot and bring to a boil. Add the lobsters and cover, turn the heat very low—using a heat-diffusing pad if necessary—and simmer gently for about one hour. Stir often, scraping the bottom of the pot. The sauce will be thick, but light and delicate in taste and enhanced by the flavor of the lobsters. About 10 minutes before the sauce is done, start cooking the linguini or spaghettini in boiling salted water. Cook for four or five minutes, or until it is *al dente*, then drain it quickly. Place the pasta on hot plates. Remove the lobsters from the pot and pour some of the sauce over the pasta. Split or chop the lobsters, remove their entrails and veins, and serve the lobster pieces with the pasta, spooning the remaining sauce over them.

HOWARD MITCHAM
THE PROVINCETOWN SEAFOOD COOKBOOK

Lobster with Whiskey

To serve 4

two 2 lb.	lobsters, poached for 10 minutes, split, the meat extracted and cut into 1-inch [2½-cm.] chunks, the tomalley, coral (if any) and body shells reserved	two 1 kg.
2 tbsp.	olive oil	30 ml.
4 tbsp.	Cognac	60 ml.
¾ cup	bourbon whiskey	175 ml.
¼ cup	finely chopped shallots	50 ml.
¼ cup	chopped onion	50 ml.
	salt and pepper	
1½ cups	dry white wine	375 ml.
2 tbsp.	chopped fresh tarragon leaves	30 ml.
4 cups	heavy cream	1 liter
½ cup	mayonnaise (recipe, page 165)	125 ml.
¼ cup	chopped fresh parsley	50 ml.
¼ cup	freshly grated Parmesan cheese	50 ml.
2 tbsp.	butter, melted	30 ml.

Heat the olive oil in a large saucepan over medium-high heat. Add the lobster meat, tomalley and coral, if any, and sauté the mixture only until warm. Pour 2 tablespoons [30 ml.] of the Cognac and ⅓ cup [75 ml.] of the whiskey over the lobster and ignite the spirits. When the flame dies, remove the pan from the heat and add the shallots, onion, salt and pepper. Return the pan to medium-low heat and, stirring constantly, cook for eight minutes, or until the onion is tender. Remove the lobster and vegetables from the pan.

Add the white wine to the pan and cook over high heat until the wine is reduced to about ¼ cup [50 ml.]. Reduce the heat to medium and add the tarragon and heavy cream. Stirring constantly, cook slowly until this sauce thickens and is reduced to about 1½ cups [375 ml.]. Add the remaining Cognac and whiskey to the pan. Bring the sauce to a boil and once more reduce it to about 1½ cups.

Remove the sauce from the heat. Blend in the mayonnaise and parsley. Blend all of the ingredients with a whisk to obtain a smooth, creamy sauce. Mix the lobster meat with this cream sauce. Taste and adjust the seasoning. Spoon the lobster mixture back into the lobster shells. Dust the tops with the Parmesan cheese and sprinkle them with the melted butter. Broil under a preheated broiler for three to five minutes, or until the sauce is bubbly and the surface brown. Serve immediately.

DOMINIQUE D'ERMO
DOMINIQUE'S FAMOUS FISH, GAME & MEAT RECIPES

Lobster Thermidor

This recipe is from Wheeler's restaurant in London. The technique of cutting a lobster in half and extracting its meat is demonstrated on pages 30-31.

To serve 2

one 1½ lb.	lobster, poached in boiling water or court bouillon (recipe, page 162), split, the meat extracted and body shell reserved	one ¾ kg.
4 tbsp.	butter	60 ml.
1	medium-sized shallot, chopped	1
1 tbsp.	flour	15 ml.
1 tbsp.	dry sherry	15 ml.
1 tbsp.	dry white wine	15 ml.
½ cup	fish stock (recipe, page 163)	125 ml.
⅔ cup	freshly grated Parmesan cheese	150 ml.
1 tbsp.	chopped fresh parsley	15 ml.
1 tbsp.	heavy cream	15 ml.
1 tsp.	dry mustard	5 ml.
	salt and pepper	

Cut the lobster meat into pieces about 1 inch [2½ cm.] square. Melt 3 tablespoons [45 ml.] of the butter in a large, nonreactive skillet and lightly fry the chopped shallot, but do not brown it. Stir in the flour, then add the sherry, white wine, lobster meat and stock, and simmer for three or four minutes, stirring all the time. Add about half of the grated cheese, all of the parsley, and the cream. Take the skillet off the heat, add the dry mustard and salt and pepper to the lobster mixture and mix well. Spoon the lobster pieces into the reserved lobster shell.

To the sauce left in the pan, add the remaining butter and the rest of the cheese. Mix, coat the lobster pieces with the sauce, and brown the assembly lightly by sliding it under a hot broiler.

MACDONALD HASTINGS AND CAROLE WALSH
WHEELER'S FISH COOKERY BOOK

Lobster Stuffed with Crab Meat

To serve 4

four 1 to 1½ lb.	lobsters	four ½ to ¾ kg.
1 lb.	crab meat, picked over	½ kg.
16	soda crackers, finely crushed	16
	salt and pepper	
6 tbsp.	butter, melted	90 ml.
¼ cup	clam broth or milk	50 ml.
2 tbsp.	dry sherry	30 ml.
¼ cup	freshly grated Parmesan cheese	50 ml.
	paprika	

Place each lobster on its back, and use a sharp knife to split it in half. Remove the stomach and intestinal vein, but leave intact all of the meat, fat, liver (tomalley) and juices. Arrange the lobster halves, cavities upward, in large, shallow baking pans. Combine the crab meat, the crackers, 4 tablespoons [60 ml.] of the melted butter, the broth or milk, the sherry, and salt and pepper to taste. Pile this stuffing mixture into the cavities in the body shells and over the tail meat of the lobsters. Sprinkle the remaining melted butter over the tops of the stuffed lobsters, and then sprinkle them with the grated Parmesan cheese and paprika. Bake the lobsters in a preheated 450° F. [230° C.] oven for 18 to 20 minutes, or until the tops are golden brown.

MIKE LINZ AND STAN FUCHS
THE LOBSTER'S FINE KETTLE OF FISH

Lobster Soufflé

If the lobster claws can be broken with a hammer on one side only, small quantities of the soufflé mixture can be stuffed into them and baked while the bodies are being served.

To serve 6

three 1¾ lb.	cold poached lobsters, split, with meat removed and diced; body shells cleaned and reserved	three 875 g.
4 tbsp.	butter	60 ml.
5 tbsp.	flour	75 ml.
1½ cups	milk	375 ml.
6	eggs, separated	6
	salt and pepper	

Melt the butter in a heavy saucepan. Stir in the flour until smooth. Then add the milk and cook, stirring constantly for about three minutes, until the sauce is thickened and smooth. Reduce the heat and simmer for about 15 minutes, stirring occasionally. Set this sauce mixture aside to cool.

Add the diced lobster meat to the cooled sauce mixture. Beat the egg yolks and add them, too. Season with salt and pepper to taste. Whip the egg whites until they are stiff and fold them into the lobster mixture. Place the lobster shells on a baking sheet and stuff them with the mixture.

Bake the stuffed shells in a preheated 375° F. [190° C.] oven for 20 to 25 minutes, or until the soufflés are puffed and brown. Do not open the oven door during the first 15 minutes of baking. Serve at once.

LILLIAN LANGSETH-CHRISTENSEN AND CAROL STURM SMITH
THE SHELLFISH COOKBOOK

Lobster Flamed with Pernod

To serve 6

six 1½ lb.	lobsters	six ¾ kg.
½ cup	olive oil	125 ml.
8 tbsp.	butter	120 ml.
2 tbsp.	chopped onion	30 ml.
2½ tbsp.	chopped shallot	37 ml.
1	garlic clove, finely chopped	1
2 tbsp.	Cognac	30 ml.
¼ cup	puréed tomato	50 ml.
1	medium-sized tomato, peeled, seeded and chopped	1
¼ tsp.	chopped fresh thyme leaves	1 ml.
1	bay leaf	1
¾ cup	dry white wine	175 ml.
⅔ cup	heavy cream	150 ml.
3 tbsp.	fresh lemon juice	45 ml.
2 tbsp.	Pernod or other anise-flavored liqueur	30 ml.

Split the lobsters into halves. Remove and reserve the coral, if any, and the creamy parts from the heads. Crack the claws. Sauté the lobster halves in the oil—two or three at a time—until the shells turn red. Remove the oil from the pan.

Add to the pan half of the butter, the onion, shallots and garlic. Brown lightly. Deglaze the pan with the Cognac and ignite the Cognac. When the flame dies, add the puréed tomato, chopped tomato and herbs. Bring the mixture to a boil.

Remove the lobster pieces. Extract the meat from the tails and claws. Cut the meat into chunks and reserve the tail shells. Strain the cooking liquid and boil it down to reduce it by half. Mix the coral and creamy parts of the lobsters with the remaining butter; stir in the cream, lemon juice and Pernod. Combine this sauce with the reduced cooking liquid. Add the lobster meat. Fill the tail shells with the mixture. Brown the stuffed tails under a preheated broiler—about five minutes—and serve them with rice.

JEAN F. NICOLAS
THE COMPLETE COOKBOOK OF AMERICAN FISH AND SHELLFISH

Stuffed Lobster

To serve 2

two 2 lb.	lobsters, poached, split, the meat extracted and chopped, the tomalley and coral (if any) reserved and the body shells reserved	two 1 kg.
½ lb.	fresh mushrooms, thinly sliced	¼ kg.
2 tbsp.	butter	30 ml.
1 tbsp.	flour	15 ml.
	salt and pepper	
1 cup	heavy cream	¼ liter
3 tbsp.	dry sherry	45 ml.
2 tbsp.	chopped fresh parsley	30 ml.

In the top part of a double boiler set over simmering water, melt the butter and cook the mushrooms until browned. Sift the flour over the mushrooms, adding a dusting of salt and pepper, and stir until smooth. Remove the pan from the water. Blend in the cream and place the pan over the water for seven or eight minutes, stirring often. Remove the pan from the water and blend in the sherry. Sieve the tomalley and coral, if any, and blend them into this sauce. Add the lobster meat. Fill the shells with the mixture. Before serving, place the lobsters under a preheated broiler for a few minutes to brown the tops. Garnish the lobsters with the parsley.

FRANCES MAC ILQUHAM
FISH COOKERY OF NORTH AMERICA

Lobster and Asparagus in Aspic

Le Favori

To serve 4

1	large spiny lobster, poached in court bouillon *(recipe, page 162)*, the tail shelled and cut into ½-inch [1-cm.] slices	1
½ lb.	asparagus tips, cut into ¼-inch [6-mm.] slices and parboiled for 1 minute	¼ kg.
6 tbsp.	green mayonnaise *(recipe, page 165)*	90 ml.
	liquid fish aspic *(recipe, page 163)*, chilled until syrupy	

Tomato vinaigrette

3	medium-sized tomatoes, chopped and puréed	3
2 tbsp.	wine vinegar	30 ml.
½ cup	olive oil	125 ml.
	salt and white pepper	

To make the tomato vinaigrette, first drain the tomato purée in a sieve lined with dampened cheesecloth for about five

hours. Refrigerate the drained purée until well chilled—about two hours. Mix the purée with the vinegar, oil, salt and white pepper.

Mix the asparagus tips with the green mayonnaise. Place the lobster slices side by side on a rack over a plate. Place spoonfuls of the asparagus and mayonnaise on top of each slice and glaze each assembly with the liquid aspic. Refrigerate until the aspic sets—about one to two hours. Glaze the assemblies with a second coat of aspic and refrigerate them for several hours, or until well chilled.

Place the garnished lobster slices on a serving platter and spoon the tomato vinaigrette around them. Serve cold.

ÉDOUARD NIGNON
ÉLOGES DE LA CUISINE FRANÇAISE

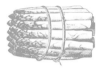

Fisherman's Spiny Lobster

Langouste Pêcheur

To serve 2

one 2 lb.	female spiny lobster, the tail shelled and cut into pieces, the tomalley and coral reserved	one 1 kg.
¼ cup	olive oil	50 ml.
1	large onion, finely chopped	1
2	large tomatoes, peeled, seeded and chopped	2
½ cup	water	125 ml.
	salt and pepper	

Coral-and-tomalley mayonnaise

	reserved lobster tomalley and coral	
1	egg yolk	1
1 cup	olive oil	¼ liter

Heat the oil in a sauté pan, add the onion and tomatoes, and cook over medium heat until the onion is soft and the tomato liquid has evaporated. Add the lobster pieces, mix well into the sauce, and cook for a few minutes; then add the water, salt and pepper. Cover and simmer the lobster very gently for about 10 minutes.

Meanwhile, pound the coral and tomalley to a paste in a mortar. Add the egg yolk and beat with the pestle, gradually adding the oil until the mixture thickens into a mayonnaise.

When the lobster is cooked, remove the pan from the heat. Mix some of the hot sauce into the mayonnaise, then pour the mayonnaise into the pan. Mix well. Serve the lobster pieces with the sauce on a hot serving dish.

EUGÈNE BLANCARD
METS ET PRODUITS DE PROVENCE

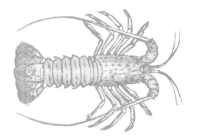

Spiny Lobster with Tomato, Herb and Wine Sauce

Langouste à l'Américaine

To serve 10

three 2 lb.	female spiny lobsters, tails shelled and cut into pieces, and the coral reserved	three 1 kg.
1 cup	olive oil	¼ liter
	salt and pepper	
14 tbsp.	butter	210 ml.
⅔ cup	shallots, finely chopped	150 ml.
1	garlic clove, crushed to a paste	1
⅓ cup	Cognac	75 ml.
2 cups	dry white wine	½ liter
6	medium-sized tomatoes, peeled, seeded and coarsely chopped	6
	cayenne pepper	
½ tsp.	chopped fresh chervil leaves	2 ml.
½ tsp.	chopped fresh tarragon	2 ml.
2 tbsp.	chopped fresh parsley	30 ml.

Heat the oil in a very large nonreactive sauté pan, season the lobster pieces and toss them into the pan. Stir over high heat until the pieces are red, about five minutes.

Drain off the oil, leaving the lobster in the sauté pan, and add 4 tablespoons [60 ml.] of the butter. Add the shallots and garlic. Sauté for a few minutes over low heat. Heat the Cognac in a small nonreactive pan and ignite it, and when the flames die, add the Cognac to the sauté pan, along with the white wine, the tomatoes and a pinch of cayenne pepper. Mix everything over high heat. When the mixture comes to a boil, reduce the heat, cover the pan and cook for 20 minutes.

Crush the coral in a bowl, add the rest of the butter and beat the coral and butter together. Remove the lobster pieces from the pan and put them in a warmed, deep serving dish.

Boil the sauce uncovered until the liquid is reduced to about 2 cups [½ liter]. Reduce the heat, add the coral butter and stir thoroughly. Add the chervil and tarragon and heat the sauce, without allowing it to boil. Pour the sauce over the lobster pieces. Sprinkle with the parsley and serve at once.

ODETTE KAHN
LA PETITE ET LA GRANDE CUISINE

Galician Lobster

Langosta a la Gallega

To serve 2

one 2 to 2½ lb.	lobster, poached, shelled, the meat cut into pieces and the cooking liquid reserved	one 1 to 1¼ kg.
2	medium-sized onions, finely chopped	2
2	garlic cloves, finely chopped	2
1 tbsp.	chopped fresh parsley	15 ml.
4 tbsp.	olive oil	60 ml.
2 tbsp.	wine vinegar	30 ml.
1 tsp.	paprika	5 ml.
1	whole clove, crushed	1
3 or 4	saffron threads, crumbled and steeped in 2 tbsp. [30 ml.] hot water	3 or 4
	salt and pepper	
½ cup	dry white wine	125 ml.

In a heavy skillet, mix the onions, garlic and parsley; add the olive oil, wine vinegar, paprika, clove, saffron, salt and pepper. Bring the mixture to a boil over high heat; add 1 cup [¼ liter] of the lobster cooking liquid and the wine. Cook uncovered over moderate heat for 10 minutes, or until the liquid has reduced to a light sauce. Stir in the lobster meat and heat it through. Serve the lobster at once.

JEANNETTE AGUILAR
THE CLASSIC COOKING OF SPAIN

Lobster in Black-Bean Sauce

To serve 4

2	medium-sized lobster tails, shelled and cut into segments	2
1½ tbsp.	fermented black beans	22½ ml.
2	garlic cloves, crushed to a paste, plus ½ tsp. [2 ml.] finely chopped garlic	2
1 tsp.	sugar	5 ml.
¼ cup	peanut oil	50 ml.
1 tsp.	finely chopped fresh ginger	5 ml.
¾ cup	hot water	175 ml.
1 tsp.	cornstarch, dissolved in 1 tbsp. [15 ml.] cold water	5 ml.
2 tbsp.	chopped scallions, white parts only	30 ml.
1	egg, lightly beaten	1

Rinse the black beans in a strainer under cold water for a few seconds, then drain them. Mash the beans to a paste with the crushed garlic and the sugar.

Heat the oil in a wok or skillet, and fry the chopped garlic and ginger until they start to brown. Add the lobster segments, increase the heat and stir fry them for four or five minutes, turning them constantly. Remove the lobster from the pan, add the black-bean mixture to the oil and fry for one minute. Return the lobster to the pan, add the hot water, stir well, cover the pan and cook for three minutes. Stir in the cornstarch mixture, then stir until the sauce boils and thickens slightly. Add the scallions and egg, and stir until the egg sets. Serve the lobster at once, accompanied by hot rice.

CHARMAINE SOLOMON
CHINESE DIET COOKBOOK

Lobster Tails Skorpios

The technique of removing lobster meat from the tail in one piece is demonstrated on page 30.

To serve 4

8	small lobster tails	8
3 tbsp.	olive oil	45 ml.
1 cup	finely chopped onion	¼ liter
1	garlic clove, finely chopped	1
2 cups	peeled and chopped fresh tomatoes or drained and chopped canned plum tomatoes	½ liter
½ cup	tomato sauce (recipe, page 165)	125 ml.
¼ tsp.	dried oregano	1 ml.
¼ tsp.	sugar	1 ml.
⅛ tsp.	dry mustard	½ ml.
	freshly ground black pepper	
¼ cup	finely chopped fresh parsley	50 ml.
3 tbsp.	butter	45 ml.
	flour	
¼ lb.	feta cheese, thinly sliced	125 g.

In a saucepan, heat the olive oil and sauté the onion without browning it. Add the garlic, tomatoes, tomato sauce, oregano, sugar, mustard, black pepper and parsley. Cook the mixture, uncovered, for about 30 minutes, or until it is reduced to a moderately thick sauce.

Shell the lobster tails, taking care to remove the meat from each of them in one piece. In a skillet, heat the butter. Dust the lobster with flour and sauté the tails briskly—stirring them constantly—for about two minutes, or just until firm. Transfer the lobster tails to a shallow baking dish. Pour the sauce over them. Cover them with the slices of feta cheese and bake in a preheated 425° F. [220° C.] oven for about 10 minutes, or until the cheese melts. Serve with rice and green salad.

THE GREAT COOKS COOKBOOK

Lobster in Fried-Onion Sauce
Bara Jheenga Do-piaza

To serve 6

5 cups	diced cooked lobster meat	1¼ liters
½ cup	vegetable oil	125 ml.
2	medium-sized onions, sliced lengthwise into thin shreds	2
1½ cups	finely chopped onions	375 ml.
2 tsp.	finely chopped garlic	10 ml.
1 tbsp.	peeled and finely chopped fresh ginger	15 ml.
1 tbsp.	ground coriander	15 ml.
½ tsp.	ground turmeric	2 ml.
¼ tsp.	fennel seeds, crushed	1 ml.
½ tsp.	cayenne pepper	2 ml.
1½ tsp.	paprika	7 ml.
3	medium-sized tomatoes, peeled, seeded and chopped, or substitute 1 cup [¼ liter] drained canned tomatoes, chopped	3
2 cups	boiling water	½ liter
1½ tsp.	coarse salt	7 ml.
¼ cup	heavy cream	50 ml.
2 tbsp.	finely chopped fresh coriander leaves	30 ml.

In a large shallow pan—preferably one with a nonstick surface—heat the oil over medium-high heat. When the oil is very hot, add the onion shreds, and fry, stirring them until they turn dark brown—about nine minutes. Take the onions out with a slotted spoon, and spread them on paper towels to drain.

Add the chopped onions to the same oil, and—stirring constantly—fry them until they turn caramel brown—about 15 minutes. Add the garlic and ginger and fry for an additional two minutes. Reduce the heat to medium, and add the coriander, turmeric, fennel, cayenne pepper and paprika. Stir rapidly for five seconds, and then add the tomatoes. Cook the mixture, uncovered, until it reduces to a thick pulpy sauce and the oil begins to separate from the tomatoes—about four minutes. Add the boiling water and salt. Reduce the heat, cover and simmer for 15 minutes. If the sauce looks thin and runny, increase the heat and boil it rapidly, uncovered, until it is reduced to a thick gravy.

Add the lobster meat and simmer until heated through. Stir in the cream and chopped coriander leaves. Check for salt and transfer to a serving platter. Serve the lobster garnished with the fried-onion shreds and, if desired, more chopped coriander leaves.

JULIE SAHNI
CLASSIC INDIAN COOKING

Octopus and Squid

Galician Octopus Pie

This version of a famous Galician dish, the like of which I have not met elsewhere in the world, is that given to me by Señora Pilar Bustamante, whose home in Galicia is at La Coruña. Before I give her instructions, let me make clear that the resulting "pie" is as wide and flat and thin as a pizza.

To serve 4

1 lb.	octopus, cleaned and skinned	½ kg.
2	bay leaves	2
	salt	
2	large onions, chopped	2
3 tbsp.	olive oil	45 ml.
4	large tomatoes, peeled, seeded and chopped	4
1	red pepper, halved, seeded, deribbed and chopped	1
	Olive-oil pastry	
2	eggs	2
½ tsp.	salt	2 ml.
½ cup	milk	125 ml.
½ cup	olive oil	125 ml.
1 tbsp.	rendered pork fat or melted lard	15 ml.
3 cups	flour	¾ liter

To make the pastry, mix together in a large bowl the eggs, salt, milk, oil and melted fat. Then add the flour, little by little, so as to form a soft dough *(masa blanda)*. You will know when it is right because the dough will no longer stick to your fingers, although it will still be quite moist. Knead it very briefly, form it into a ball, cover, and let it rest while you cook the octopus and prepare the rest of the pie filling.

Fill a fireproof casserole with boiling water and drop two bay leaves into it. Take hold of one octopus tentacle and dip the octopus three or four times into the water, which must continue to boil hard, until the octopus curls. Once it has curled, reduce the heat and leave the octopus in the water to simmer for about half an hour. Toward the end of cooking, add a little salt. Remove the octopus, let it cool, then cut it into small pieces.

Meanwhile, fry the onions very gently in the oil, covered, for about 10 minutes, taking care that they do not brown. Add the tomatoes and let them cook, too. Then add the red pepper and the pieces of octopus, and continue cooking for 10 to 15 minutes more. Let the mixture cool before using it.

Divide the pastry dough in two. Take a wide and shallow baking pan—for example, a round one 12 inches [30 cm.] in diameter or a rectangular one 10 by 13 inches [25 by 32 cm.]. Lightly oil the pan. Roll out half of the dough so that it will cover the bottom of the pan. Place the rolled dough in the pan so that the dough comes up the sides and overlaps the edges. Spread the filling over this. Roll out the remaining dough to make the top of the pie, and put this in place, rolling the edges over and crimping them to make a tight seal all the way round. Cook the pie in a preheated 350° F. [180° C.] oven for about 30 minutes, until it is a light golden brown.

ALAN DAVIDSON
NORTH ATLANTIC SEAFOOD

Octopus in Red Wine
Oktapothi Krasato

The ink from octopus may also be sizzled in olive oil in a skillet, combined with lemon juice and used as a bread dip.

To serve 5 or 6

2 lb.	octopus, cleaned and skinned, ink sac reserved	1 kg.
⅓ cup	olive oil	75 ml.
1	large onion, chopped	1
2	garlic cloves, crushed	2
½ cup	dry red wine	125 ml.
	ink from octopus (optional)	
4	tomatoes, peeled, seeded and chopped	4
	salt	
	freshly ground black pepper	
2 tbsp.	finely chopped fresh parsley	30 ml.

Place the octopus in a pan without any liquid, cover and simmer over medium heat for 15 minutes. The octopus will exude its own juice and simmer in it. Drain the octopus and allow it to cool slightly. Cut the head and tentacles into small pieces, stripping off any suckers if desired.

Heat the oil in a skillet and gently fry the onion until it is transparent, about 10 minutes. Add the garlic and octopus pieces and stir over medium heat for five minutes longer. Add the wine and let the stew cook, uncovered, until most of the wine has evaporated, about 10 minutes.

Reduce the heat and add the ink from the sac if desired, along with the tomatoes and salt and pepper to taste. Cover the pan, and simmer gently over low heat for one and one half hours, or until the octopus is tender. Add water during cooking, if the mixture looks as if it is scorching. Add most of the parsley, cook for a minute more, then serve the stew hot with pasta or rice. Sprinkle the remaining parsley on top.

TESS MALLOS
THE COMPLETE MIDDLE EAST COOKBOOK

Octopus and Fennel in Wine, Cretan-Style

Oktapodi Maratho Krasato

To serve 4

1½ lb.	octopus, cleaned and skinned	¾ kg.
5 to 6 tbsp.	olive oil	75 to 90 ml.
1	medium-sized onion or 5 scallions, chopped	1
1 cup	red wine	¼ liter
1	fennel bulb, chopped	1
3 or 4	tomatoes, peeled, seeded and chopped	3 or 4
	salt and freshly ground pepper	

Using a sharp knife, slice the octopus into rounds the thickness of a little finger. Heat the oil in a heavy, nonreactive pot, add the onion or scallions, and cook over low heat until translucent and soft. Add the octopus slices to the onion or scallions, pour in the wine, cover, and simmer for 15 minutes. Put the fennel and tomatoes on top of the octopus, season with salt and pepper to taste, and give the pot a shake to mix the contents. Cover and simmer until the octopus is fork-tender—45 to 50 minutes or longer, depending on the size and age of the octopus. Serve warm or cold.

VILMA LIACOURAS CHANTILES
THE FOOD OF GREECE

Octopus with Potatoes and Peas

Pulpo con Patatas y Guisantes

To serve 4

2 lb.	octopus, cleaned and skinned	1 kg.
	salt	
⅔ cup	olive oil	150 ml.
1	large onion, chopped	1
3 or 4	garlic cloves, chopped	3 or 4
1	large tomato (or 2 small ones), peeled, seeded and chopped	1
¼ tsp.	cayenne pepper	1 ml.
4	medium-sized potatoes, peeled and cut into chunks or thick slices	4
1½ cups	cooked peas	375 ml.

Put the octopus in a large saucepan without adding any water. Sprinkle it with salt, cover the pan, and let the octopus cook in its own juices over low heat for about 45 minutes.

Three or four times during the cooking, lift the octopus out, using a fork, and dip it into a pan of boiling water; then run the octopus under cold water and return it to the saucepan to continue cooking.

Heat the olive oil in a fireproof casserole and gently fry in it the onion, garlic, tomatoes and cayenne for 10 minutes, or until the onion is soft and most of the liquid has evaporated. Add the potatoes and cook for about five minutes. Then add the octopus and enough of its cooking liquid to cover the contents of the casserole. Add salt if necessary, and let the dish cook gently, uncovered, for about 30 minutes, or until the potatoes are tender and the sauce is smooth and thick. Finally, add the peas and heat the mixture through. Serve straight from the casserole.

LEONORA RAMIREZ
EL PESCADO EN MI COCINA

Stewed Octopus

Poulpe à la Marseillaise

To serve 4

2 lb.	octopus, cleaned, skinned and cut into small pieces	1 kg.
⅓ cup	olive oil	75 ml.
	salt and pepper	
1	leek, trimmed to 1 inch [2½ cm.] above the white part, washed and chopped	1
1	onion, chopped	1
1	bouquet garni of thyme, fennel, bay leaf and celery	1
4	medium-sized tomatoes, peeled, seeded and chopped	4
¼ tsp.	powdered saffron	1 ml.
1	garlic clove, crushed to a paste	1
3 to 4 cups	water	¾ to 1 liter
¾ cup	white rice	175 ml.

Heat the oil in a heavy enameled casserole. When the oil is very hot, toss in the pieces of octopus and sauté them over high heat, adding salt and pepper. When the pieces are golden, add the leek, onion and bouquet garni. When the leek starts to turn golden, add the tomatoes, saffron and garlic.

Add enough water to cover the contents of the casserole by about ½ inch [1 cm.]. Cover and cook over low heat for one hour, adding more water from time to time to keep the level of the liquid constant. About 20 minutes before serving, add the rice. Serve straight from the casserole, or from a warmed serving dish.

H. HEYRAUD
LA CUISINE À NICE

Octopus Fritters

To serve 4

1½ cups	coarsely chopped octopus meat, parboiled for 15 minutes and drained	375 ml.
⅔ cup	flour	150 ml.
1 tsp.	baking powder	5 ml.
	salt and freshly ground black pepper	
1	egg, lightly beaten	1
⅓ cup	milk	75 ml.
	vegetable or peanut oil for deep frying	

Sift the flour, baking powder and a pinch each of salt and pepper into a bowl. Blend the beaten egg and milk and gradually stir this mixture into the flour. Beat this batter until smooth. Add the chopped octopus.

Heat the oil to 375° F. [190° C.]. Drop the batter-coated octopus into the oil, a few pieces at a time. Fry them until they are golden brown—about one minute. Drain the fritters on paper towels.

DOMINIQUE D'ERMO
DOMINIQUE'S FAMOUS FISH, GAME & MEAT RECIPES

Squid Stew

Calamari in Zimino

To serve 4

3 lb.	squid, cleaned and skinned	1½ kg.
1 lb.	Swiss chard or spinach, stems and large ribs removed, leaves chopped	½ kg.
	salt and pepper	
3	medium-sized tomatoes, peeled, seeded and chopped	3
Sofrito		
1	onion, finely chopped	1
1 tbsp.	finely chopped fresh parsley	15 ml.
1 tbsp.	finely cut fresh fennel leaves	15 ml.
1 tbsp.	finely chopped celery leaves	15 ml.
1	garlic clove, finely chopped	1
3 to 4 tbsp.	olive oil	60 to 75 ml.

Make the *sofrito* by frying the onion, parsley, fennel and celery leaves, and garlic in the oil in a heavy, enameled pot. When the mixture has cooked for a minute or two, add the chard or spinach. Let the mixture simmer for a few minutes in the covered pot, then add the squid, salt, pepper and tomatoes, and continue cooking until the squid is tender—30 to 45 minutes.

GUELFO CAVANNA
DONI DI NETTUNO

Squid Stewed with Green Olives

Seiches à la Mode de l'Estaque

The original version of this recipe calls for cuttlefish, which is not available in America. Squid is a suitable substitute.

To serve 4

2 lb.	squid, cleaned, skinned and cut into small pieces	1 kg.
6	medium-sized tomatoes, peeled, seeded and chopped	6
3	garlic cloves, lightly crushed	3
1	bouquet of fennel leaves and bay leaf	1
3 tbsp.	olive oil	45 ml.
	salt and pepper	
¾ cup	dry white wine	175 ml.
½ cup	green olives, pitted	125 ml.

Put the squid into a fireproof, earthenware casserole with the tomatoes, garlic, herb bouquet, oil, salt and pepper. Bring to a boil, then add the wine and olives. When the sauce returns to a boil, reduce the heat, cover and simmer for one hour. Remove the herb bouquet before serving.

C. CHANOT-BULLIER
VIEILLES RECETTES DE CUISINE PROVENÇALE

Small Squid, Neapolitan-Style

To serve 4

1½ lb.	small squid, cleaned and skinned	¾ kg.
3 tbsp.	olive oil	45 ml.
1	garlic clove, sliced	1
4	medium-sized tomatoes, peeled, seeded and coarsely chopped	4
½ tsp.	salt	2 ml.
½ tsp.	pepper	2 ml.
1 tbsp.	pine nuts	15 ml.
10	ripe olives, pitted and chopped	10
1 tbsp.	seedless raisins	15 ml.
½ cup	water	125 ml.
4	thin slices Italian bread, toasted	4

In a skillet, brown the garlic in the oil. Remove the garlic, and add the tomatoes, salt, pepper and squid. Cook over medium heat for 10 minutes, then add the pine nuts, olives, raisins and water. Cover and simmer for 20 minutes, or until the squid is tender. Place one slice of toast in each of four warmed, shallow bowls, pour in the squid and serve at once.

ADA BONI
THE TALISMAN ITALIAN COOK BOOK

Squid with Peas, Roman-Style

Seppie coi Piselli alla Romana

Leaving the skin on the squid, as the authors suggest, will enhance the color of this dish. The volatile oils in chilies may irritate your skin. Wear rubber gloves when handling them.

To serve 6

3 lb.	squid, cleaned, the tentacles cut off and the pouches cut into rings	1½ kg.
3 tbsp.	olive oil	45 ml.
1	garlic clove	1
1	dried hot red chili, seeded	1
1 cup	dry white wine	¼ liter
2 tbsp.	chopped fresh parsley	30 ml.
1 tsp.	salt	5 ml.
2½ cups	freshly shelled peas	625 ml.

Put the olive oil in a big, wide skillet set over medium heat. Add the garlic and the chili. When the garlic is golden and the chili a deep brown, remove and discard them, and put in the squid. Cook for three minutes, or until the squid have changed their color to pink and purple. Add the wine and continue cooking until almost all of it has evaporated. Reduce the heat to low, add the parsley and salt, and cook for about 15 minutes. Add the peas, and simmer again until everything is tender. Taste for seasoning. Serve the squid piping hot, with Italian bread.

MARGARET AND G. FRANCO ROMAGNOLI
THE ROMAGNOLIS' TABLE

Squid Stewed in Their Own Ink and Red Wine

Calamares en su Tinta

To serve 6

2½ lb.	small squid, cleaned and skinned, ink sacs reserved	1¼ kg.
1 cup	red wine	¼ liter
3 tbsp.	olive oil	45 ml.
1	garlic clove, crushed lightly	1
3	medium-sized onions, chopped	3
⅔ cup	almonds, blanched and peeled	150 ml.
½ cup	fish stock *(recipe, page 163)* or water	125 ml.
	salt and pepper	

Pour the squid ink into a bowl. Discard the sacs and intestines. Wash the squid thoroughly, turn them inside out, snip off the eyes with sharp scissors and wash the squid again.

Cut off the heads and tentacles and chop these into small pieces; slice the bodies into rings. In a nonreactive bowl, mix the squid ink with 3 tablespoons [45 ml.] of the wine and reserve it. Cover all the squid flesh with the remaining wine and let it marinate for a few hours in a nonreactive bowl.

Heat the oil; fry the garlic in it until brown and then discard the garlic. Fry the onions in the oil until soft, remove them and set them aside.

Drain the squid flesh, but keep the liquid in which it marinated. Fry the squid in the oil for two to three minutes, stirring constantly. Add the onions, the ink mixed with wine, the liquid in which the squid marinated, the almonds, the fish stock or water, and salt and pepper to taste. Cover and simmer over low heat for one hour, or until the flesh is easily pierced with a small, sharp knife. Serve the squid with plain boiled rice.

MARINA PEREYRA DE AZNAR AND NINA FROUD
THE HOME BOOK OF SPANISH COOKERY

Squid with Prosciutto

Calamares a la Bilbaina

To serve 6

8 to 10	small squid, cleaned and skinned, and the ink reserved	8 to 10
3 tbsp.	olive oil	45 ml.
2	medium-sized onions, finely chopped	2
2	garlic cloves, chopped	2
1 tbsp.	chopped fresh parsley	15 ml.
2	tomatoes, peeled, seeded and chopped	2
2 to 3 oz.	sliced prosciutto, cut into small pieces	60 to 90 g.
	salt and pepper	
2 tbsp.	fresh bread crumbs	30 ml.
½ cup	dry white wine	125 ml.

In a skillet, heat the olive oil over medium heat and add the onion, garlic, parsley, tomatoes, prosciutto and squid. Season, and cook uncovered until the squid is tender—up to 10 minutes. Remove the squid from the skillet. Purée the sauce through a sieve into a clean pan. Place the ink in a mortar with the soft bread crumbs and 2 tablespoons [30 ml.] of the white wine. Pound the mixture together and add it to the sauce. Add the remaining wine. Bring the sauce to a boil and add the squid. Allow the mixture to come to a boil again and serve immediately.

JEANNETTE AGUILAR
THE CLASSIC COOKING OF SPAIN

Squid with Swiss Chard

Seppie in Zimino

To serve 6

3 lb.	small squid, cleaned and skinned; the body pouch sliced into rings and tentacles halved lengthwise	1½ kg.
1	onion, chopped	1
¾ cup	chopped fresh parsley	175 ml.
1	celery rib, chopped	1
¼ cup	olive oil	50 ml.
2 lb.	Swiss chard, tough stems removed, leaves trimmed and cut into large pieces	1 kg.
⅔ cup	crushed plum tomatoes	150 ml.
1½ tsp.	salt	7 ml.
	freshly ground pepper	

In a large pot, sauté the onion, parsley and celery together in the olive oil for three or four minutes, or until golden green. Add the chard to the pot and cook it for about five minutes, or until wilted. Add the tomatoes, salt, pepper and squid. Stir, cover, and cook at a gentle boil for 10 minutes. Uncover and continue cooking for another 10 to 15 minutes, or until the squid is tender. Taste for salt, and add more if desired. Serve with hot slices of toasted or fried Italian bread.

MARGARET AND G. FRANCO ROMAGNOLI
THE ROMAGNOLIS' MEATLESS COOKBOOK

Squid in Their Own Ink

Calamares en su Tinta

To serve 4

2½ lb.	tiny squid, cleaned and skinned, ink sacs reserved	1¼ kg.
¼ cup	olive oil	50 ml.
2	onions, chopped	2
2	tomatoes, peeled, seeded and chopped	2
2	garlic cloves, finely chopped	2
1 tbsp.	chopped fresh parsley	15 ml.
2 tbsp.	fresh bread crumbs	30 ml.
¼ cup	brandy	50 ml.
	water	
	salt	

Remove the stomach and the backbone from each of the squid, and cut off the tentacles. Push the tentacles into the body of each squid.

Heat the oil in a large skillet, and gently cook the onions and tomatoes. When the onions begin to soften, add the squid and cook until they become opaque—about 15 minutes. Remove the squid and put them into a shallow, fireproof, earthenware dish. Make a sauce in the skillet by adding the garlic, parsley, bread crumbs, brandy, a few tablespoons of water, and salt. Cook for a few minutes and add the ink from the sacs. Pour this sauce over the squid.

Cover, and cook gently either on top of the stove or in a preheated 325° F. [160° C.] oven for one hour, or until the squid are tender. Serve in the same dish, with triangles of fried bread and boiled white rice.

ANNA MAC MIADHACHÁIN
SPANISH REGIONAL COOKERY

Squid with Rice Stuffing

Kalamarakia Yemista

To serve 4 or 5

2½ lb.	medium-sized squid, cleaned and skinned	1¼ kg.
⅓ cup	olive oil	75 ml.
½ cup	white wine	125 ml.
1½ cups	tomato juice, heated	375 ml.

Rice stuffing

1	large onion, finely chopped	1
6 tbsp.	olive oil	90 ml.
½ cup	white rice	125 ml.
¼ cup	pine nuts	50 ml.
¼ cup	dried currants, soaked in warm water for 15 minutes and drained	50 ml.
2 tbsp.	chopped fresh parsley	30 ml.
	salt and pepper	

Rub the squid with salt and rinse well under running water.

To make the stuffing, cook the onion in the oil over medium heat until it is soft—about 10 minutes. Add the rice, pine nuts, currants, parsley, and salt and pepper to taste.

Partially fill the squid with the stuffing, leaving room for the rice to swell. Sew up the openings. Heat the oil in a large skillet and, over high heat, sauté the stuffed bodies and the tentacles for about five minutes, until the flesh is firm. Arrange these in a nonreactive fireproof casserole. Add the wine, the hot tomato juice and salt to taste. Cover the casserole, and cook the mixture over very low heat or bake in a preheated 350° F. [180° C.] oven for about one and one half hours, or until the squid is tender and the sauce is thick. Serve hot or cold.

CHRISSA PARADISSIS
THE BEST OF GREEK COOKERY

Stuffed Squid

Calamares Rellenos

To serve 3 or 4

2 lb.	squid, cleaned and skinned, the tentacles finely chopped, the ink extracted and reserved	1 kg.
3	slices boiled ham, chopped	3
3	eggs, 2 hard-boiled and chopped	3
1	slice firm-textured white bread, soaked in water and squeezed dry	1
	salt and pepper	
1 tbsp.	olive oil	15 ml.

Ink sauce

1	medium-sized onion, finely chopped	1
2	garlic cloves, finely chopped	2
½ cup	finely chopped green pepper	125 ml.
1 tbsp.	olive oil	15 ml.
1 cup	tomato sauce *(recipe, page 165)*	¼ liter
	reserved squid ink	
	salt and pepper	

Combine the chopped squid tentacles with the ham and hard-boiled eggs. Add the bread and the raw egg and blend well. Season with a little salt and pepper. Sauté this mixture in the olive oil until lightly browned. Stuff the squid with the mixture, using a teaspoon. Set the stuffed squid aside.

For the sauce, first warm the olive oil in a large skillet set over medium heat, and sauté the onion, garlic and green pepper in the oil for 10 minutes, or until they are tender. Add the tomato sauce and the squid ink, and season the mixture with a pinch each of salt and pepper. Simmer this sauce for 15 minutes.

Add the stuffed squid to the skillet, bring the sauce to a boil, reduce the heat, cover the skillet and simmer the squid gently for 45 minutes.

ANN ROGERS
A BASQUE STORY COOK BOOK

Stuffed Squid in Piquant Sauce

Les Touteno Farcies en Sauce Piquante

To serve 4

2 lb.	squid, cleaned, skinned and the tentacles reserved	1 kg.
2 tbsp.	olive oil	30 ml.
½ cup	brandy	125 ml.
1	garlic clove, crushed to a paste	1
2 tbsp.	chopped fresh parsley	30 ml.
2	salt anchovies, filleted, soaked in water for 30 minutes, drained, patted dry and chopped	2
2 tbsp.	chopped capers	30 ml.
1 tbsp.	flour	15 ml.
1 cup	white wine	¼ liter

Tomato stuffing

¼ cup	olive oil	50 ml.
1	onion, chopped	1
	finely chopped squid tentacles	
3	tomatoes, peeled, seeded and chopped	3
3	slices firm-textured white bread, crusts removed, soaked in milk and squeezed dry	3
1	garlic clove, crushed to a paste	1
2 tbsp.	finely chopped fresh parsley	30 ml.
2 or 3	egg yolks	2 or 3

To make the stuffing, sauté the onion briefly in the oil. Add the chopped tentacles and sauté for five to 10 minutes. Remove from the heat, add the tomatoes, soaked bread, garlic, parsley and egg yolks, and mix thoroughly. Stuff the squid with this mixture, leaving some room for the stuffing to swell during cooking. Sew up the squid.

Heat the olive oil in a heavy, nonreactive pot and sauté the stuffed squid for a minute or two. Pour the brandy over the squid, set the brandy alight and, when the flames die, add the garlic, parsley, anchovies and capers. Sprinkle in the flour, stir well and moisten with the wine. Bring the wine to a boil, cover the pot and cook over low heat or in a preheated 325° F. [170° C.] oven for one hour, or until the squid is easily pierced with a small, sharp knife.

RENÉ JOUVEAU
LA CUISINE PROVENÇALE

Grilled Squid from Setubal

Lulas Grelhadas à Setubalense

This recipe is from a Portuguese fishing town near Lisbon.

To serve 4

1½ lb.	small squid, cleaned and skinned	¾ kg.
1	sprig fresh parsley, chopped	1
	salt and pepper	
1 tbsp.	butter, softened	15 ml.
2 tbsp.	olive oil	30 ml.

Cut off the squid tentacles and chop them up. Mix them with the parsley, salt, pepper and butter. Stuff the bodies of the squid with this mixture and close the open end of each squid with a wooden pick. Season with salt and pepper, brush them with olive oil, and broil them, turning once, for 15 minutes.

Serve the squid with boiled potatoes sprinkled with melted butter, lemon juice and chopped parsley.

MARIA ODETTE CORTES VALENTE
COZINHA REGIONAL PORTUGUESA

Squid Fritters

To serve 4

¾ lb.	small squid, cleaned, skinned, the body pouches tenderized by pounding, finely chopped	350 g.
½ cup	flour	125 ml.
1 tsp.	salt	5 ml.
1 tsp.	baking powder	5 ml.
2	eggs, the yolk of 1 separated from the white	2
⅓ cup	milk	75 ml.
	oil for deep frying	

Blend the flour, salt and baking powder. In another bowl, mix together the whole egg, egg yolk and milk. Stir this into the dry mixture. Beat the egg white to the soft-peak stage. Fold it into the batter. Let the batter rest in the refrigerator for a half hour. Fold in the chopped squid. Deep fry the mixture by spoonfuls in oil that has been heated to 375° F. [190° C.] until the fritters are golden. Serve with tartar sauce or cocktail sauce.

JOYCE DODSON PIOTROWSKI
THE SQUID BOOK

Mixed Fried Seafood, Italian-Style

Fritto Misto Mare

This recipe is for the classic Neapolitan version of fritto misto di mare. Even in Naples, other fish might be added. Elsewhere in Italy the choice could be quite different, but will usually include squid, cut into rings, which is deliciously crunchy when correctly fried. If desired, the seafood can be coated with batter (recipe, page 167) before it is deep fried.

To serve 6

1½ lb.	small squid, cleaned, skinned and sliced into rings	¾ kg.
	olive oil for deep frying	
6	whole mullet (5 oz. [150 g.] each), cleaned	6
	flour	
	salt	
6	sprigs fresh parsley	6
1	lemon, cut into 6 wedges	1

Heat the oil until it registers 375° F. [190° C.] on a deep-frying thermometer. As the oil is approaching the correct temperature, roll the fish and squid in flour to which a little salt has been added. Shake them free of any excess flour, and fry them in the hot oil until they are golden and crisp—about three minutes. Drain the seafood, and serve it on a warmed platter with a garnish of parsley and lemon wedges.

JEANNE CARÓLA FRANCESCONI
LA CUCINA NAPOLETANA

Fried Squid

Calamares Fritos

To serve 4

3 lb.	small squid, cleaned, skinned and sliced into rings	1½ kg.
	olive oil	
3 tbsp.	fresh lemon juice	45 ml.
3 cups	flour, seasoned with salt	¾ liter
2	eggs, beaten	2
	lemon slices	

Marinate the squid with ¼ cup [50 ml.] of olive oil and all of the lemon juice for about one hour, stirring occasionally. Pat the squid dry. Dip them in the salted flour, the beaten egg, and then in the flour again. Deep fry the squid in olive oil heated to 365° F. [185° C.]. When they are crisp and brown—after about three minutes—drain them on paper towels. Serve them hot, garnished with lemon slices.

JEANNETTE AGUILAR
THE CLASSIC COOKING OF SPAIN

Mixed Shellfish

Court Bouillon of Shrimp, Scallops and Oysters

To serve 6

1 lb.	shrimp, shelled and deveined	½ kg.
1 lb.	shucked bay scallops, rinsed	½ kg.
18	oysters, scrubbed, shucked and the liquor reserved	18
2 cups	fish stock *(recipe, page 163)*	½ liter
12 tbsp.	butter, 8 tbsp. [120 ml.] cut into small pieces and chilled	180 ml.
5 tbsp.	dry white wine	75 ml.
1	carrot, cut into julienne	1
1	celery rib, cut into julienne	1
1	leek, washed, trimmed to 1 inch [2½ cm.] above the white part, and cut into julienne	1
	sea salt	
	freshly ground white pepper	
1	large black truffle, thinly sliced, the liquid reserved if truffle is canned (optional)	1

Place the fish stock in a broad skillet and cook over high heat until half of the liquid has evaporated. Set the stock aside. In a nonreactive saucepan, bring 4 tablespoons [60 ml.] of the butter and 4 tablespoons of the wine to a boil. Add the carrot, celery and leek; cook, covered, over low heat for five minutes, shaking the pan often. Remove from the heat.

In a small, nonreactive saucepan, heat the remaining tablespoon [15 ml.] of white wine. Using a wire whisk, gradually beat the chilled butter pieces into the wine. Set the wine-butter sauce aside.

Heat the reduced fish stock. Add the shrimp, then the scallops. Season to taste with salt and pepper. Simmer, stirring, for one minute. Add the oysters, the oyster liquor and the julienned vegetables. Simmer gently for one minute longer to allow the flavors to blend. Scatter the truffle slices, if using, on top and sprinkle with a few drops of truffle liquid. Pour the reserved wine-butter sauce over the seafood and swirl to combine. Serve hot with steamed rice.

TOM MARGITTAI AND PAUL KOVI
THE FOUR SEASONS

Shellfish with Peppers and Saffron

To serve 4

2 dozen	mussels, scrubbed and debearded	2 dozen
2 dozen	littleneck clams, scrubbed	2 dozen
¾ lb.	medium-sized shrimp, shelled with the tails left intact, and deveined	350 g.
1	onion, chopped	1
2 tbsp.	olive oil	30 ml.
3	garlic cloves, finely chopped	3
2	green peppers, halved, seeded, deribbed and cubed	2
1½ tbsp.	finely chopped fresh parsley	22½ ml.
¼ tsp.	saffron threads	1 ml.
½ cup	fish stock *(recipe, page 163)*	125 ml.
½ cup	dry white wine	125 ml.
	salt and freshly ground pepper	
8	slices French bread	8
1	garlic clove, halved	1
¼ cup	olive oil	50 ml.
	cayenne pepper	

Soften the chopped onion in the olive oil in a 6-quart [6-liter] nonreactive pot. Stir in the chopped garlic and cook for one minute, or until it colors to a pale gold. Add the cubed peppers, and stir and cook for four to five minutes until they turn tender-crisp. Sprinkle on the parsley and saffron; stir both in. Pour in the fish stock and wine and bring the liquid to a boil, stirring all the while. Season the liquid with salt and pepper to taste. Cook the contents at a lively simmer for three to four minutes.

Add the mussels and clams to the pot, hinge side down, increase the heat to high, cover, and cook for three minutes, or until the mussels and clams are not quite fully opened. Add the shrimp, reduce the heat slightly, and cook until the shrimp have just turned opaque and the clams and mussels have opened all the way—about two minutes.

Meanwhile, rub both sides of the bread slices with the garlic and brush them with a light film of olive oil. Sprinkle both sides with a few grains of cayenne pepper. Arrange the slices on a baking sheet lined with foil, and bake them in a preheated 350° F. [180° C.] oven until golden brown on both sides—eight to 10 minutes—turning the slices once.

Serve the shellfish in wide bowls with a few bread slices secured amid the shellfish in each bowl.

LISA YOCKELSON
THE EFFICIENT EPICURE

Scallops and Oysters with Truffles
Saint-Jacques et Belons aux Truffes

To serve 2

6	shucked scallops, rinsed	6
6	shucked oysters, with their liquor	6
1 tsp.	oil	5 ml.
1 oz.	canned truffles, cut into julienne, with ½ tsp. [2 ml.] truffle juice	30 g.
	pepper	
¼ cup	low-fat milk	50 ml.
1 tsp.	crème fraîche	5 ml.
1	large fresh mushroom, sliced, poached in water and lemon juice for 1 minute, drained and puréed through a sieve	1
2	1½-inch [4-cm.] pieces of small carrot, cut into thin julienne	2
2	1½-inch [4-cm.] pieces of small leek or large scallion, white part only, cut into thin julienne	2
2	1½-inch [4-cm.] pieces of celery rib, cut into thin julienne	2
1	medium-sized mushroom, stem trimmed and cap cut into thin julienne	1

In one saucepan, heat the oil, add the julienned truffles, sauté them briefly, and add the pepper and the milk, *crème fraîche* and truffle juice. Simmer all together for two minutes and set aside.

Through a cloth-lined sieve, filter the oyster liquor into another saucepan. Bring to a simmer, and poach the scallops in the oyster liquor for four minutes, turning them each over once. Remove them with a slotted spoon and keep them warm. Poach the oysters in the liquor for 20 seconds on each side, remove, and keep them warm with the scallops.

Add the mushroom purée and the poaching liquid to the truffle mixture to season the dish. This is meant to be a thin sauce. Keep it hot but do not let it boil.

Just before serving, in a skillet with a nonstick surface, sauté the vegetable julienne for two minutes. Apportion the scallops and oysters between two warmed soup plates, cover them with the sauce and sprinkle on the hot vegetables.

MICHEL GUERARD
MICHEL GUERARD'S CUISINE MINCEUR

Shellfish Sausages
Boudins de Fruits de Mer

The technique of making shellfish sausages is demonstrated on pages 36-37. A somewhat simpler version of the shellfish sauce can be made by combining 3 cups [¾ liter] of fish stock with the reserved shrimp shells, simmering the mixture for about 25 minutes, then boiling it down to reduce it to ½ cup [125 ml.] before removing the pan from the heat and whisking in 10 tablespoons [150 ml.] of butter pieces.

To serve 6 to 10

½ lb.	shucked scallops, rinsed and cut into ¼-inch [6-mm.] slices	¼ kg.
½ lb.	shrimp, shelled, deveined and cut into ½-inch [1-cm.] pieces, the shells reserved	¼ kg.
1 lb.	sole fillets, preferably gray or lemon sole, skinned and cut into ½-inch [1-cm.] pieces, the carcasses and trimmings reserved	½ kg.
1½ cups	heavy cream	375 ml.
1 tsp.	salt	5 ml.
¼ tsp.	freshly ground white pepper	1 ml.
1 tbsp.	finely chopped mixed fresh tarragon leaves, parsley, chives and chervil leaves	15 ml.
Shellfish sauce		
	sole carcasses and trimmings	
	shrimp shells	
½ cup	celery leaves	125 ml.
¾ cup	onion, thinly sliced	175 ml.
1	bay leaf	1
¼ tsp.	fresh thyme leaves	1 ml.
½ tsp.	salt	2 ml.
½ tsp.	crushed peppercorns	2 ml.
½ cup	dry sherry	125 ml.
3 cups	fish stock (recipe, page 163) or water	¾ liter
10 tbsp.	unsalted butter, cut into small pieces	150 ml.

Purée the sole fillets in a food processor for a few seconds. Push pieces of fish back into the purée with a rubber spatula, and blend again for a few seconds until you have a smooth mixture. Add ½ cup [125 ml.] of the cream and blend for a few seconds more. Whip the remaining cream until it holds a soft peak. Whisk the fish purée into the whipped cream. Fold in the scallops, shrimp, salt, pepper and herbs.

Cut three pieces of aluminum foil, each about 14 inches [34 cm.] long, and butter them. Place one third of the mixture in a strip about 8 inches [20 cm.] long down the center of each piece of foil. Roll the foil pieces to enclose the mixture and twist the ends of the foil tight. Place the sausages in a large skillet. Cover with cold water and use a small lid as a weight to hold down the sausages and keep them immersed. Cover the skillet with its lid, bring the water just to a simmer, and cook the sausages gently over low heat for about 15 to 20 minutes, or until the sausages are firm when pressed. Remove the skillet from the heat and let the sausages cool in the water for about 10 minutes.

Remove the sausages from the water and unwrap them carefully. Discard any liquid that accumulated in the foil. Transfer the sausages to a buttered casserole dish, cover them with wax paper, and keep them warm in a 160° F. [70° C.] oven while you make the sauce.

Put the trimmings from the sole in a saucepan. Place the shrimp shells in the food processor, purée them for a few seconds and add them to the saucepan. Add the celery leaves, onion, bay leaf, thyme, salt, peppercorns, sherry and fish stock. Bring to a boil, and boil gently for 20 to 25 minutes. Strain, then simmer the liquid until all but ½ cup has evaporated. Reduce the heat and add the butter, piece by piece, beating after each addition. Taste for seasoning. Coat the sausages with the sauce and serve immediately.

JACQUES PÉPIN
LA MÉTHODE

Steamed Egg Custard with Seafood

Chawan Mushi

To make the dashi called for in this recipe, you will need the dried kelp (kombu) and dried flaked bonito (katsuobushi) sold at Japanese food markets. Bring 3 cups [¾ liter] of water to a boil in a small pan. Add a 2-inch [5-cm.] square of the kelp and boil it for three minutes. Remove the kelp from the pan and add 1½ tablespoons [22½ ml.] of the bonito. Return the liquid to a boil, then let it cool before straining it.

To serve 4

4	small shrimp, shelled and deveined	4
4	shucked oysters	4
4	dried Japanese mushrooms	4
1 tbsp.	Japanese soy sauce	15 ml.
1 tbsp.	sugar	15 ml.
	Custard	
4	eggs	4
2½ cups	*dashi,* or substitute fish stock *(recipe, page 163),* cooled to room temperature	625 ml.
1 tbsp.	Japanese soy sauce	15 ml.
2 tbsp.	*sake, mirin* or dry sherry	30 ml.

Soak the mushrooms in hot water for 30 minutes, cut off and discard the stems, and simmer the caps in a small saucepan with 1 tablespoon [15 ml.] of the soy sauce and the sugar for eight to 10 minutes. Meanwhile, for the custard, beat the eggs, then mix in all of the other ingredients.

Put a mushroom into each of four custard cups or ramekins; add a shrimp and an oyster. Fill the cups with the custard mixture. Skim off any bubbles that appear on top of the custard. Put the cups in a saucepan with enough hot water to come halfway up the sides of the cups. Cover each cup with foil, pressing it close to the outside of the cup. Cover the saucepan with a folded tea towel, then with a lid, and bring the water to a boil. Reduce the heat and simmer for 15 minutes, or until the custard is set. Serve hot or cold.

CHARMAINE SOLOMON
THE COMPLETE ASIAN COOKBOOK

Chesapeake Bay Fish Stew

The techniques of cleaning and cutting up live crabs are demonstrated on pages 20-21.

To serve 6

1 dozen	soft-shell clams, scrubbed	1 dozen
1 dozen	cherrystone clams, scrubbed	1 dozen
6	hard-shell blue crabs, scrubbed, cleaned and cut into pieces	6
½ lb.	sea bass fillets, cut into 2-inch [5-cm.] pieces	¼ kg.
two 2 lb.	striped bass, filleted and cut into 2-inch [5-cm.] pieces	two 1 kg.
1	small butterfish, filleted and cut into 2-inch [5-cm.] pieces	1
¼ lb.	Norfolk spot fillets, cut into 2-inch [5-cm.] pieces	125 g.
¾ lb.	catfish, skinned, filleted and cut into 2-inch [5-cm.] pieces	350 g.
½ lb.	sea trout fillets, cut into 2-inch [5-cm.] pieces	¼ kg.
8 cups	court bouillon *(recipe, page 162)*	2 liters
⅛ tsp.	whole saffron threads	½ ml.
	salt and freshly ground black pepper	
	buttered, thin French-bread slices, baked until brown	

Place the clams and ¼ cup [50 ml.] of water in a heavy pan or casserole. Cover, and heat until the clams open—about eight minutes. Discard those that do not open. Add the liquid from the clams to the court bouillon and, when the clams are cool enough, cut off and discard the siphons of the soft-shell clams. Reserve six cherrystones for garnish; remove the remaining clams from their shells and set the meat aside.

Bring the court bouillon to a simmer. Add the crabs and simmer them for 15 minutes. Add the sea bass and cook for three minutes. Add the butterfish and spot; cook for three minutes longer. Add the catfish, sea trout and saffron, and cook for five minutes, or until all of the fish are cooked. Add the clams, those in and those out of the shells, and reheat them. Serve the stew immediately in deep bowls either over the crisp bread slices or with the bread passed separately.

JEAN HEWITT
THE NEW YORK TIMES SOUTHERN HERITAGE COOKBOOK

Braised Mixed Seafood

Zarzuela de Pescado

In its original title, this famous Spanish dish is called a musical comedy of seafood because so many kinds of fish and shellfish are combined. The fish suggested by the author can be replaced with substitutes according to what is available; for example, halibut instead of angler. But a mixture is essential, and all of the fish must have firm flesh that will not disintegrate in the cooking. The zarzuela is best served in a heatproof earthenware casserole, which should be warmed if you have not used it for the cooking.

	To serve 4	
10 oz.	squid, cleaned, skinned and sliced into rings	300 g.
1 dozen	mussels, scrubbed, debearded, steamed open and left on the half shell	1 dozen
2 dozen	small hard-shell clams, scrubbed, steamed open and left on the half shell	2 dozen
1 lb.	large shrimp, shelled and deveined	½ kg.
1 lb.	angler fillets, thinly sliced	½ kg.
¾ cup	olive oil	175 ml.
1	onion, chopped	1
1	garlic clove, finely chopped	1
1	sprig fresh parsley, finely chopped	1
1	large tomato, peeled, seeded and finely chopped	1
	salt	
2 tsp.	fresh lemon juice	10 ml.
2	peppercorns	2
⅓ cup	sherry	75 ml.
1 tbsp.	Cognac	15 ml.
¼ cup	pitted black olives (optional)	50 ml.

Put all but about 2 tablespoons [30 ml.] of the oil in a skillet. Add the onion, garlic, parsley and tomatoes, and cook the mixture over low heat for about 15 minutes. The frying should be gentle and light.

Sprinkle the squid rings lightly with salt. Fry them, covered, in a large, heavy enameled pot over low heat, using the remaining oil and adding a little lemon juice.

After about 10 minutes, when the squid are cooked, add the mussels, clams, shrimp and fish and the fried tomato mixture. Season with salt and cook, covered, over gentle heat for about 15 minutes. Add the peppercorns, sherry and Cognac, and remove from the heat without delay. A typical finishing touch is to add a handful of pitted black olives.

LEONORA RAMIREZ
EL PESCADO EN MI COCINA

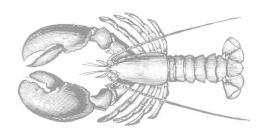

Cioppino

	To serve 8	
1 lb.	shrimp, shelled with the tails left intact, deveined	½ kg.
2 dozen	clams or mussels, scrubbed, the mussels debearded, steamed open, and the cooking liquid strained and reserved	2 dozen
one 2 lb.	Dungeness crab, scrubbed, cleaned, cut up and the claws cracked, or lobster, cleaned and cut into pieces	one 1 kg.
½ cup	olive oil	125 ml.
1	large onion, chopped	1
2	garlic cloves, chopped	2
3 tbsp.	chopped fresh parsley	45 ml.
¼ lb.	Italian dried mushrooms, soaked in warm water for 30 minutes, drained and the stems cut off	125 g.
1	green pepper, halved, seeded, deribbed and chopped	1
3 or 4	tomatoes, peeled, seeded and chopped	3 or 4
1 cup	tomato sauce (recipe, page 165), strained and boiled to reduce it to ⅓ cup [75 ml.]	¼ liter
2 cups	red wine	½ liter
	salt and freshly ground black pepper	
1	whole sea bass or striped bass, cleaned, boned and cut into serving pieces	1

Place the olive oil in a deep, nonreactive pot; when it is hot, add the onion, garlic, parsley, mushrooms and green pepper and cook for three minutes. Next add the chopped tomatoes and the reduced tomato sauce, the wine and the reserved mussel or clam liquid. Salt and pepper the mixture to taste, cover and let it simmer for 30 minutes. Add the cut-up fish, the shrimp and the crab or lobster, and cook until done. Serve with plenty of wine and garlic bread.

JAMES BEARD
JAMES BEARD'S NEW FISH COOKERY

Squid Cioppino

To serve 6

2 lb.	squid, cleaned, skinned, the body pouches tenderized by pounding, and sliced into rings	1 kg.
1 dozen	clams, scrubbed	1 dozen
1 lb.	large shrimp, shelled and deveined	½ kg.
½ cup	olive oil	125 ml.
4	garlic cloves	4
6	large tomatoes, peeled and seeded	6
½ tsp.	crushed red pepper	2 ml.
	salt and freshly ground pepper	

Heat the olive oil in a large heavy pan. Sauté the garlic over medium heat until it just begins to color—about five minutes. Add the tomatoes to the pan. Add the red pepper, some pepper and a teaspoon [5 ml.] of salt. Cook over high heat until the mixture is reduced to a thick purée—about 15 minutes. Add the squid, clams and shrimp. Cook for exactly three minutes, with a lid covering the pan.

JOYCE DODSON PIOTROWSKI
THE SQUID BOOK

Deep-fried Squid and Shrimp

Fritto di Calamari e Gamberi

To serve 4

1 lb.	squid, cleaned, skinned and sliced into rings	½ kg.
½ lb.	medium-sized shrimp, shelled and deveined	¼ kg.
	salt	
2 cups	flour	½ liter
3	eggs	3
1 lb.	solid vegetable shortening for frying	½ kg.
	lemon wedges	

Soak the squid and shrimp in cold water, with a pinch of salt, for 10 to 15 minutes, then drain on paper towels.

Put the flour into a plastic bag, then drop in the slightly damp fish pieces and shake very well. The pieces should be fully, but lightly, covered with flour.

Beat the eggs in a bowl with a pinch of salt and set aside while you heat the vegetable shortening in a deep fryer. While the shortening is getting hot, cover a serving dish with a layer of paper towels.

When the shortening is very hot (375° F. [190° C.]), dip each piece of floured squid or shrimp into the beaten eggs and fry until golden brown, about three minutes. Transfer to a serving dish lined with a paper towel to absorb the grease.

When all of the fish is cooked, remove the paper towels from the bottom of the serving dish, sprinkle the fish with salt, and garnish with lemon wedges. Serve hot.

GIULIANO BUGIALLI
THE FINE ART OF ITALIAN COOKING

Seafood à la Mediterranée

To serve 4

¾ lb.	large shrimp, rinsed	350 g.
1 dozen	cherrystone clams, scrubbed	1 dozen
4	lobster tails	4
½ cup	olive oil	125 ml.
3	garlic cloves, finely chopped	3
4	large, fresh tomatoes, peeled, seeded and chopped, or 2 cups [½ liter] drained and chopped canned plum tomatoes	4
¾ cup	dry white wine	175 ml.
1	bay leaf	1
½ tsp.	dried oregano	2 ml.
	salt and pepper	
2 tbsp.	finely chopped fresh parsley	30 ml.

Slit the shells of the shrimp lengthwise down the entire back; devein and dry the shrimp, but do not remove the shells. Wash the lobster tails and, with a large kitchen knife, cut the tails crosswise, shells and all, into 1-inch [2½-cm.] slices.

In a large, deep skillet over medium heat, heat the olive oil with the garlic and cook for one minute, taking care that the garlic does not brown. Add the shrimp and lobster-tail slices and cook for two minutes. Stir in the tomatoes and wine. Add the bay leaf, oregano, salt and pepper. Increase the heat and cook briskly for about five to six minutes. Add the clams; cover the skillet and continue to cook briskly—shaking and stirring—for 10 to 12 minutes, or until the clams open. Remove the skillet from the heat; sprinkle the shellfish with the chopped parsley, and serve it hot with pasta or rice and a crispy green salad.

THE GREAT COOKS COOKBOOK

Mussels and Shrimp Judy

To serve 4

1 dozen	mussels, scrubbed and debearded	1 dozen
1 lb.	shrimp, shelled and deveined	½ kg.
2 tbsp.	unsalted butter	30 ml.
3	shallots, chopped	3
1 tbsp.	brandy	15 ml.
2 tbsp.	light cream	30 ml.
½ cup	dry Marsala wine	125 ml.
3 tbsp.	chopped fresh flat-leafed parsley	45 ml.

Place the mussels in a large pot. Add 1 cup [¼ liter] of water and steam the mussels for about five minutes, until all of the shells are open. Discard the shells; there should be about 1 cup of mussels. Melt the butter in a nonreactive skillet and add the shrimp and shallots to the pan. Sauté the shrimp and shallots for three minutes. Add the brandy and cream and simmer for a few minutes. Add the mussels, then the Marsala, and cook for three minutes. Sprinkle with the parsley or stir it in. Serve with hot boiled rice or pasta.

ELISA CELLI AND INEZ M. KRECH
NATURALLY ITALIAN

Scallops and Shrimp, Chinese-Style

To serve 8

1 lb.	shucked sea scallops, rinsed and cut into thick round slices	½ kg.
1¼ lb.	shrimp, shelled, deveined, and cut lengthwise into halves	600 g.
1 tsp.	peeled and grated fresh ginger	5 ml.
1 tsp.	honey	5 ml.
2 tsp.	soy sauce	10 ml.
¼ cup	chicken stock *(recipe, page 166)*	50 ml.
3 tbsp.	oil	45 ml.
2	large green peppers, halved, seeded, deribbed and cut into julienne	2
6	scallions, cut into julienne	6
12	water chestnuts, sliced	12
6	dried black mushrooms, soaked in warm water for 30 minutes, the stems cut off and the caps sliced, the liquid strained and reserved	6
	watercress leaves	

In a bowl, combine the ginger, honey, soy sauce and chicken stock; set aside.

In a wok or a large skillet, heat the oil until it is very hot. Put in the green pepper julienne and half of the julienned scallions and stir fry for one minute. Add the water chestnuts and mushrooms and stir fry for another minute. Push the vegetables to the side and add the scallops and shrimp. Stir fry for two minutes, then mix the vegetables and seafood together. Add the reserved liquid mixture and the mushroom soaking liquid; cook, stirring, until the seafood pieces are just firm (vegetables should still be crunchy). Garnish each serving with some of the remaining julienned scallions and a sprinkle of watercress leaves.

A. J. MC CLANE
MC CLANE'S NORTH AMERICAN FISH COOKERY

Oyster and Lobster, Cuisine Nouvelle

To serve 6

6	lobster tails, poached for five minutes, shelled and the meat cut into cubes	6
1 dozen	oysters, shucked	1 dozen
1	carrot, cut into julienne	1
1	leek, trimmed to 1 inch [2½ cm.] above the white part, washed and cut into julienne	1
6 tbsp.	butter, 4 tbsp. [60 ml.] cut into small pieces	90 ml.
4	shallots, chopped	4
1 tbsp.	oil	15 ml.
¼ cup	brandy, warmed	50 ml.
1	bunch fresh parsley, half chopped, half reserved for garnish	1
1½ cups	heavy cream	375 ml.
	salt and pepper	

Sauté the carrots and leeks in 2 tablespoons [30 ml.] of the butter for two minutes. Remove the vegetables from the pan and set them aside. Add the oil to the pan and sauté the shallots for two minutes. Add the lobster cubes and oysters. Stir until the edges of the oysters curl—about two minutes. Remove the lobster and oysters from the pan and set them aside. Add the brandy to the pan juices and ignite it. When the flame dies, add the chopped parsley and the cream. Season with salt and pepper and cook until the liquid is reduced to one third its original volume. Add the butter pieces and stir until this sauce is smooth and creamy. Add the lobster and oysters. Simmer for one minute.

To serve, pour the mixture onto a warmed serving plate. Sprinkle the julienne vegetables on top. Garnish with the sprigs of parsley.

SANDI BROWN AND JOYCE LAFRAY
FAMOUS FLORIDA! RESTAURANTS & RECIPES

Shellfish Pilaf

If no mussels are available, use clams. The fish stock may be replaced by chicken stock.

	To serve 6	
2 dozen	mussels, scrubbed, debearded, steamed open, and the cooking liquid strained and reserved	2 dozen
1 cup	diced poached and peeled shrimp	¼ liter
1 cup	diced poached scallops	¼ liter
1	onion, finely chopped	1
about 4 tbsp.	butter	about 60 ml.
1½ cups	white rice	375 ml.
about 1½ cups	fish stock (recipe, page 163)	about 375 ml.
	pepper	

Sauté the onion in the butter until tender but not browned. Add the rice and sauté until the kernels are white. Mix the mussel cooking liquid with enough fish stock to make 3 cups [¾ liter] liquid, add the mixture to the rice, and bring it to a boil. Cover and cook for 18 to 20 minutes. Add the mussels, shrimp and scallops to the cooked rice and stir until the shellfish is heated through. Add as much additional butter as you allow yourself. Season with pepper—no salt.

MADELEINE M. KAMMAN
THE MAKING OF A COOK

Soufflé Neptune

	To serve 6	
½ cup	diced crab meat	125 ml.
½ cup	diced cooked lobster meat	125 ml.
2 tbsp.	butter	30 ml.
1½ cups	thick white sauce (recipe, page 164)	375 ml.
6	eggs, the yolks separated from the 6 whites, plus 1 additional egg white	

Anchovy sauce		
2 cups	white sauce (recipe, page 164)	½ liter
3 tbsp.	shellfish butter (recipe, page 164), made with crayfish or shrimp	45 ml.
8	flat oil-packed anchovy fillets, rinsed and patted dry	8
	heavy cream (optional)	

Melt the butter in a large saucepan and in it sauté the crab meat and lobster over medium heat for two or three minutes. Stir in the white sauce. Add the egg yolks, one by one, mix-

ing well. Beat the seven egg whites until stiff and fold them gently into the seafood mixture. Butter a 2-quart [2-liter] mold and pour in the soufflé mixture. Bake in a preheated 375° F. [190° C.] oven for approximately 40 minutes.

Meanwhile, mix all of the sauce ingredients except the cream, and cook uncovered over medium heat for five minutes. Strain the sauce; it should be thick but still pourable. If necessary, add a little cream. When the soufflé is puffed and brown, serve it immediately, accompanied by the sauce.

CHARLOTTE ADAMS
THE FOUR SEASONS COOKBOOK

Scallop and Shrimp Brochettes

Brochettes de Coquilles St. Jacques et Crevettes

Mussels, crayfish tails, pieces of fish fillet and mushrooms are other possibilities for seafood brochettes. The brochettes can be served on a bed of boiled rice or rice pilaf. If possible, use only fresh herbs in the marinade.

	To serve 4	
1 lb.	shucked scallops, rinsed	½ kg.
1 lb.	shrimp, shelled and deveined	½ kg.
	melted butter	
	freshly ground black pepper	
½ tsp.	paprika	2 ml.
	lemon wedges (optional)	
1½ cups	white butter sauce (recipe, page 164) (optional)	375 ml.

Herb marinade		
1 cup	dry white wine	¼ liter
2 tbsp.	oil	30 ml.
1 tbsp.	chopped fresh tarragon	15 ml.
2 tsp.	chopped fresh mixed herbs (thyme, oregano, basil, parsley)	10 ml.

Place the scallops and shrimp in a nonreactive bowl. Make the marinade: Combine the wine, oil and herbs and pour this over the shellfish. Mix well, cover, and refrigerate for at least two and, if possible, up to eight hours.

Drain the marinated scallops and shrimp and thread them on long metal skewers. Scallops are threaded through their diameter. Brush them generously with melted butter, sprinkle with black pepper and paprika, and broil or grill them about 3 inches [8 cm.] from the heat for four or five minutes, or until they are browned and tender. Turn them once during cooking and baste often with melted butter.

Serve the brochettes on a dish garnished with lemon wedges, or serve white butter sauce in a separate container.

ANNE WILLAN
THE OBSERVER FRENCH COOKERY SCHOOL

Avocados Stuffed with Seafood

Avocats Farcis aux Fruits de Mer

To serve 8

½ lb.	shrimp or crayfish, poached, shelled and deveined	¼ kg.
½ lb.	crab meat	¼ kg.
4	large, ripe avocados	4
⅓ cup	fresh lime juice	75 ml.
¼ lb.	fresh mushrooms, trimmed	125 g.
¾ cup	pitted green olives	175 ml.
3 tbsp.	chopped fresh parsley and basil or parsley and chervil, plus several whole sprigs	45 ml.
½ cup	chopped walnuts plus 8 halves, or sliced or slivered toasted almonds	125 ml.
¾ cup	long-grain white rice	175 ml.
¼ cup	olive oil	50 ml.
2 to 2½ tsp.	salt	10 to 12 ml.
	freshly ground pepper	
	Tabasco sauce	

Slice the avocados in half, remove the pits and scoop out the flesh. Dice the flesh coarsely and sprinkle it with a few drops of the lime juice. Reserve the avocado shells.

Slice the mushrooms thin and put them to marinate in the lime juice. If you are using crayfish tails, slice them in half lengthwise. Pick over the crab meat, discarding any bits of shell and shredding the meat with your fingers.

Slice the olives into fine slivers. Reserve for garnishing a spoonful of the olives, a spoonful of the chopped herbs, the walnut halves or a few of the almonds, and a few of the shellfish tails.

Bring 2 quarts [2 liters] of water with a tablespoon [15 ml.] of salt to a boil and stir in the rice. Boil for 15 to 18 minutes, or until just tender. Drain, and rinse briefly under cold running water. Drain again thoroughly.

In a large bowl, combine the rice, avocado, raw mushrooms in their marinade, shellfish, olives, olive oil, and herbs and seasonings, along with the nuts. Stir the mixture together well and correct the seasoning, adding extra lime juice as needed. Heap the mixture into the avocado shells, smoothing it into a generous mound. Once filled, the avocados may wait for an hour or two in the refrigerator before serving. If you wish to prepare the dish a day in advance, it would be best to store the filling in a covered bowl, and then fill the avocado shells just before serving. Decorate the dish with the reserved garnish and sprigs of herbs, and serve slightly chilled (but not too cold).

SIMONE BECK WITH MICHAEL JAMES
NEW MENUS FROM SIMCA'S CUISINE

Standard Preparations

Court Bouillon

The amount of wine in this recipe may be varied according to taste. Instead of wine, you can use ½ cup [125 ml.] of wine vinegar; add it at the start of cooking. An unpeeled garlic clove may also be included.

To make about 2 quarts [2 liters] court bouillon

1	large onion, sliced	1
1	large carrot, sliced	1
1	large leek, sliced	1
1	celery rib, diced	1
12	sprigs parsley	12
2	sprigs thyme	2
2	sprigs dill (optional)	2
1	bay leaf	1
6 cups	water	1½ liters
	salt	
2 cups	dry white or red wine	½ liter
5 or 6	peppercorns	5 or 6

Put the vegetables, herbs and water into a large pan, and season with a pinch of salt. Bring to a boil, then reduce the heat, cover, and simmer for approximately 15 minutes. Pour in the wine and simmer for an additional 15 minutes, adding the peppercorns during the last few minutes of cooking. Strain the court bouillon through a sieve into a bowl or a clean pan before using it.

Crab or Shrimp Boil

To make about ¾ cup [175 ml.] seasoning

⅓ cup	mustard seeds	75 ml.
3 tbsp.	coriander seeds	45 ml.
1 tbsp.	crushed red pepper	15 ml.
1 tbsp.	bay leaf, chopped or crumbled	15 ml.
¼ tsp.	dill seeds	1 ml.
10	whole allspice	10
2	whole cloves	2
1 tbsp.	coarse salt	15 ml.

Combine all of the ingredients and mix well. Stored in a tightly covered jar, the seasoning may be kept safely in a cool, dry place for up to one year.

To use the seasoning, allow about 3 tablespoons [45 ml.] of the mixture, 3 cups [¾ liter] of water and one eighth of a whole lemon for each pound [1 kg.] of shellfish. For more pungency, replace the water and lemon with 1½ cups [375 ml.] of beer or vinegar mixed with 1½ cups of water. Bring the liquid to a boil in a nonreactive pot; tie the seasoning in cheesecloth and drop it into the pot. Add the lemon, if using, and simmer the mixture for 10 minutes. Add the crabs or shrimp and simmer uncovered—one to three minutes for the shrimp, 20 minutes for the crabs.

Fish Stock

For a richer-flavored stock, up to 1 cup [¼ liter] of coarsely crushed crab, lobster and shrimp shells can be added.

To make about 2 quarts [2 liters] stock

2 lb.	fish heads, bones and trimmings, rinsed and broken up	1 kg.
1	onion, sliced	1
1	carrot, sliced	1
1	leek, sliced	1
1	celery rib, diced	1
1	bouquet garni	1
2 quarts	water	2 liters
2 cups	dry white wine	½ liter

Place the fish, vegetables and bouquet garni in a large, non-reactive pot. Add the water. Bring to a boil slowly over low heat. Skim the top until no more scum rises, then cover the pot and simmer the mixture for 15 minutes. Add the wine and simmer, covered, for another 15 minutes. Strain the stock into a deep bowl through a colander lined with muslin or a double thickness of cheesecloth. Cool the stock, then cover it and chill it overnight, or until the stock has set to an aspic. With a spoon, remove any fat from the surface.

Fish Aspic

To make about 4 cups [1 liter] aspic

4 cups	fish stock (recipe, above)	1 liter
2 or 3 tbsp.	unflavored powdered gelatin	30 or 45 ml.
2	egg whites	2
2	eggshells, finely crushed	2
2 to 4 tbsp.	dry white wine	30 to 60 ml.

Strain the stock into a bowl through a sieve lined with damp-ened cheesecloth or muslin. Chill the stock for several hours to allow the fine solids in it to settle. Decant the clear liquid into a pan and warm it over low heat.

In a small bowl, soften 2 tablespoons [30 ml.] of the gela-tin in ½ cup [125 ml.] of cold water; add a little stock. Add the softened gelatin to the stock in the pan and stir until the gelatin is dissolved. Remove the pan from the heat. Refriger-ate a spoonful of stock. If it does not set within 10 minutes, soften the remaining gelatin in ¼ cup [50 ml.] of water, warm the stock again and stir in the gelatin.

To clarify the stock, beat the egg whites until they form soft peaks and add them to the saucepan with the eggshells. Place the pan over high heat and whisk the stock to thor-oughly incorporate the egg whites. Cook without stirring so that the whites will separate from the stock and rise to its surface. When a few bubbles begin to break the egg-white layer, remove the pan from the heat and set it aside for 10 minutes. Bring the stock to a boil two more times, letting it stand off the heat for 10 minutes between each boil.

Strain the liquid aspic into a bowl through a cloth-lined sieve. When all of it has dripped through the cloth, test a spoonful in the refrigerator and add more softened gelatin if necessary. Let the aspic cool to room temperature. Taste for salt and add the wine. The aspic is now ready for use.

Fish Velouté Sauce

To make about 1 cup [¼ liter] sauce

2 cups	fish stock (recipe, left)	½ liter
2 tbsp.	butter	30 ml.
2 tbsp.	flour	30 ml.

Melt the butter in a heavy saucepan over low heat. Stir in the flour to make a roux and cook, stirring, for two to three minutes. Pour the stock into the pan, whisking constantly. Raise the heat and continue to whisk until the sauce comes to a boil. Reduce the heat to low, and move the saucepan half off the heat so that the liquid on one side of the pan simmers. A skin of impurities will form on the still side. Remove the skin periodically with a spoon. Cook the sauce for about 40 minutes to reduce it and to eliminate the taste of flour.

Bercy Sauce

To make 1¼ cups [300 ml.] sauce

¼ cup	dry white wine	50 ml.
¼ cup	fish stock (recipe, above, left)	50 ml.
1 tsp.	very finely chopped shallots	5 ml.
1 cup	fish velouté sauce (recipe, above)	¼ liter
4 tbsp.	butter, cut into small pieces	60 ml.
1 tsp.	chopped fresh parsley	5 ml.

In a heavy saucepan, boil the wine and fish stock with the shallots until the liquid is reduced to two thirds of its origi-nal volume. Stir in the velouté sauce and bring the mixture to a boil. Reduce the heat and simmer for five minutes to allow the flavors to mingle. Off the heat, whisk in the butter, a few pieces at a time. When all of the butter has been incor-porated, whisk in the parsley.

White Butter Sauce

Beurre Blanc

To make 1 to 1 ½ cups [250 to 375 ml.] sauce

⅓ cup	dry white wine	75 ml.
⅓ cup	white wine vinegar	75 ml.
3	shallots, very finely chopped	3
	salt and pepper	
½ to ¾ lb.	unsalted butter, chilled and cut into ¼-inch [6-mm.] dice	250 to 375 g.

In a heavy stainless-steel or enameled saucepan, boil the wine and vinegar with the shallots and a pinch of salt until only enough liquid remains to moisten the shallots. Remove the pan from the heat and allow it to cool for a few minutes. Season the mixture with pepper.

Place the pan on a heat-diffusing pad over very low heat and whisk in the butter, a handful at a time, until the mixture has a creamy consistency. Remove the sauce from the heat as soon as all of the butter has been incorporated.

Shellfish Butter

A more strongly flavored butter may be produced by substituting ¼ pound [125 g.] of whole crayfish, shrimp or prawns for the crushed shells called for in this recipe. Poach the shellfish in their shells, then drain and chop them—shells and all. Pound the meat and shells in a large mortar until they form a coarse-textured paste. Pound the paste with the beaten butter, sieve the mixture and season it to taste.

To make about 1 cup [125 ml.] butter

8 tbsp.	unsalted butter, chilled	120 ml.
1 cup	finely crushed cooked crustacean shells	¼ liter
	fresh lemon juice, strained (optional)	

Set the butter on a work surface, and use a rolling pin or kitchen mallet to pound the butter until it softens enough to be easily dented with a finger. Put the butter in a bowl, and beat it with a wooden spoon or whisk until light and fluffy.

In a large mortar, combine the beaten butter with the crushed shells and pound the mixture to a fine paste. Force the paste through a fine-meshed sieve into a bowl. Season the flavored butter to taste. Covered, the butter can be safely refrigerated for one week.

Cocktail Sauce

The volatile oils in chilies may irritate your skin. Wear rubber gloves when handling them.

To make about 4 cups [1 liter] sauce

9 lb.	tomatoes, peeled, seeded and finely chopped	4½ kg.
2 cups	chopped onions	½ liter
2	dried hot chilies, stemmed, seeded and chopped	2
2	sweet red peppers, halved, seeded, deribbed and chopped	2
½ tsp.	ground cinnamon	2 ml.
½ tsp.	freshly ground black pepper	2 ml.
¼ tsp.	ground allspice	1 ml.
¼ tsp.	ground mace	1 ml.
⅛ tsp.	ground cloves	½ ml.
2 tsp.	dry mustard	10 ml.
½ cup	brown sugar	125 ml.
1 cup	vinegar	¼ liter
¼ cup	prepared horseradish	50 ml.

In a heavy, nonreactive saucepan, bring the chopped tomatoes to a boil over medium heat, stirring them frequently. Reduce the heat and simmer the tomatoes uncovered for 30 minutes. Stir in the onions, chilies, red peppers, spices and brown sugar, and—stirring frequently—simmer the mixture for one hour, or until it is reduced to half its original volume. Stir in the vinegar and let the mixture return to a simmer. Remove the pan from the heat and purée the mixture through a food mill. Stirring frequently, simmer the purée for 30 minutes, or until the mixture is firm enough to hold its shape on the spoon. Let the sauce cool to room temperature, then stir in the horseradish. Chill before serving.

White Sauce

To make about 1 cup [¼ liter] sauce

2 tbsp.	butter	30 ml.
2 tbsp.	flour	30 ml.
2 cups	milk	½ liter
	salt and white pepper	
	grated nutmeg (optional)	
	heavy cream (optional)	

Melt the butter in a heavy saucepan. Stir in the flour and cook, stirring, over low heat for two to five minutes. Pour in all of the milk at once, whisking constantly to blend the mixture smoothly. Increase the heat and continue whisking while the sauce comes to a boil. Season with a very little salt. Reduce the heat to very low, and simmer for about 40 minutes, stirring every so often to prevent the sauce from sticking to the bottom of the pan.

When the sauce thickens to the desired consistency, add white pepper and a pinch of nutmeg if you like; taste for seasoning. Whisk again until the sauce is perfectly smooth, then add cream if you prefer a richer and whiter sauce.

Thick white sauce for soufflé bases. Make the sauce as above, but use half the amount of milk. Cook the sauce until it is almost too thick to pour—about five minutes—stirring constantly to prevent sticking.

Cheese sauce (Mornay sauce). Make the sauce a little thinner than usual to allow for it thickening when cheese is added. Remove the pan from the heat, add 3 tablespoons [45 ml.] each of grated Gruyère and Parmesan cheese, and stir until the cheese melts completely and the sauce is smooth.

Crayfish-butter sauce (Nantua sauce). Cut 3 tablespoons [45 ml.] of crayfish butter *(recipe, opposite)* into small bits and stir them into the sauce, a few at a time.

Tomato Sauce

When fresh ripe tomatoes are not available, use drained, canned Italian-style tomatoes or home-canned tomatoes.

	To make about 1 ¼ cups [300 ml.] sauce	
6	medium-sized very ripe tomatoes, quartered	6
1	bay leaf	1
1	large sprig dried thyme	1
	coarse salt	
1	onion, sliced	1
2	garlic cloves, lightly crushed (optional)	2
2 tbsp.	butter, cut into small pieces (optional)	30 ml.
	freshly ground black pepper	
1 to 2 tsp.	sugar (optional)	5 to 10 ml.
1 tbsp.	finely chopped fresh parsley (optional)	15 ml.
1 tbsp.	fresh basil leaves, torn into small pieces (optional)	15 ml.

Place the tomatoes in an enameled, tinned or stainless-steel saucepan with the bay leaf, thyme and a pinch of coarse salt. Add the onion and the garlic, if using. Bring to a boil, crushing the tomatoes lightly with a wooden spoon, and cook, uncovered, over fairly brisk heat for 10 minutes, or until the tomatoes have disintegrated into a thick pulp. Tip the tomatoes into a plastic or stainless-steel sieve placed over a pan. Using a wooden pestle, press the tomatoes through the sieve. Cook, uncovered, over low heat until the sauce is reduced to the required consistency. Remove the pan from the heat. If you like, whisk in the pieces of butter to enrich the sauce. Season the sauce with pepper and, if desired, with sugar, chopped parsley and basil.

Chunky tomato sauce. Peel and seed the tomatoes, and cut them into chunks. Lightly sauté a finely chopped onion and a chopped garlic clove in a little oil and butter. Add the tomatoes and cook over brisk heat, stirring occasionally, for 10 minutes, or until they are reduced to a pulp. Season and add herbs to taste. About 2 tablespoons [30 ml.] of butter can be added at the end of the cooking to enrich the sauce.

Mayonnaise

To prevent curdling, the egg yolks, oil and vinegar or lemon juice should be at room temperature and the oil should be added very gradually at first. The prepared mayonnaise will keep for several days in a covered container in the refrigerator. Stir it well before use.

	To make about 1 ½ cups [375 ml.] mayonnaise	
2	egg yolks	2
	salt and white pepper	
2 tsp.	wine vinegar or strained fresh lemon juice	10 ml.
1 to 1 ½ cups	oil	250 to 375 ml.

Put the egg yolks in a warmed dry bowl. Season with salt and pepper, and whisk for about a minute, or until the yolks become slightly paler in color. Add the vinegar or lemon juice and whisk until thoroughly mixed.

Whisking constantly, add the oil, drop by drop to begin with. When the sauce starts to thicken, pour in the remaining oil in a thin, steady stream, whisking rhythmically. Add only enough oil to give the mayonnaise a soft but firm consistency. It should just hold its shape when lifted in a spoon. If the mayonnaise is too thick, whisk in 1 to 2 teaspoons [5 to 10 ml.] of additional vinegar or lemon juice, or warm water.

Green mayonnaise. Parboil ¼ pound [125 g.] of spinach leaves for two minutes; drain the spinach in a strainer, plunge it into cold water to stop the cooking, and squeeze the spinach dry with your hands. Finely chop the spinach, then purée it in a food mill or a food processor. Stir the purée into the prepared mayonnaise, along with 1 tablespoon [15 ml.] of fines herbes.

Tartar sauce. Add 1 tablespoon [15 ml.] each (or more to taste) of finely chopped sour gherkins, capers and fines herbes to 1½ cups [375 ml.] of prepared mayonnaise.

Hollandaise Sauce

To make about 1 cup [¼ liter] sauce

3	large egg yolks	3
1 tbsp.	cold water	15 ml.
12 tbsp.	unsalted butter, chilled and cut into small pieces	180 ml.
	salt and white pepper	
	cayenne pepper	
1 tsp.	strained fresh lemon juice	5 ml.

Pour water to a depth of about 1 inch [2½ cm.] into the bottom of a double boiler—or a large pan or fireproof casserole if you are making a water bath. Heat the water until it simmers, then reduce the heat to low. Place the top of the double boiler over the bottom, or set a rack or trivet into the pan or casserole and place a smaller pan on the rack or trivet. Put the egg yolks and the cold water in the upper pan, and beat the yolks until they are smooth. Whisk a handful of the butter into the yolks and beat until the butter has been absorbed; continue adding butter in this way until all of it has been used. Beat until the sauce becomes thick and creamy. Season the sauce to taste with salt, white pepper and cayenne pepper. Then add the lemon juice.

Cold Shellfish Mousse

The cooked meat of any other crustacean—lobster, shrimp, prawn or crayfish—may be substituted for the crab meat called for in this recipe.

To make an 8-cup [2-liter] mousse

2 lb.	crab meat, picked over	1 kg.
4 tbsp.	butter	60 ml.
1	carrot, finely chopped	1
1	celery rib, finely chopped	1
1	onion, finely chopped	1
½ cup	dry white wine	125 ml.
¼ cup	brandy	50 ml.
	freshly grated nutmeg	
	cayenne pepper	
	white pepper	
	fresh thyme leaves	
1 cup	fish velouté sauce *(recipe, page 163)*	¼ liter
1½ cups	heavy cream, lightly whipped	375 ml.
1 cup	fish aspic *(recipe, page 163)*	¼ liter

Melt the butter in a skillet and add the chopped carrot, celery and onion. Cook over very low heat for about 30 minutes, stirring occasionally; the vegetables should soften, but not brown. Stir in the wine. Warm the brandy in a heavy ladle held over low heat. Ignite the brandy; when the flames die, stir the brandy into the vegetable mixture. Stir in the seasonings, add the crab meat, and simmer for one minute.

Purée the mixture in a food processor or with a mortar and pestle. A small batch at a time, force the purée through a fine-meshed sieve into a glass or nonreactive metal bowl. Discard any solids left on the mesh. Place the bowl of purée in a larger bowl partly filled with crushed ice. Stir the velouté sauce into the purée, then fold in the whipped cream. Add the aspic, stirring until the mixture is smooth.

Rinse an 8-cup [2-liter] mold with cold water and spoon into it the crab meat mixture. Cover the mold with plastic wrap, pressing it down onto the mousse to prevent a skin from forming. Refrigerate the mousse for at least six hours, or until it is very firm. To serve, run a knife around the inside edge of the mold to loosen the mousse. Set an inverted serving platter over the mold, and turn both platter and mold over together to unmold the mousse.

Basic Meat Stock

This stock may be made, according to your taste and recipe needs, from beef, veal, pork or chicken—or a combination of these meats. For the beef, use such cuts as shank, short ribs, chuck and oxtail; for the veal, use neck, shank and rib tips; for the pork, use hocks, Boston shoulder and back ribs; for the chicken, use backs, necks, wings and carcasses. Adding gelatinous elements such as calf's feet, pig's feet or pork rind will make the finished stock set to a clear, firm jelly that can serve as an aspic if prepared carefully enough.

To make about 2 quarts [2 liters] stock

4 to 5 lb.	meat, bones and trimmings of beef, veal, pork and/or chicken	2 to 2½ kg.
1 lb.	pig's, calf's or chicken feet, pig's ears or fresh pork rind (optional)	½ kg.
12 to 16 cups	water	3 to 4 liters
4	carrots	4
2	large onions, 1 stuck with 2 or 3 whole cloves	2
1	celery rib	1
1	leek, split and washed	1
1	large bouquet garni	1

Put the bones on a rack in a heavy stockpot, and place the meat and trimmings on top of them. Add cold water to cover by 2 inches [5 cm.]. Bring to a boil over low heat, starting to skim before the liquid reaches a boil. Keep skimming, occasionally adding a glass of cold water, until no scum rises—up to 30 minutes. Do not stir, lest you cloud the stock.

Add the vegetables and bouquet garni to the pot, pushing them down into the liquid. Continue skimming until a boil is reached again. Reduce the heat to very low, partially cover the pan, and cook at a bare simmer for two hours if using only chicken trimmings—otherwise for five hours—skimming off the surface fat three or four times.

Strain the stock by pouring the contents of the pot into a large bowl through a colander lined with a double layer of cheesecloth or muslin. Discard the bones and meat trimmings, vegetables and bouquet garni. Cool the strained stock and remove the last traces of fat from the surface with a folded paper towel. If there is residue at the bottom of the bowl, pour the clear liquid slowly into another container.

Refrigerate the stock if you do not plan to use it immediately; it will keep safely for three to four days. To preserve the stock longer, refrigerate it for only 12 hours—or until the last bits of fat solidify on the top—then scrape off the fat and warm the stock enough so that it may be poured into four or five pint-sized freezer containers. Be sure to leave room in the containers to allow for expansion, and cover the containers tightly. The stock will keep in the freezer for six months.

Batter for Deep Frying

To coat about 12 to 15 pieces

1 cup	flour	¼ liter
	salt and pepper	
1 tbsp.	olive oil	15 ml.
1 cup	beer, water or milk	¼ liter
2	egg whites	2

Sift the flour into a bowl and season with salt and pepper. Make a well in the center of the flour. Add the oil, and gradually whisk in the beer, water or milk—working from the center outward. Whisk for only as long as it takes to produce a smooth batter: Do not overwork the mixture. Let the batter rest for about one hour at room temperature. Beat the egg whites until they form soft peaks, and fold them gently into the batter mixture just before using it.

Short-Crust Dough

This recipe makes enough dough for a two-crust, 8- or 9-inch [20- or 23-cm.] pie.

To make 1 pound [½ kg.] dough

2 cups	flour	½ liter
½ tsp.	salt	2 ml.
10 tbsp.	unsalted butter, cut into pieces	150 ml.
3 to 4 tbsp.	ice water	45 to 60 ml.

Into a large bowl, sift the flour and salt. Add the butter. Rub together the butter and flour, using the tips of your fingers, or cut the butter into the flour with two knives or a pastry blender, until the mixture has a coarse, mealy texture.

Stirring lightly with a knife or fork, sprinkle the water over the mixture a spoonful at a time until the dough begins to cohere. Gather the dough into a ball, pressing it together with your hands. Cover the dough with plastic wrap, wax paper or foil, and refrigerate it for one or two hours before using it. The dough can safely be kept in the refrigerator for two days, in the freezer for one month. If frozen, let the dough defrost in the refrigerator for one day before using it.

To roll out dough: Unwrap the dough and put it on a cool, floured surface (a marble slab is ideal). Divide the ball, if necessary; rewrap the excess portion and return it to the refrigerator. Partially press out the dough with your hand, then give it a few gentle smacks with the rolling pin to flatten it and render it more supple. Roll out the dough from the center, turning it 90 degrees clockwise after each roll, until it forms a round, an oblong or a rectangle—depending on the shape called for in the recipe—about ⅛ inch [3 mm.] thick. Roll the dough onto the rolling pin, lift it up and unroll it over the piepan. Press the dough firmly against all surfaces and trim the edges. If using the dough to cover a pie, trim the pastry to within ½ inch [1 cm.] of the rim of the piepan, turn under the dough edges around the rim to form a double layer, and press the dough firmly to the rim with thumb and forefinger to crimp the edges.

Puff-Pastry Dough

To make 2 pounds [1 kg.] dough

3 cups	all-purpose flour	¾ liter
1 cup	cake flour	¼ liter
2 tsp.	salt	10 ml.
1 lb.	unsalted butter	½ kg.
10 to 12 tbsp.	cold water	150 to 180 ml.

Sift the flours and salt into a bowl. Cut a quarter of the butter into small pieces and add them to the bowl. Using your finger tips, rub the butter into the flour. Add just enough cold water—a few tablespoonfuls at a time—to bind the ingredients, and work the dough into a ball. Wrap it in floured plastic wrap and refrigerate it for 30 minutes.

Meanwhile, place the remaining butter between two sheets of parchment or wax paper and, with a rolling pin, flatten the butter into a slab about 6 inches [15 cm.] square and ½ inch [1 cm.] thick. Chill the butter for 30 minutes.

Place the dough on a lightly floured board and roll it into a 12-inch [30-cm.] square. Place the square of butter diagonally in the center of the dough and fold the corners of the dough over the butter so that they meet in the center. Roll the dough into a rectangle 12 by 18 inches [30 by 45 cm.].

Fold the dough into thirds and give it a quarter turn. Roll the dough again into a rectangle and fold it again into thirds. Wrap, and chill the dough for at least one hour. Roll and turn the dough twice more, refrigerate for two hours, and repeat, giving it six turns in all. After a final turn, chill it for four hours before using. Tightly wrapped, the dough can be refrigerated for two or three days, frozen for two or three months. If frozen, defrost it in the refrigerator overnight.

Recipe Index

All recipes in the index that follows are listed by their English titles except in cases where a food of foreign origin, such as quenelles, is universally recognized by its source name. Foreign recipes are listed by country or region of origin. Recipe credits appear on pages 174-176.

General Index/ Glossary

Included in this index to the cooking demonstrations are definitions, in italics, of special culinary terms not explained elsewhere in this volume. The Recipe Index begins on page 168.

Recipe Credits

The sources for the recipes in this volume are shown below. Page references in parentheses indicate where the recipes appear in the anthology.

Académie Culinaire de France, *Cuisine Française.* © Éditions Universitaires aux droits des Éditions Le Bélier-Prisma, 1971. Published by Éditions Le Bélier-Jean-Pierre Delarge, Éditeur, Paris. Translated by permission of Éditions Le Bélier-Jean-Pierre Delarge, Éditeur(99).
Adams, Charlotte, *The Four Seasons Cookbook.* Copyright © 1971 in all countries of the International Copyright Union by The Ridge Press, Inc. and Crown Publishers, Inc. Published by permission of The Ridge Press, Inc. and Crown Publishers, Inc.(110, 161).
Aguilar, Jeanette, *The Classic Cooking of Spain.* Copyright © by Jeanette Aguilar. Reprinted by permission of Holt, Rinehart and Winston, Publishers(114, 146, 151, 154).
Alberson, Sarah D., *The Blue Sea Cookbook.* © 1968 by Sarah D. Alberson, permission by Hastings House, Publishers Inc.(104, 109).
Beard, James, *James Beard's Fish Cookery.* Copyright 1954 by James A. Beard. Published by Little, Brown and Company, Boston. By permission of Little, Brown and Company(121). *James Beard's New Fish Cookery,* A revised and updated edition. Copyright 1954, © 1976 by James A. Beard. Reprinted by permission of Little, Brown and Company(96, 158).
Beck, Simone with Michael James, *New Menus from Simca's Cuisine.* Copyright © 1979, 1978 by Simone Beck and Michael James. By permission of Harcourt Brace Jovanovich, Inc.(162).
Bennett, Victor with Antonia Rossi, *Papa Rossi's Secrets of Italian Cooking.* By permission of the authors (105, 133).
Bérard, Léone, *Poissons et Fruits de Mer.* © Robert Laffont, Paris et Marabout S.A., Verviers 1976. Published by Robert Laffont and Marabout Service. Translated by permission of S.A. Les Nouvelles Éditions Marabout(101).
Blancard, Eugène, *Souvenirs de Villégiature—Mets et*

Produits de Provence. Published by Imprimerie Bordato, Toulon, 1926(145).
Bocuse, Paul, *The New Cuisine.* © 1976 Flammarion. English translation, Copyright © 1977 by Random House, Inc. Published by Hart-Davis, MacGibbon Ltd./Granada Publishing Ltd. By permission of Hart-Davis, MacGibbon Ltd./Granada Publishing Ltd.(114). *Paul Bocuse's French Cooking.* Translated by Colette Rossant, edited by Lorraine Davis. Translation copyright © 1977 by Random House, Inc. Reprinted by permission of Pantheon Books, a division of Random House, Inc.(104, 123, 142).
Boni, Ada, *The Talisman Italian Cook Book.* Translated by Matilde La Rosa. Copyright 1950, 1977 by Crown Publishers, Inc. Published by Crown Publishers, Inc., New York. Used by permission of Crown Publishers, Inc.(150).
Brobeck, Florence and Monika B. Kjellberg, *Smörgasbord and Scandinavian Cookery.* Published 1948 by Little, Brown and Company(101).
Brown, Helen, *Helen Brown's West Coast Cook Book.* Copyright 1952 by Helen Brown. By permission of Little, Brown and Company(132).
Brown, Helen Evans, *Shrimp and Other Shellfish Recipes.* Copyright © 1966 by Philip S. Brown. Used by permission of the John Schaffner Agency(91).
Brown, Sandi and Joyce LaFray, *Famous Florida! Restaurants & Recipes.* Copyright © 1981 by LaFray Publishing Company. By permission of LaFray Publishing Company (160—Hans Eichmann, owner, "Vinton's," Coral Gables, Fla.).
Brownstone, Cecily, *Cecily Brownstone's Associated Press Cook Book.* Reprinted with permission, copyright 1972. Published by David McKay Co., Inc.(113, 132).
Bugialli, Giuliano, *The Fine Art of Italian Cooking.* Copyright © 1977 by Giuliano Bugialli. Reprinted by permission of Times Books, a division of Quadrangle/The New York Times Book Co., Inc.(159).
Carnacina, Luigi and Luigi Veronelli, *La Buona Vera Cucina Italiana.* © 1966 by Rizzoli Editore. Published by Rizzoli Editore, Milan. Translated by permission of Rizzoli Editore(137).
Cavanna, Guelfo, *Doni di Nettuno.* Privately published, Florence, 1913(150).
Celli, Elsa and Inez M. Krech, *Naturally Italian.* Copyright © 1978 by Elisa Celli and Inez M. Krech. Published by E. P. Dutton, Inc. Reprinted by permission of the

publisher(160).
Chamberlain, Narcissa G. and Narcisse Chamberlain, *The Flavor of France in Recipes and Pictures,* Volume 2. Copyright © 1964 by Hastings House, Publishers Inc. By permission of Hastings House, Publishers Inc. (141).
Chamberlain, Narcisse and Narcissa G. Chamberlain, *The Chamberlain Sampler of American Cooking in Recipes and Pictures.* Copyright © 1961 by Hastings House, Publishers Inc. Reprinted by permission of Hastings House, Publishers Inc.(102).
Chanot-Bullier, C., *Vieilles Recettes de Cuisine Provençale.* Published by Tacussel, Marseilles. Translated by permission of Tacussel, Éditeur(101, 150).
Chantiles, Vilma Liacouras, *The Food of Greece.* Copyright © 1975 by Vilma Liacouras Chantiles. Published by Atheneum, New York. By permission of Vilma Liacouras Chantiles(149).
Chekenian, Jane and Monica Meyer, *Shellfish Cookery.* Copyright © 1971 by Jane Chekenian and Monica Meyer. Reprinted with permission of Macmillan Publishing Co., Inc.(93, 95, 96, 121).
Clancy, John and Frances Field, *Clancy's Oven Cookery.* Copyright © 1976 by John Clancy and Frances Field. Reprinted by permission of Delacorte Press/Eleanor Friede(112).
Coleman, Jane S., *Gulf Coast Gourmet.* Copyright © 1962 by Jane S. Coleman. Published by Foley's Woman's Club, Foley, Ala. By permission of Jane S. Coleman (106).
Collin, Rima and Richard, *The Pleasures of Seafood.* Copyright © 1976 by Rima and Richard Collin. Reprinted by permission of Holt, Rinehart and Winston, Publishers(129, 139).
Cox, J. Stevens (Editor), *Guernsey Dishes of Bygone Days.* © James and Gregory Stevens Cox, The Toucan Press, Guernsey, 1974. Published by The Toucan Press, Guernsey. By permission of Gregory Stevens Cox, The Toucan Press(90).
La Cuisine Lyonnaise. Published by Éditions Gutenberg, 1947(128).
Curnonsky, *Cuisine et Vins de France.* Copyright © 1953 by Augé, Gillon, Hollier-Larousse, Moreau et Cie (Librairie Larousse), Paris. Published by Librairie Larousse, Paris. Translated by permission of Société Encyclopédique

Universelle(110).

Cutler, Carol, *The Six-Minute Soufflé and Other Culinary Delights.* Copyright © 1976 by Carol Cutler. By permission of Clarkson N. Potter, Inc.(110, 113, 114).

Dannenbaum, Julie, *Menus for All Occasions.* © Copyright 1974 by Julie Dannenbaum. Published by Saturday Review Press/E. P. Dutton & Co., Inc., New York. By permission of Edward Acton, Inc., New York(103).

David, Elizabeth, *French Country Cooking.* Copyright © Elizabeth David, 1951, 1958, 1966. Published by Penguin Books Ltd., London. By permission of Penguin Books Ltd.(98).

Davidson, Alan, *North Atlantic Seafood.* Copyright © 1979 by Alan Davidson. Reprinted by permission of Viking Penguin, Inc. and Penguin Books Ltd.(120, 148). *Mediterranean Seafood.* Copyright © Alan Davidson, 1972. Published by Penguin Books Ltd., London. By permission of Penguin Books Ltd.(98, 100).

De Aznar, Marina Pereyra and Nina Froud, *The Home Book of Spanish Cookery.* First published in 1956 by Faber and Faber Ltd., London. New material © Marina Pereyra de Aznar and Nina Froud 1967, 1974. By permission of Nina Froud(151).

D'Ermo, Dominique, *Dominique's Famous Fish, Game & Meat Recipes.* Copyright © 1981 by Acropolis Books Ltd. Reprinted by permission of Acropolis Books(143, 150).

De Groot, Roy Andries, *Revolutionizing French Cooking.* Copyright © 1975, 1976 by Roy Andries de Groot. Used by permission of McGraw-Hill Book Company, New York(111).

Delfs, Robert A., *The Good Food of Szechwan.* Copyright © in Japan 1974 by Kodansha International Ltd. By permission of Kodansha International Ltd.(117).

Le Duc, *Crustacés, Poissons et Coquillages.* © 1977 by Éditions Jean-Claude Lattès, Paris. Reprinted by permission (98, 110).

Ellison, J. Audrey (Editor), *The Great Scandinavian Cook Book.* © Wezäta Förlag, Göteborg, Sweden, 1963. English translation © J. Audrey Ellison, 1966. Reprinted by permission of Crown Publishers, Inc.(105, 122).

Feast of Italy. Translated from the Italian edition published by Arnoldo Mondadori Editore. Copyright © 1973 by Arnoldo Mondadori Editore. Reprinted by permission of A & W Publishers, Inc.(102, 119).

Finn, Molly, *Summer Feasts.* Copyright © 1979 by Molly Finn. Reprinted by permission of Simon & Schuster, a division of Gulf & Western Corporation(126).

Foods of the World, *American Cooking: The Northwest; Pacific and Southeast Asian Cooking; The Cooking of Japan.* Copyright © 1970 Time Inc.; Copyright © 1970 Time Inc.; Copyright © 1976 Time-Life Books, Inc.; Published by Time-Life Books, Alexandria(97, 139; 116; 136).

Francesconi, Jeanne Caròla, *La Cucina Napoletana.* Copyright 1965 by Casa Editrice Fausto Fiorentino, Napoli. Published by Casa Editrice Fausto Fiorentino, Naples, 1965. Translated by permission of Jeanne Caròla Francesconi(154).

Frederick, J. George and Jean Joyce, *Long Island Seafood Cook Book.* Copyright 1939 by Business Bourse, New York. Reprinted in 1971 by Dover Publications, Inc., New York. Used by permission of Dover Publications, Inc.(97, 108).

Froud, Nina and Tamara Lo, *International Fish Dishes.* Copyright © 1974 by Nina Froud and Tamara Lo. By permission of Hippocrene Books, Inc.(137).

Ghedini, Francesco, *Northern Italian Cooking.* Copyright © 1973 by Paola Schiavina Ghedini, Gabriella Martelli Ghedini and Anita Ghedini Gardini. Reprinted by permission of the publisher, E. P. Dutton, Inc.(125).

Gin, Margaret and Alfred E. Castle, *Regional Cooking of China.* © 1975 Margaret Gin and Alfred Castle. Published by 101 Productions, San Francisco, Calif. Reprinted by permission of 101 Productions(104).

Glidden, Helene, *Pacific Coast Seafood Chef.* Copyright © 1953 by Helene Glidden. Published by Binford & Mort, Publishers. Used by permission of the publisher(102).

Gouffé, Jules, *Le Livre de Cuisine.* Published by Librairie Hachette, Paris, 1867(122).

The Grand Central Oyster Bar & Restaurant Seafood Cookbook. Copyright © 1977 by Jerome Brody, and Joan and Joseph Foley. Published by Crown Publishers, Inc., New York. Used by permission of Crown Publishers, Inc.(103).

The Great Cooks Cookbook. Copyright © 1974 by The Good Cooking School, Inc. Used by permission of J. G. Ferguson Publishing Company, Chicago, Ill.(119, 140, 147, 159).

Greene, Bert, *Bert Greene's Kitchen Bouquets.* © 1979 by Bert Greene. Published by Contemporary Books, Inc. By permission of the publisher(95, 112).

Grigson, Jane, *Fish Cookery.* Copyright © Jane Grigson, 1973. Published by Penguin Books Ltd., London. By permission of Pitman Publishing Limited(105).

Guérard, Michel, *Michel Guérard's Cuisine Minceur.* English translation. Copyright © 1976 by William Morrow and Company, Inc. Originally published in French under the title La Grande Cuisine Minceur. Copyright © 1976 by Éditions Robert Laffont, S.A. By permission of William Morrow and Company(106, 156).

Hargreaves, Barbara (Editor), *The Sporting Wife.* Copyright © H. F. & G. Witherby Ltd., 1971. By permission of Anthony Witherby(128).

Hastings, Macdonald and Carole Walsh, *Wheeler's Fish Cookery Book.* © 1974 by Macdonald Hastings and Carole Emmanuel. Published by Michael Joseph Ltd., London 1974. By permission of Michael Joseph Ltd.(143).

Hewitt, Jean, *The New York Times Large Type Cookbook.* Copyright © 1968, 1971 by the New York Times Company. Reprinted by permission of Times Books, a division of Quadrangle/The New York Times Book Co., Inc.(130). *The New York Times Southern Heritage Cookbook.* Copyright © 1976 by the New York Times. Published by G. P. Putnam's Sons. Reprinted by permission of G. P. Putnam's Sons(107, 157).

Heyraud, H., *La Cuisine à Nice.* Privately published, Nice, 1922(149).

Houston, Alice Watson, *The American Heritage Book of Fish Cookery.* © 1980 American Heritage Publishing Co., Inc. Reprinted by permission of the publisher(91, 120).

Hunt, Peter, *Peter Hunt's Cape Cod Cookbook.* Copyright © 1962 by The Stephen Greene Press. Reprinted by permission of The Stephen Greene Press(106).

Janvier, Emmanuelle, *Les Meilleures Recettes aux Fruits de Mer.* Copyright Elsevier Séquoia, Bruxelles, 1977. Published by Elsevier Séquoia, Bruxelles. Translated by permission of Elsevier Séquoia(100).

Jensen, Ingeborg Dahl, *Wonderful Wonderful Danish Cooking.* Copyright © 1965 by Ingeborg Dahl Jensen. Reprinted by permission of Simon & Schuster, a division of Gulf & Western Corporation(126).

Jouveau, René, *La Cuisine Provençale.* Copyright © Bouquet & Baumgartner, Flamatt, Switzerland. Published by Éditions du Message, 1962, Berne. Translated by permission of Bouquet & Baumgartner(153).

The Junior League of Charleston, *Charleston Receipts.* © 1950 by The Junior League of Charleston, Inc. Published by the Junior League of Charleston, Inc., South Carolina. By permission of the Junior League of Charleston(118, 141).

The Junior League of New Orleans, *The Plantation Cookbook.* Copyright © 1972 by The Junior League of New Orleans, Inc. Published by Doubleday & Company, Inc., New York. Reprinted by permission of Doubleday & Company, Inc.(107).

Kahn, Odette, *La Petite et la Grande Cuisine.* © Calmann-Lévy, 1977. Published by Éditions Calmann-Lévy, Paris. Translated by permission of Éditions Calmann-Lévy(99, 146).

Kamman, Madeleine, *The Making of a Cook.* Copyright © 1976 by Madeleine Kamman. Published by Atheneum Publishers. By permission of the publisher(161). *When French Women Cook.* Copyright © 1976 by Madeleine M. Kamman. Published by Atheneum Publishers. By permission of the publisher(112, 131).

Kennedy, Diana, *Recipes from the Regional Cooks of Mexico.* Copyright © 1978 by Diana Kennedy. Reprinted by permission of Harper & Row, Publishers, Inc.(127).

Lane, Lilian, *Malayan Cookery Recipes.* © Lilian Lane, 1964. Published by Eastern Universities Press Sdn. Bhd., Singapore, in association with Hodder & Stoughton, Educational, London. By permission of Eastern Universities Press Sdn. Bhd.(125).

Langseth-Christensen, Lillian and Carol Sturm Smith, *The Shellfish Cookbook.* Copyright © 1967 by the authors. Used with the permission of the publisher, Walker & Company(116, 144).

Leung, Mai, *The Classic Chinese Cook Book.* Copyright © 1976 by Yuk Mai Leung Thayer. Reprinted by permission of Harper & Row, Publishers, Inc.(115, 130).

Linz, Mike and Stan Fuchs, *The Lobster's Fine Kettle of Fish.* Copyright © 1958 by The Citadel Press. Published by arrangement with The Citadel Press(94, 104, 120, 144).

London, Sheryl and Mel, *The Fish-Lovers' Cookbook.* © 1980 by Sheryl and Mel London. Permission granted by Rodale Press, Inc., Emmaus, Pa.(116, 133, 135, 138).

McClane, A. J., *The Encyclopedia of Fish Cookery.* Copyright © 1977 by A. J. McClane and Arie deZanger. Published by Holt, Rinehart & Winston. Used by permission of Holt, Rinehart & Winston(92). *McClane's North American Fish Cookery.* Copyright © 1981 by A. J. McClane and Arie deZanger. Reprinted by permission of Holt, Rinehart and Winston, Publishers(90, 160).

MacIlquham, Frances, *Fish Cookery of North America.* Copyright © 1974 by Frances MacIlquham. Published by Winchester Press, New York. Reprinted by permission of Winchester Press, Tulsa, Okla.(92, 118, 134, 145).

MacMiadhacháin, Anna, *Spanish Regional Cookery.* Copyright © Anna MacMiadhacháin, 1976. Published by Penguin Books Ltd., London. By permission of Penguin Books Ltd.(152).

A Maine Cookbook. Copyright 1969 by Twin City Printery. Published by Twin City Printery, Lewiston, Me., 1969. By permission of Twin City Printery(94).

Mallos, Tess, *The Complete Middle East Cookbook.* Copyright © 1979 by Tess Mallos. By permission of the publisher, Summit Books, Sydney, Australia(148).

Margittai, Tom and Paul Kovi, *The Four Seasons.* Copyright © 1980 by Tom Margittai and Paul Kovi. Reprinted by permission of Simon & Schuster, a division of Gulf & Western Corporation(121, 155).

Maryland Seafood Marketing Authority, *Maryland Seafood Cookbook 1.* Reprinted by permission of Office of Seafood Marketing, Annapolis, Md.(115).

Mason, Phillip, *Shellfish Cookbook.* © 1974 by Phillip Mason. Reprinted by permission of Sterling Publishing Co., Inc., New York, N.Y.(90, 94, 115, 122).

Minchelli, Jean and Paul, *Crustacés, Poissons et Coquillages.* Published by Éditions Jean-Claude Lattès. Translated by permission of Éditions Jean-Claude Lattès(99).

Mitcham, Howard, *The Provincetown Seafood Cookbook.* Copyright © 1975 by Howard Mitcham. Published by Addison-Wesley, Reading, Mass. By permission of the author(97, 142).

Morris, Dan and Inez, *The Complete Fish Cookbook.* Copyright © 1972, by Dan and Inez Morris, used with permission of the publisher. The Bobbs-Merrill Company, Inc.(92, 109, 142).

Mosimann, Anton, *Cuisine à La Carte.* © Anton Mosimann 1981. Published by Northwood Books, London. Translated by permission of Northwood Books(100, 124).

Nicolas, Jean F., *The Complete Cookbook of American Fish and Shellfish.* Copyright © CBI Publishing Company, 1981. Reprinted with permission of the publisher(140, 144).

Nignon, Édouard, *Éloges de la Cuisine Française.* Copyright 1933, by H. Piazza & Cie. Published by Éditions d'Art H. Piazza, Paris, 1933. Translated by permission of Éditions Daniel Morcrette, B.P. 26, 95270-Luzarches, France(145).

Ortiz, Elisabeth Lambert, *The Complete Book of Caribbean Cooking.* Copyright © 1973 by Elisabeth Lambert Ortiz. Reprinted by permission of the publisher, M. Evans & Co., Inc., New York, N.Y.(91).

Paradissis, Chrissa, *The Best of Greek Cookery.* Copyright © 1976 P. Efstathiadis & Sons, Athens. By permission of P. Efstathiadis & Sons(152).

Pépin, Jacques, *La Méthode.* Copyright © 1980 by Jacques Pépin. Published by Times Books, a division of

Quadrangle/The New York Times Book Co., Inc. By permission of the publisher(156).
Peter, Madeleine, *Favorite Recipes of the Great Women Chefs of France.* Translated and edited by Nancy Simmons. Copyright © 1977 by Éditions Robert Laffont S.A. Copyright © 1979 by Holt, Rinehart and Winston. Published by Holt, Rinehart and Winston, Publishers. By permission of the publisher(109).
Petits Propos Culinaires, © 1979, Prospect Books. Published by Prospect Books, Washington, D.C. By permission of the publisher(123).
Piotrowski, Joyce Dodson, *The Squid Book.* © 1980 by permission of the author(154, 159).
Pohren, D. E., *Adventures in Taste: The Wines and Folk Food of Spain.* Copyright © 1972 by Donn E. Pohren(93, 132, 134).
Point, Fernand, *Ma Gastronomie.* © Flammarion. Translated and adapted by Frank Kulla and Patricia Shannon Kulla. English language edition © 1974, Lyceum Books, Inc. Published by Lyceum Books, Inc., Wilton, Ct. By permission of Lyceum Books, Inc.(136).
Les Princes de la Gastronomie. © 1.2.1975—Les Éditions Mondiales. Published by Modes de Paris. Translated by permission of Les Éditions Mondiales(111, 141).
Quillet, Aristide, *La Cuisine Moderne.* Copyright Librairie Aristide Quillet, 1946. Published by Librairie Aristide Quillet. Translated by permission of Librairie Aristide Quillet(124).
Ramirez, Leonora, *El Pescado en mi Cocina.* Published by Editorial Molino. Translated by permission of Editorial Molino(149, 158).
Robinson, Robert H. and Daniel G. Coston, Jr., *The Craft of Dismantling a Crab.* By permission of Sussex Prints(94).
Rogers, Ann, *A Basque Story Cook Book.* Copyright © 1968 by Ann Rogers. Reprinted by permission of Curtis Brown, Ltd. All rights reserved(153).

Romagnoli, Margaret and G. Franco, *The Romagnolis' Meatless Cookbook.* Copyright © 1976 by Margaret and G. Franco Romagnoli. Reprinted by permission of Atlantic-Little, Brown and Company(152). *The Romagnolis' Table.* Copyright © 1974, 1975 by Margaret and G. Franco Romagnoli. Reprinted by permission of Atlantic-Little, Brown(151).
Sahni, Julie, *Classic Indian Cooking.* Text Copyright © 1980 by Julie Sahni. By permission of William Morrow & Company(126, 127, 128, 147).
Sarvis, Shirley, *Crab & Abalone: West Coast Ways with Fish & Shellfish.* Copyright © 1968 by Shirley Sarvis and Tony Calvello. Published by Bobbs-Merrill Company Inc. By permission of Shirley Sarvis(117, 118).
Simms, A. E., *Fish and Shell-Fish.* © 1969 Zomer & Keunig Boeken B.V. Ede/The Netherlands, English Language Edition © 1973. By permission of Virtue & Co. Ltd.(140).
Singh, Dharam Jit, *Classic Cooking From India.* Copyright © 1956 by Dharam Jit Singh. Reprinted by permission of Houghton Mifflin Company(103, 135).
Solomon, Charmaine, *Chinese Diet Cookbook.* Copyright © 1979 Lansdowne Press, Sydney, Australia. Used by permission of Lansdowne Press(146). *The Complete Asian Cookbook.* Copyright © 1981 Lansdowne Press, Sydney, Australia. Used by permission of Lansdowne Press(124, 157).
Spear, Ruth A., *Cooking Fish and Shellfish.* Copyright © 1980 by Ruth A. Spear. Reprinted by permission of Doubleday & Company, Inc.(120, 136).
Steinmetz, Emma W. K., *Onze Rijsttafel.* © Unieboek b.v./C. A. J. van Dishoeck, Bussum. Published by C. A. J. van Dishoeck, Bussum. Translated by permission of Unieboek b.v./C. A. J. van Dishoeck(133).
Szathmáry, Louis, *The Chef's Secret Cook Book.* Copyright © 1971 by Louis Szathmáry. Published by Times Books, a division of Quadrangle/The New York Times Book Co., Inc. By permission of the author(125, 138).

Tada, Tatsuji, *Japanese Recipes.* Published by Charles E. Tuttle Company, Inc. of Tokyo, Japan. By permission of Charles E. Tuttle Company, Inc.(131).
Tracy, Marian, *The Shellfish Cookbook.* Copyright © 1965 by Marian Tracy, used with permission of the publisher, The Bobbs-Merrill Company, Inc.(102, 119).
Troisgros, Jean and Pierre, *The Nouvelle Cuisine of Jean & Pierre Troisgros.* English translation copyright © 1978 by William Morrow and Company, Inc. Originally published under the title *Cuisiniers à Roanne.* Copyright © 1977 by Éditions Robert Laffont, S.A. Used by permission of William Morrow and Company, Inc.(108).
Ungerer, Miriam, *Good Cheap Food.* Copyright © 1973 by Miriam Ungerer. Reprinted by permission of Viking Penguin, Inc.(96).
Valente, Maria Odette Cortes, *Cozinha Regional Portuguesa.* Published by Livraria Almedina, Coimbra, 1973. Translated by permission of Livraria Almedina(154).
Van Es, Ton, *Het Volkomen Visboek.* © 1975 Meijer Pers b.v., Amsterdam, Holland. Published by Meijer Pers b.v. Translated by permisssion of Meijer Pers(134).
Willan, Anne, *The Observer French Cookery School.* Copyright © 1980 by Anne Willan and Jane Grigson. Reprinted by permission of La Varenne, Paris and Harold Ober Associates Incorporated(161).
Willan, Anne (Editor), *Grand Diplôme Cooking Course Volumes 3 and 14.* Copyright © BPC Publishing 1971 and Phoebus Publishing 1972. By courtesy of Macdonald & Company (Publishers) Ltd.(117, 138).
Wolfert, Paula, *Mediterranean Cooking.* Copyright © 1977 by Paula Wolfert. Reprinted by permission of Times Books, a division of Quadrangle/The New York Times Book Co., Inc. from *Mediterranean Cooking* by Paula Wolfert(129, 135).
Yockelson, Lisa, *The Efficient Epicure.* Copyright © 1982 by Lisa Yockelson. Reprinted by permission of Harper & Row, Publishers, Inc.(130, 155).

Acknowledgments

The indexes for this book were prepared by Louise W. Hedberg. The editors are particularly indebted to Pat Alburey, Hertfordshire, England; Dr. George J. Flick, Dept. of Food, Science and Technology, Virginia Polytechnic Institute and State University, Blacksburg; John D. Kaylor, National Marine Fisheries Service, Gloucester, Massachusetts; John B. Richards, Marine Advisory Programs, University of California, Santa Barbara; Frank S. Taylor, Marine Resources Research Institute, Charleston, South Carolina and Jeremiah Tower, San Francisco.

The editors also wish to thank the following: Sharon Archer, Falls Church, Virginia; Paul E. Bauerfeld, Beth Beville, John C. DeVane Jr., National Marine Fisheries Service, Charleston, South Carolina; John Bridge, Estuary Products, Essex, England; Jacqueline Cattani, Bethesda, Maryland; Dr. Marion Clarke, Marine Advisory Programs, University of Florida, Gainesville; Mark Claxton, R. W. Claxton, Inc., Washington, D.C.; John A. Dassow, National Marine Fisheries Service, Seattle, Washington; Jennifer Davidson, London; Pamela Davidson, London; Christopher M. Dewees, Marine Advisory Programs, University of California, Davis; Cecile Dogniez, Paris; J. Audrey Ellison, London; Jeffrey A. Fisher, Institute of Food and Agricultural Sciences, University of Florida, Key West; Bertha V. Fontaine, National Marine Fisheries Service, Pascagoula, Mississippi; Dorothy Frame, London; Diana Grant, London; Maggie Heinz, London; Phillip E. Hoke, Seafood Specialties, Santa Barbara, California; Marion Hunter, Surrey, England; Elisabeth Lu Kissel, National Marine Fisheries Service, Washington, D.C.; Martin A. Moe, Aqualife Research Corporation, Marathon Shores, Florida; Agneta Munktell, London; C. J. Newnes, Fish Merchant, London; Hank Pennington, Marine Advisory Programs, University of Alaska, Kodiak; Dr. Robert Price, Dept. of Food Science and Technology, University of California, Davis; Liz Roy, Southern Seafood Company, Cape Canaveral, Florida; E. B. Smith, Norfolk, England; J. M. Turnell & Co., Vegetable Merchants, London; Eileen Turner, Sussex, England; Edward Ueber, National Marine Fisheries Service, Tiburon, California.

Picture Credits

The sources for the pictures in this book are listed below. Credits for each of the photographers and illustrators are listed by page number in sequence with successive pages indicated by hyphens; where necessary, the locations of pictures within pages are also indicated—separated from page numbers by dashes.

Photographs by Aldo Tutino: cover, 4, 13—bottom, 14-17, 18—bottom, 19—top and bottom, 20-21, 25—top and bottom, 26-27—bottom, 30-37, 39-47, 50, 53-62, 63—top, 64-66, 68-69—top, 70-75, 76-77—bottom, 78-88. Other photographs (alphabetically): Tom Belshaw, 12, 13—top, 23—bottom left, 24—bottom right, 25—center, 28, 38, 48—bottom, 49, 76-77—top. Alan Duns, 18—top, 19—center, 22—top and bottom left, 23—top and bottom right, 24—center and bottom left, 26—top left, 48—top, 51-52, 63—bottom, 68-69—bottom. John Elliott, 22—bottom right, 26—top right, 27—top. Louis Klein, 2. Illustrations (alphabetically): Biruta Akerbergs, 8-11. From the Mary Evans Picture Library and private sources and *Food & Drink: A Pictorial Archive from Nineteenth Century Sources* by Jim Harter, published by Dover Publications, Inc., 1979, 90-167. Endpapers: Designed by John Pack.

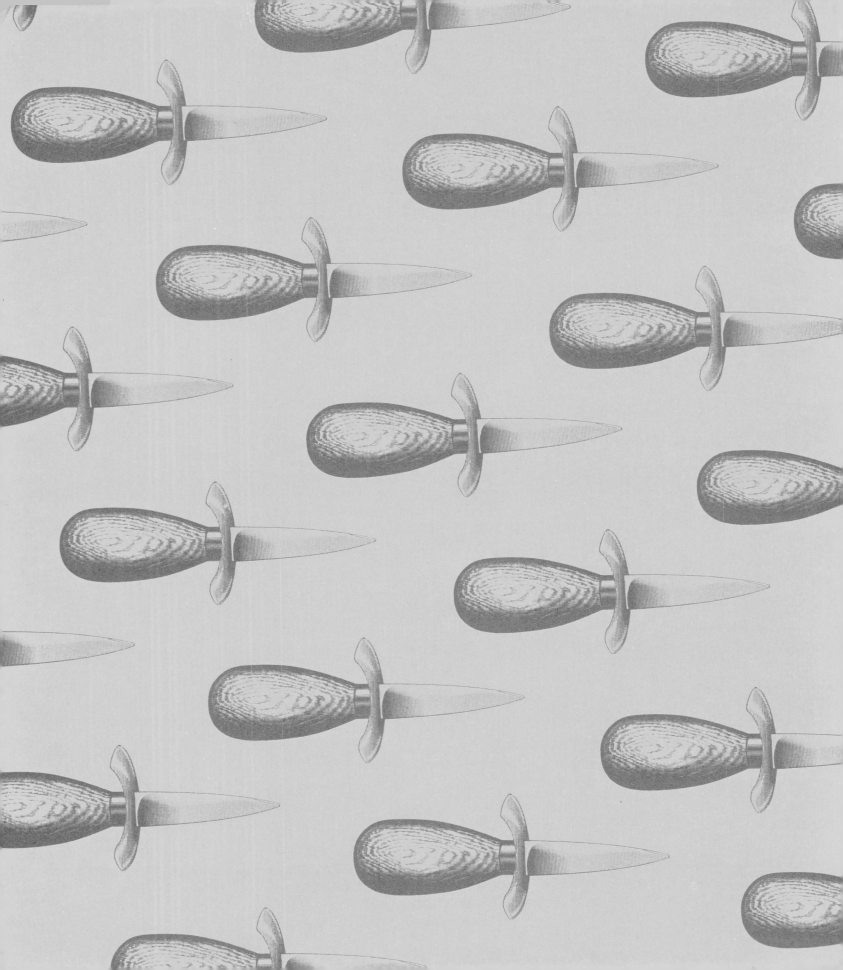